Who Will You Become?

Who Will You Become?

An Ignatian Introduction to Catholic Theology

RYAN G. DUNS, SJ
CONOR M. KELLY

GEORGETOWN UNIVERSITY PRESS | WASHINGTON, DC

The publisher is not responsible for third-party websites or their content. URL links were active at time of publication.

Cataloging-in-Publication data is on file with the Library of Congress.

ISBN 9781647126407 (hardcover)
ISBN 9781647126414 (paperback)
ISBN 9781647126421 (ebook)

∞ This paper meets the requirements of ANSI/NISO Z39.48-1992 (Permanence of Paper).

26 25   9 8 7 6 5 4 3 2   First printing

Printed in the United States of America

EU GPSR Authorized Representative
LOGOS EUROPE, 9 rue Nicolas Poussin, 17000, LA ROCHELLE, France
E-mail: Contact@logoseurope.eu

Cover design by Erin Kirk
Interior design by Westchester Publishing Services

To my parents, Robert and Michele,
who gave their children the gift of freedom to discern
who they would become. To my Jesuit mentors in Ignatian discernment:
Ben Fiore, SJ, Howard Gray, SJ, Bill Verbryke, SJ, Walter Farrell, SJ,
and Karl Kiser, SJ. And to the members of Alpha Sigma Nu (ΑΣΝ),
the only honor society allowed to bear the name Jesuit.

—RGD, SJ

To my parents, Peter and Geraldine,
for their beautiful witness to discernment
(both explicitly and implicitly Ignatian) in action.

—CMK

CONTENTS

ACKNOWLEDGMENTS

The origins of this text trace back to a large-format Foundations in Theology course that we developed for the Department of Theology at Marquette University and co-taught for multiple years. Convinced that we could serve our students better if we had a coherent narrative to link our lectures together, we focused on theology's prospects for discernment and crafted this book. As a result, our first thank-you belongs to the undergraduate students who joined us in the various iterations of the course and helped us refine our approach to introducing Catholic theology from an Ignatian perspective.

We could not have delivered a single session of that course without the assistance of our team of graduate co-instructors, so we also wish to thank all the graduate students who served with us over the years in Marquette's team-taught THEO 1001 class. Their willingness to engage with the ideas found in this book and to wrestle with them in the classroom yielded invaluable insight into what works (and what does not work) for college students, and we are grateful for their honest feedback throughout our drafting process.

We owe an immense debt of gratitude to Brian Bajzek, Deirdre Dempsey, Jen Henery, Jon Metz, and Sean Larsen, our friends and colleagues at Marquette who courageously used portions—or, in some cases, the entirety—of initial drafts of this text in their own classes and provided detailed input that shaped our revisions. We want to acknowledge their generosity in incorporating this material into their classrooms and express our appreciation to all the students in those classes who wrestled with the text in development. Hopefully, teachers and students alike will see the fruit of their thoughtful guidance in the finished product.

We are delighted this text comes to print through Georgetown University Press and are especially grateful to Al Bertrand, the director, for his keen editorial guidance and to two anonymous reviewers for their insightful suggestions that strengthened the text. We also extend our gratitude to Elizabeth Sheridan-Drake, our production coordinator, Francys Reed and the marketing team, and all those at Westchester Publishing Services—particularly our project manager, Sudeshna Dasgupta, and copyeditor, Gillian Dickens—who helped make this finished book a reality.

I (Conor) want to give a note of thanks to a few people who have been especially formative in my own Ignatian journey. Sr. Mary Lynch, SSJ, guided me through the nineteenth annotation—often referred to as Ignatius's *"Spiritual Exercises* in daily life"—when I was a master's student, opening my mind to the breadth of Ignatian spirituality and its prospects for discernment. At Marquette, I have had fruitful conversations about Ignatian spirituality with many of my Jesuit colleagues as well as Michael Dante, director of the university's Faber Center for Ignatian Spirituality, and I thank them all for their accompaniment.

Finally, my family has been a source of Ignatian inspiration for me. My parents demonstrated the power of pausing to prayerfully discern God's call throughout their lives (my late mother even completed certification as a spiritual director) and taught me much of what I know about embracing theology as a way of life. My brother, meanwhile, has quietly been teaching a master class on how to answer the questions at the heart this book through the ways he has consistently established a clear sense of the ultimate values that deserve his priority and has unwaveringly worked to live up to those values in each moment. My wife, Kate, has been a true partner in discernment, and I am grateful for her perpetual efforts to help me live up to my telos as the man God calls me to be. She and our children, Clare and Ryan, provide the only proof I need that the divine can indeed be found when we follow Ignatius's advice and seek God in all things.

I (Ryan) owe an enormous debt of gratitude to my Jesuit brothers. Since entering the Society of Jesus in 2004, I have been blessed to know and be mentored by many good and holy priests. Many pages would be required to thank each one, but the Jesuits mentioned in the dedication have left important traces on my heart and life. I sincerely hope that were these men to read this book, they would see their influence on the text. This book, in a concrete sense, is a way for me to "pay forward" in a small way what I have been given by so many great-souled companions.

Readers will find mentions of the communities to which I belong: the Duns and Hagan families from Cleveland, the worldwide network of Irish musicians and dancers, the Jesuits, and the sisters of the Ladies Ancient Order of Hibernians, whom I serve as chaplain. I am also a member of Alpha Sigma Nu (AΣN), the only honor society permitted to bear the name "Jesuit." Alpha Sigma Nu proudly recognizes and celebrates students who distinguish themselves by embodying the values of scholarship, loyalty, and service. At Marquette University where I teach, five women stand out as embodying Alpha Sigma Nu's values: Deirdre Dempsey, Lynn Griffith, Brigid Kinsella-Alba, Kate Trevey, and AΣN's executive director, Clara Dwyer. When I look at the way these colleagues discerningly serve Marquette's community, I am inspired by the way they are animated by Ignatian spirituality and committed to the values of Jesuit education. So, as a member of Marquette's community, I want to acknowledge them for their leadership and witness to all things Ignatian. They are witnesses to the way Ignatian discernment not only cultivates flourishing and excellence but also empowers one to call forth flourishing and excellence from others. I know this firsthand, so from the bottom of my heart, thank you for your counsel, your witness, your humor, and for allowing me to call you by the greatest of names: friend.

Introduction

Why Bother with Theology?

Life is full of choices. Some are inconsequential, like what to have for lunch. Others are monumental and life-altering, like whether to get married and to whom. What all these choices have in common, however, is that they contribute to making us who we are.

At first glance, this may sound absurd. One can easily imagine how selecting a fiancé(e) could affect one's course of life, but a sandwich? Yet the truth is that every decision shapes us. Obviously, an "I do" at the altar makes someone a spouse, but a BLT at the diner just as convincingly makes a patron something other than a vegetarian. Although not all our choices are equally significant, each one has an impact on the person we become. This is, at a fundamental level, part of what it means to be a human being. As creatures endowed with free will, we have the power to decide who we want to be, and we enact this decision not in one definitive pronouncement but through a whole series of choices that unfold over a lifetime. The task for a human life, then, is to learn how to recognize the power that our choices hold and to use that power purposefully to become the person we most fully long to be.

Great people—the kind who will be remembered by history and admired by generations for the lives they live, the kind we want our kids to grow up to become—are the ones who understand this power and refuse to take their free will for granted. They know that their choices define their lives, and they act accordingly, making sure that they like who they are about to become. By working to align their choices with their deepest convictions, these exemplary humans not only shape themselves but also transform the world around them.

Consider Rosa Parks. In one fateful decision, she helped to spark a movement that dismantled legalized racial segregation in the United States. By all accounts, Parks did not act to start a protest that day. As an active member of the NAACP in Montgomery, Alabama, she likely knew about the possibility of a bus boycott, but other African American women had been arrested for similarly refusing to yield their seats to white passengers, and the boycott had not materialized. Yet Parks did act, and with great courage, because she knew what was at stake aboard that bus on December 1, 1955: Rosa Parks. Convinced by years of resistance to systemic oppression at the hands of white citizens and institutions that she was worth more than the infinitesimal value that US society ascribed to Black persons, Parks said simply, "No, I am not" when asked if she was going to follow the bus driver's order to move. As we now know, this was a choice with profound consequences, but for Parks, it was first and foremost a choice about herself, and she decided that she was, in her own words, "tired of giving in."[1] As a result of this decision, Parks embodied her convictions and became the model of resistance to injustice that we commemorate today.

With respect to the power of choices, Parks's story is illuminating for two reasons. First, she was able to have a powerful impact precisely because she realized her own identity was on the line with the decision she would make. Second, once she recognized the stakes, she was determined to be the person she always believed she could be—a decision that meant aligning her actions with her most strongly held commitments. Practically speaking, then, an effective reaction to the power of our choices requires not only realizing that we shape ourselves through our decisions but also establishing a clear sense of what we value most. Fred Rogers, the Presbyterian minister and icon of kindness behind *Mister Rogers' Neighborhood*, once captured this connection when he acknowledged, "You rarely have time for everything you want in this life, so you need to make choices. And hopefully your choices can come from a deep sense of who you are."[2] His point was that in our exercise of free will, we humans always reveal our priorities because we will never be able to choose every single thing we would like at all times. To make good choices, we need to know our true priorities; otherwise, we will muddle through life, contradicting ourselves at every turn.

The Two Choices Behind Every Choice

The best way to think about the significance of our decisions in light of all these pieces is to say that there are really two choices we need to make in life if we are going to make a difference for ourselves and others in this world. First, we need to decide what matters most to us, so that we will have the "deep sense" of who we are that Mister Rogers emphasized. Second, we need to decide how to act in a fashion consistent with those values. Hence, each time we must make a particular choice, whether about marriage or marshmallows, we are required to make *two* choices that respond to the following questions:

1. What do I really value?
2. How do I live up to those values in this moment?

These questions constitute the two choices behind every choice. They are vital questions, and they are challenging questions, but we seldom give them the consideration they deserve. Instead, we typically plow ahead with each decision without contemplating the connections between them. The main reason for this oversight is that few people feel equipped to answer these questions in a productive fashion.

To answer these questions well, so that we can make good choices and build a life of meaning and purpose, we need two things: theology and discernment.

Granted, this list is a bit self-serving for two theologians to propose, but hear us out. We genuinely believe that theology and discernment are crucial to a well-formed life because no one can answer the first question sufficiently without theology, and no one can answer the second question effectively without discernment. The source of our confidence comes from the nature of these questions and the particular meaning of these two terms.

To begin, consider the first question. When understood as an assessment not just of a person's values in general but as an account of one's most strongly held commitments, this question is basically the question theology was designed to answer. Theology is, after all, the study (-*ology*) of God (*theos*). Although one might be tempted to insist that the study of God can only help someone decide their deepest values if they are already a committed believer and not, say, an atheist or an agnostic, this need not be the case. In fact, such an interpretation presumes an unnecessarily narrow view of God that is not consistent with the way theology conceives its object of study.

The Lutheran theologian Paul Tillich famously defined God in the context of theological reflection as the human person's "ultimate concern."[3] With this formulation, he meant that whatever functions as a person's most fundamental concern—the thing they care about most, the value (or set of values) that motivates their actions—operates as a "god" in their lives. Tillich, as a practicing Lutheran, of course defended the claim that the Christian God ought to be the human person's ultimate concern, but his understanding of the theological role of God in human life is instructive regardless of one's religious affiliations. His definition reveals that every human person, even the atheist and the agnostic, has a "god" in their lives, because we all have something that serves as our ultimate concern.

Now, I realize this assertion is probably going to generate even more skepticism than my opening declaration that every choice forms us, so let me address the objection head-on with a thought experiment. Think for a minute about the career you would like to pursue as an adult. Can you explain why you want to work as a doctor, a lawyer, a teacher, or in some other chosen profession? I suspect you can give a fairly succinct answer: I want to help people, or I want to make a lot of money, or something else. Fair enough. But now, can you explain why you want that outcome? Why do you want to help people, for instance? This is harder to defend, but it is usually still possible to identify something else you value, perhaps the conviction that no one should have to suffer unnecessarily. This is a great commitment, but if I push things a little further and ask why you hold that value, the answer becomes harder to pinpoint and even more difficult to articulate. All the more so if we keep asking why. The difficulty arises because we all eventually get to a point where we do not have additional reasons for the things we think are important; we just know that they are. Or, more accurately, we firmly *believe* that they are important. The value of this conviction is self-evident to us. It needs no justification. We take it as a matter of faith. And this conviction, whatever it is, is our ultimate concern.

The point of theology, as the study of God, is to push us not simply to identify the thing that functions as our ultimate concern but, even more significantly, to determine whether this thing is worth being an ultimate concern at all. This makes theology an essential resource for human decision-making, because it invites a person to identify *and* assess their ultimate concern, ensuring that we are actually serving the God we really want to serve and not some false idol of convenience. In this way, theology introduces critical scrutiny into the first choice behind every choice, replacing the unexamined life that the Greek philosopher Socrates famously insisted was not worth living with a life of meaning through intentionality.

Theology can empower this intentional examination because it exists within an established tradition, a set of common convictions and practices formed over time as people grappled with the question of what is genuinely worthy of humanity's ultimate concern. In this book, we rely on the religious tradition that has shaped us, the authors. We are both Catholic theologians teaching at Marquette University. Conor is a husband and father of two children; Ryan is a Catholic priest (a Jesuit). We thus explore how Christianity defines the most appropriate ultimate concern—the God revealed in Jesus Christ—providing what is essentially an introduction to Catholic Christian theology along the way because this vision of ultimate concern is the one that inspires us and allows us to provide a satisfactory answer to that first choice.

We want to be clear about how we appeal to this tradition in the context of this book. The point of walking through the ins and outs of this theological tradition is not to convince anyone that it presents the "right" answer. Instead, we offer this vision so that you can test the adequacy of your own answer to the first choice behind every choice. We think Catholic Christianity offers the most coherent response to the question of what should matter before all else, and we will explain that coherence so you can develop an answer that is at least equally as persuasive.

This may seem like a lofty task, but it is an indispensable one, because the only way to be the person you want to become is to have a clear sense of what your ultimate, guiding concern is going to be. And the only way to have a clear sense of that ultimate concern is to subject your various options to critical scrutiny. Insofar as theology invites and empowers this scrutiny, it is an essential resource for those who would like to use their choices to construct the life of meaning and purpose that constitutes the fullness of our human potential.

Significantly, this critical analysis represents only half of the work required to make good choices. Once we have established our core convictions, we also need to determine how to live a life that matches those values. If we fail to do this, the thing we call our God will not be our *ultimate* concern but a conditional concern that we freely dismiss to pursue some other value. As the Jesuit priest and theologian Howard Gray explained, one of the things that makes God *God* is that God always asks us to do something: God is always calling us to become ourselves in a more full and complete way. Thus, if one has an ultimate concern that does not lead to action, it is hardly worth calling this thing "God." Or, as Ryan is fond of telling our students, a spirituality without consequences—a spirituality that does not call you to put "skin in the game" of life—is, ultimately, an inconsequential spirituality.

How, then, do we move from identifying our God to determining what this God is asking us to do? How do we go from knowing what we really value (question 1) to ascertaining how we live up to those values in a given moment (question 2)? Well, we need another tool that theology offers. We need discernment.

What Is Discernment? The Ignatian B.U.T.

To get a sense of discernment and its importance, just think about the choices that emerge in the transitions occasioned by the end of high school. The months between graduation and the start of college are filled with questions. The graduate may wonder anxiously, "Did I pick the right college? Will I like it? Will I succeed?" Friends and family add to the anxiety. It seems that at every graduation party, family gathering, and during small talk, someone asks, "So, where are you going to college? When do you leave? What are you going to major in?" It is this last question that is most perilous. Because once it is answered, the most anxiety-provoking question follows: *What're you going to do with that?* It is as though we're expected to have our futures totally figured out . . . before ever setting foot on campus! It's as though everyone expects you to be able to answer the two questions behind every choice: *What do I really value?* and *How do I live up to those values?*

A story. A few years ago, I (Ryan) attended a graduation party where family and friends had been invited. Amid the typical awkwardness, and while I waited at the grill for a burger, I overheard a remarkable exchange. Aunt Sissy stepped into the midst of a group of graduates. She introduced herself and asked the young man to her right an unexpected question: *So, who will you be when you graduate?* The poor kid was caught off-guard and stammered out an answer. She posed this question to every student in the group, and then, for the next thirty minutes, they had a real conversation.

Aunt Sissy dared to raise a question most of us never think to ask others, let alone to pose to ourselves: *Who will you be?* This is not, to be sure, an everyday sort of question. Every day we make a ton of decisions about what to eat, where to go, and how to spend our time. But there are some decisions that, as Conor mentioned, are more impactful. Some decisions ask us to take a stand and to commit ourselves to an ultimate concern. I started with my story about Aunt Sis because she was asking the question at the heart of discernment. Because "discernment" isn't an everyday sort of word, let me tell you *what* it is, *how* Conor and I understand it, and *why* we want to share some ideas about it with you.

First, a Latin lesson. "Discern" comes from the Latin *discernere* and means "to separate, or to distinguish." To *discern* requires one to examine and evaluate a reality. When we *discern*, we sift the good from the bad and distinguish the better from the worse. One would expect a restaurant's head chef to have a *discerning* palate, meaning her experience enables her to judge the quality of a dish's flavor. A talent scout has a *discerning* ear that can hear the promise in a singer's voice. A recruiter needs a *discerning* eye to recognize the next "star" among a field of players. A *discerning* judge sifts through and evaluates the legal issues to apply the law wisely and fairly. It should be obvious from these examples that *discernment* isn't an abstract formula or one-size-fits-all calculation. After all, discerning the next great wide receiver and discerning the next break-out artist are two different things. What these examples of discernment *do* have in common is that they are all skills that make those who have them good at their jobs. Discernment is an art or a skill in making informed decisions. And, like any skill, discernment can be practiced and developed.

In its typical use, *discernment* refers to a way of making decisions in a fashion that aligns our choices with our deepest convictions. This is a skill everyone needs to develop to respond to the question, "How do I live up to my values in this moment?" Conor and I, however, use the word *discernment* in a way that reflects our experiences as theologians. Conor and I both have been deeply formed by the spirituality of Saint Ignatius of Loyola (1491–1556), who was the founder and first General Superior of the Society of Jesus (the Jesuits). Consequently, we describe ourselves as having an *Ignatian* spirituality. Ignatius, we believe, is a reliable guide who can assist us in developing a decision-making process for negotiating life's choices. He believed that Jesus Christ was calling every person to the fullness of human existence: a life lived in relationship with God. He developed discernment as a way of listening for and responding to this call. Ignatian discernment is therefore a spiritual exercise that looks at the heart's movements—its joys and hopes and fears and doubts—and tries to distinguish where and how God is at work in a person's life and where God is leading. Concisely, *discernment is a prayerful method for discovering and accepting who God calls you to become.*

As Conor mentioned, life presents us with a series of choices. Yet not every choice, not every career, not every calling, is right for everyone. Not everyone is called to double-major in chemistry and theology (although it helps a med school application!). Not everyone is called to be a physical therapist or a teacher or to do a year of service. Sometimes it feels as if we are paralyzed by choice because we know that if we choose one thing, it means closing ourselves off to other options. But at some point, we must commit to something. Such is the lesson Harry Potter learns from Professor Dumbledore: "It is our choices, Harry, that show us what we truly are, far more than our abilities."[4] We hope this book helps readers to make the kinds of choices that show who they are and assist them in becoming who they are called to be. We do this by introducing, and inviting readers to practice, the exercise of discernment.

Let us go back to Saint Ignatius and Ignatian spirituality. Saint Ignatius was an organizational genius. His years as General Superior of the Jesuits were spent writing the *Constitutions* (the Jesuits' organizational playbook), overseeing missionary efforts, negotiating political and church conflicts, composing and responding to thousands of letters, and helping develop the network of schools for which the Jesuits are best known (for academic excellence and, in the United States, basketball). Ignatius was also a spiritual master and offered a carefully constructed way of making good decisions. He called these the "Rules for the Discernment of Spirits." We will talk about these rules later in the book. Right now, let us look at how he introduces the "Rules" or "Guidelines" for practicing discernment. Here is Father Timothy Gallagher's translation of Ignatius's introduction: "Rules for *becoming aware* and *understanding* to some extent the different movements which are caused in the soul, the good, *to receive them*, and the bad *to reject them*."[5] In this sentence, Father Gallagher traces Ignatian discernment's threefold paradigm. Conor and I find his way of putting things helpful, and we have structured our book to follow this model. Ignatian discernment, Father Gallagher writes, involves three steps:

BE AWARE
UNDERSTAND
TAKE ACTION (ACCEPT/REJECT)[6]

Because I have a bad memory, and because I think this is a good paradigm, let me try to make it "stick" by calling it the "Ignatian B.U.T." Before you think I'm being sophomoric, give me a chance to explain.

Have you ever been so excited about an idea or opportunity that your mind whirls with enthusiasm? You start to formulate elaborate plans and then, suddenly, you second-guess yourself. You pause and ponder, *"But what if it doesn't work? But what if this is too good to be true?"* Or perhaps you have been overwhelmed by fear as you face a task you have never done before. You assume there is no way you can possibly manage, so you resign yourself to giving up. Before you walk away, however, you find yourself asking, *"But what if I can do this? But what if I am supposed to give it a try?"* That one word—*but*—causes us to pause, invites us to reexamine the situation, and gives us an opportunity to rethink the viability of our ideas and assumptions. The *but* does not necessarily squash one's enthusiasm or eliminate one's doubts, but it does give one a chance to face squarely the reality of the situation.

What we call the Ignatian B.U.T. describes a disciplined practice of embracing the pause that this "but what if . . ." instinct invites. It allows us to step back from the frenzy of our daily lives, take stock of the situation, and act in a way that is consistent with the sort of person we desire to become. With this practice, we deliberately "step back" before we "step forward." This process entails *becoming aware* of our context and situation, *understanding* how God might be at work in this moment, and *taking action* by responding to the way God is calling us in our lives. As we see it, the Ignatian B.U.T. is a crucial part of any good decision-making process. This book will explore how Christian theology can contribute to and inform the decisions we make using this model.

Let me assure you that our goal is not to indoctrinate you or—as students often fear—to shove religion down your throat. Our goal, instead, is to help you raise and then to better answer two deeply human questions every one of us must grapple with: *Who am I?* and *Why am I here?* We think that Christian theology has a great deal to offer in this process because it gives compelling and exciting answers to these questions, so we want to briefly outline how we understand the theological dimensions of the Ignatian B.U.T. in a broadly accessible fashion and how that informs the structure of this book.

The Theological Structure of This Book

A good way to read this book is to approach it as a text that can help to shape how you live. As Conor and I see it, theology should not be taught as just "one more subject" a student must take to get credits. Theology, for us, is a way of life that helps us identify how God is at work in the world and then to discern how to live a life consistent with the values that God reveals. This is because theology reflects on the nature of human reality from the perspective of Christian faith. Every aspect of our human reality, as a result, is open to theological interpretation. Thus, by drawing on the resources of Christian faith, we explore how theology can assist readers in (1) *becoming aware* of God's presence in one's life, (2) gaining an *understanding* of how God stirs within and moves the heart, and (3) *taking action* to become who one is called to be. At its core, this is a book about discerning and embracing a life that will allow you to flourish as a human being. Theological reflection, we believe, can supply resources to help you toward this goal.

We are aware that students begin their study of theology with a wide variety of backgrounds. Some believe in God (theists), some do not (atheists), and others are uncertain (agnostics). Some have had positive experiences studying and practicing religion; others have had negative experiences. Some readers may even expect—or fear—that Conor and I are going to get on our theological soapboxes and proclaim, "This is the truth!" Sorry to disappoint, but we're not going to do that. To be sure, Conor and I are committed Roman Catholics. But this book is not an attempt to tell you how we're right and other traditions are wrong. Instead, it is our effort to share with readers *why* we find Roman Catholic theology meaningful and compelling. For us, our faith is not something extra, something we dedicate an hour to each week. Faith—complete with its lights and shadows, its doubts and commitments—is an integral part of our lives because it helps us understand who we are. I am who I am—Fr. Ryan Duns, SJ, and not Dr. Ryan Duns, MD—because of my faith. No doubt, I could have been a Catholic medical doctor. But as I prayed and discerned the deepest desires of my heart . . . another path appeared, and I felt called to try it out. Even if it is not always easy or without sacrifice, I can't imagine my life any other way. If we can help students to appreciate how the study of theology might help them to embrace their callings, then our efforts in writing this book will be rewarded.

This book has three parts. In part I, we explore Ignatian spirituality through practices of *becoming aware*. In these chapters, we ask readers to reflect on their context—*where* they are—and to examine their spiritual experiences—*how* they are. Throughout, we introduce theological narratives and themes to supply a framework for these reflections. Although we want to inform readers about theology, we also want to suggest how theology can be formative. To this end, in each chapter, we offer a "spiritual exercise" aimed at cultivating awareness or, to use another word, *attentiveness*. Father Howard Gray used to say that being attentive means allowing reality to be fully present on its terms, not ours.[7] Attentiveness demands courage because it requires one to look *at* realities people often look *past*.

In part II, we consider the practices that contribute to growth in *understanding*. Here we draw on Saint Ignatius's *Spiritual Exercises*, especially the sections reflecting on the life of Jesus, to suggest how one might sift through the movements of the heart and deepen a sense of how God works in one's life. The exercises accompanying these chapters are meant to develop an attitude of *reverence*. Once we have grown attentive to reality and welcome it on its terms, we can discover and reverence God's presence there. As Jesus's own life shows, God is no less present in moments of boundless joy and beauty than in moments of great sorrow and injustice. By developing an attitude of reverence, one can grow proficient in recognizing God's presence in all things.

In part III, we draw on St. Ignatius's "Rules for Discernment" and look at concrete ways discernment leads one to *take action*. Having *become aware* of one's context and spiritual experiences and having gained an *understanding* of these movements, one can become who God is calling one to be. The exercises in these chapters explore, then, what it means to *devote* oneself to accepting one's vocation. Good discernment enables one to grow more integrated and to remain steadfast in one's vocation even when faced with difficulty and opposition. Devotion does not require a person to commit oneself to *this* or *that* task but, rather, to embrace and live out one's God-given mission, even when it brings difficult or unpleasant pieces with it.

Conor and I are sensitive to the pressures and stresses students confront daily. We know something about these anxieties, doubts, hopes, and dreams. We have accompanied students through breakdowns and breakups, as well as seen remarkable breakthroughs as they take steps to become who they are called to be. We wrote this book because we are convinced that Ignatian discernment can transform lives for the better. We cannot tell readers whether to major in business or biology, go to graduate school, or do a year of service. We can, however, suggest how techniques of Ignatian discernment might contribute to what Christians would recognize as a well-lived life. Discernment, we hope to show, does not tell us *what* to choose but tutors us *how* to make decisions aimed at accepting *who* we should become. For those ready and willing to undertake this pilgrimage: Welcome.

Facts, Opinions, and Theological Beliefs

We now want to give you our first practical exercise. You can think of it as some light stretching, or a warm-up, to be done in preparation for the weightier practices in the subsequent chapters. For this first exercise to work, however, we need to discuss an important theological distinction: the relationship between facts, opinions, and beliefs.

Many students are taught to distinguish between facts and opinions. These are helpful categories because there is a genuine difference between the two, and we can get into significant difficulties if we confuse them. A fact is something we can verify or prove based on hard evidence. Facts must correspond to reality, or they will be disproven and therefore shown not to be a fact. It is a fact that Abraham Lincoln was the sixteenth president of the United States, but it is *not* a fact that Abraham Lincoln had the first Twitter account because one of these claims is true and the other is false. To claim that something is a fact is to assert that it is a faithful representation of the real world, a claim that others can interrogate and decide whether it is right or wrong.

Opinions, meanwhile, are statements of preference or taste. When we offer our opinion on a matter, we share our subjective view of a thing. Opinions are personal, and for that reason, they are not easily proven or disproven in the way that facts are. If someone says, "I think that chocolate is the best ice cream flavor," we can counter with our own opinion that "mint chocolate chip is obviously superior," but we will never settle this argument in the same way that a quick Google search can resolve a dispute about whether Lincoln was born in Illinois (as Ryan incorrectly assumes—but that's not why it's called the "Land of Lincoln!") or Kentucky (true fact). We can muster evidence to support our opinions, but they remain subjective claims that correspond to our internal thoughts and personal preferences rather than a shared external reality. No matter how much someone might disagree with me about mint chocolate chip, it will remain the case that *for me*, it is the best ice cream flavor. I can continue to hold this position even if everyone else in the world disagrees with me because it is my opinion. This is a key difference from facts. Two people can hold contradictory opinions and carry on just fine, but two contradictory *facts* cannot apply at the same time, because for one to be true, the other must logically be false and thus not a fact.

As we said, this distinction between facts and opinions is important, but it can become problematic when we assume it applies to every possible truth claim. Unfortunately, this seems to be a most prevalent assumption, and it leads to the conclusion that anything that is not a fact must therefore be an opinion. The result is that whenever people hear a truth claim, they quickly try to group it into one of these two categories by asking, "Can I prove or disprove that?" If the answer is yes, they decide it is a fact and then look for the evidence to verify or debunk the claim. If the answer is no, they assume it is an opinion and then imagine that whether it is true or not does not make much difference because you can have "your truth" (chocolate ice cream is better) and I can have "my truth" (mint chocolate chip ice cream is better) at the same time.

The world and its truth claims are not so neatly divided into facts and opinions, however. Some truth claims cannot be proved or disproved like a fact but also cannot be left in the your truth/my truth space of opinion because the assertions they make matter a great deal. For instance, if a married man says, "My wife loves me," we do not respond by saying, "Well, that's your opinion." He would not be much consoled by the idea that this is "his truth," because it leaves open the possibility that his wife could have her truth and it might just involve the opposite claim (i.e., that she does not love her husband). And yet, it would not be quite right to call "my wife loves me" a fact either. How would one measure, test for, and prove or disprove love? Certainly, spouses demonstrate their affection for each other in meaningful ways: thoughtful gifts, kind words, and tender embraces. These actions create a record of "evidence" to support the conviction that their spouse loves them, but there is no objective "standard" of love, no quantitative "love meter" to measure the love a couple shares. That a wife loves her husband is something the husband can ultimately only accept as an act of faith because it is an act that expresses a fundamental trust, a belief, in the relationship. It is not a demonstrable fact, like the acceleration of gravity (-9.8 m/s^2), but neither is it an opinion. Instead, the nature of love points to the need for a third category that transcends this distinction: belief.

Beliefs are judgments informed by experience that shape how we live our lives. They are based on and take account of facts, which means that we can evaluate whether a particular belief is justified, but they are not simply facts. Hence, a husband's belief that his wife loves him can be called into question by the fact that his wife cheated on him, but that fact alone does not define the belief. Perhaps the couple has worked through this betrayal and now has a stronger relationship than before, making his belief fully justified despite the history of infidelity. The facts matter, but belief involves more than just the facts.

Meanwhile, beliefs are more significant than opinions because beliefs make truth claims that have real consequences. A husband who believes his wife loves him will behave much differently than one who has come to believe that his wife hates his guts. No one would be surprised by this difference because we recognize that beliefs impact behavior. In fact, if there were no difference, we would doubt that the husband in the former example truly believed that his wife loved him as he claimed! People who believe something make a claim that this conviction corresponds to reality, and they act accordingly. The assumption that we can learn something about a person's beliefs from their behaviors (and vice versa) demonstrates that there is something more than opinion at stake, for it matters a great deal if a person's belief matches reality, but if one maintains a skewed opinion (and thinks that rocky road is the best ice cream flavor, God forbid!), it is no skin off my nose or anyone else's.

In this book, we will be talking about a considerable number of theological beliefs. These are not all demonstrably "provable" in the way that fact claims are—despite defenses from great Christian thinkers like St. Thomas Aquinas and others, there is no once and for all proof for the existence of God—but this does not mean these beliefs are false. Just as importantly, it does not mean they are opinions. On the contrary, we will be looking at the theological beliefs that Christians maintain *must* be true for their lives and the world to make any sense at all. Like all beliefs, these theological beliefs matter a great deal. They therefore have a direct impact on discernment because they make truth claims about what people ought to value above all else (the ultimate concern question) and how they ought to live their lives if that God really is the ultimate concern in their lives. These beliefs are rooted in facts and experiences, so we will be talking about both those things too, but ultimately, the study of theology asks us to transcend the simple fact/opinion dichotomy to examine questions on a much different, and much more consequential, plane. Our most basic request, then, is that you open yourself to the possibility of asking questions about belief, so that you can define the things you believe and then discern how to lead the life that flows from asserting that those convictions are true.

To prepare you for this task, we can now offer the first of the spiritual exercises we mentioned earlier in this introduction. You will find one like it at the end of every chapter, and the point, again, is not to coerce you into believing something but instead to demonstrate how theology can be a useful tool for you in your own life. Many academic books tell readers about the book's topic; this book is different in that it invites—or challenges—you to experience some of the content for yourself. As far as we're concerned, it's one thing to read a book about football or soccer but another thing entirely to get out on the field to play. To get the ball rolling, then, let's start with a brief exercise on trust and the matter of belief.

Meditation: The Grounds for Belief

1. Use your imagination to see your best friend. Think back on your times together.
2. What proof would you offer that they are your friend? Is there any *one* thing that proclaims, "This is proof. Nothing more is needed." Or, perhaps, you find yourself taking account of a host of experiences.
3. Think about how these experiences converge and confirm your belief. It's probably not *one* experience of honesty, or *one* good time, or *one* act of forgiveness, that testifies to your friendship. More likely, it is a series of small things that, singly, don't mean much. But add them up and you see the richness and depth of your relationship.
4. What supports the trust you have in your friendship? Is there a way to convince another person of your friend's unique qualities and character?
5. Our bet: you wouldn't give a laundry list of qualities. Instead, you'd say, "Well, you just have to get to know them if you want to see what I see. I can tell you about my beliefs, but at the end of the day, you won't know them like I do unless you take the risk of getting to know the person yourself."
6. Will you be open to studying theology in a way that includes learning *what* Christians believe but also, perhaps, coming to learn *how* and *why* they believe what they do?

Key Terms and Ideas

- Two choices behind every choice: whenever we face a practical decision, we are ultimately making two choices, one about what we really value (which we have hopefully decided in advance) and one about how we remain true to that value in the moment.
- Theology: literally the study (*-ology*) of God (*theos*), but more specifically in this book, theology is a whole way of life that involves reflection on one's most important values and deepest commitments so that one can recognize and respond to the ways God calls each person to their fullest potential.
- Ultimate concern: Paul Tillich's description of what theologians mean when they say they study "God." The idea is that whatever functions as a person's most fundamental concern, the thing they care about the most, operates as a "god" in their lives, directing their actions. Theology helps people examine whether their ultimate concern is worthy of being a god in this way.
- Discernment: the art (and skill) of making informed decisions so that these choices align with one's deepest convictions; in its more specific Ignatian sense, discernment is a prayerful method for discovering and accepting who God is calling us to become.
- Ignatian B.U.T.: *become aware, understand, take action;* the three essential steps for effective discernment based on the insights of St. Ignatius's *Spiritual Exercises.*
- Facts, opinions, beliefs: facts are objectively verifiable claims about reality; opinions are subjective assertions of taste; beliefs are judgments about reality informed, but not defined, by facts that lead to consequences in action. Theology involves the evaluation of beliefs, especially in relation to facts.

Recommended Resources

"The Olive," produced by Fairfield University Media Center, 2009 (available at https://youtu.be/MSvOPtq30Xw).

Short video recounting the life of St. Ignatius of Loyola, highlighting his own experience of discernment and explaining the roots of his unique approach to the art of making informed decisions.

Harry Potter and the Chamber of Secrets, directed by Chris Columbus, Warner Brothers, 2002.

The film includes Dumbledore's exchange with Harry cited in this chapter. Analyzed in the context of Harry's journey, the specific concerns that generate Dumbledore's response illuminate the relationship between identity and choice and thus discernment.

James Martin, SJ, *The Jesuit Guide to (Almost) Everything: A Spirituality for Real Life* (New York: Harper Collins, 2010).

The whole book provides an accessible introduction to the Jesuits' unique "way of proceeding" that underlies our text. Chapter 2, "The Six Paths," is especially helpful for students seeking to situate themselves in relation to theology and the first question behind every choice.

"Rosa Parks—Civil Rights Activist: Mini Bio," *Biography* (available at https://youtu.be/v8A9gvb5Fh0).

Short video connecting Rosa Parks's fateful decision to her faith and values, showing the two questions behind every choice in action.

Notes

1. Rosa Parks and Gregory J. Reed, *Quiet Strength: The Faith, the Hope, and the Heart of a Woman Who Changed a Nation* (Grand Rapids, MI: Zondervan, 1994), 23.
2. Fred Rogers, *The World According to Mister Rogers: Important Things to Remember* (New York: Hyperion, 2003), 32.
3. See Paul Tillich, *Systematic Theology: Reason and Revelation; Being and God*, vol. 1 (Chicago: University of Chicago Press, 1951), 11–13. Tillich is a problematic theologian to engage because reports after his death indicated that he had a history of abusive sexual relationships with women that exploited his positions of power and prestige. His own way of living thus casts a necessary suspicion on the impact of his theological claims, given the inconsistencies between his work and his life. We present his categories here because we believe they are the best way to open the theological questions at the heart of Christianity to as wide a range of believers (and nonbelievers) as possible. We also want readers to wrestle honestly with his abusive past. See Hilary Jerome Scarsella and Stephanie Krehbiel, "Sexual Violence: Christian Theological Legacies and Responsibilities," *Religion Compass* 13, no. 9 (September 2019): e12337.

4. J. K. Rowling, *Harry Potter and the Chamber of Secrets* (New York: Scholastic, 1999), 333.

5. Timothy M. Gallagher, OMV, *The Discernment of Spirits: An Ignatian Guide for Everyday Living* (New York: Crossroad, 2005), 7. Emphasis added.

6. Gallagher, *The Discernment of Spirits*, 7.

7. Howard Gray, SJ, "As I See It: Ignatius's Method for Letting God Shine through Life's Realities," *Company* 16, no. 3 (1999): 30.

PART I

Becoming Aware

1

Where Are You?

To tackle discernment's central question—*Who will you become?*—we need to step back and ask, *Where are you?* This question is discernment's bedrock. We can't move toward the future if we have no idea where we have been or how we got to where we are now. *Where are you?* is also key to theological reflection. In this chapter, we look at the personal and theological significance of posing this question.

When students arrive at our Theology 1001 course, many are nervous that it's going to be one long Bible study. We certainly *do* study the Old and New Testament, but Conor and I want students to approach the Bible in a particular way. We want them to appreciate that, for believers, the Word of God speaks to our lives because it comes from our lives. Indeed, the Bible contains many examples of the ways God has spoken, or "revealed" God's self, to people. In a book about discernment where we are trying to figure out how God moves within our hearts, we cannot skip over the scriptures. We do this, however, in an unconventional way. In what follows, I want to invite readers to begin to cultivate an "Ignatian imagination" by reflecting on a passage from the Book of Genesis. Next, I want to invite you to continue developing this imagination as we stand by the ocean and ponder life's meaning. Finally, I introduce readers to the *Examen*, a powerful spiritual tool that assists users in finding God's presence within their lives. It is a prayer technique that looks *backward* to move us *forward*.

Genesis 3:9

Fun fact: the Bible is not a single book. The word "bible" comes from the Greek word for "books," plural, and that's what we have: a collection of books gathered over many centuries. In a standard Roman Catholic Bible, there are seventy-three books: forty-six in the Old Testament, twenty-seven in the New Testament. What we believe about these books is that they are divinely inspired. By this, we mean that through the Bible's poetry and prose, its stories and its symbols, God speaks to believers. When Christians read the Bible, we are not primarily trying to extract information from it. Instead, we are opening ourselves to listen to it and to allow the Word of God to inspire us. Although we certainly can be *informed* by reading the Bible (you can, after all, take lots of classes about it), our interest in this book is how God speaks to us and *forms* us through the scriptures.

Let me say something about deciphering references to the Bible. Above you see "Genesis 3:9." The first word—Genesis—is the title of the specific book within the Bible. The first number refers to a chapter. The number after the colon refers to a verse because every chapter in the Bible has numbered verses (usually a sentence or two that constitute a complete thought). So, Genesis 1:1. This means "The Book of Genesis, chapter 1, verse 1." If you look it up, you get: "In the beginning when God created the heavens and the earth." How about Acts 2:15. This refers to the Acts of the Apostles, chapter 2, verse 15, and records Saint Peter insisting that the early Christians' enthusiasm was a sign that they were enlivened by the Holy Spirit and not intoxicated: "Indeed, these people are not drunk, as you suppose, for it is only nine o'clock in the morning." You'll often find a hyphen, which means that there's a range of verses. Although it might have been seductive in its day, let's look at "The Song of Solomon 4:1–2" for an example of how *not* to write a love poem if you want a date. The passage reads, "Your hair is a flock of goats, moving down the slopes of Gilead. Your teeth are like a flock of shorn ewes that have come up from the washing." Now, here's one that is going to take some imagination to grapple with: 2 Kings 2:23–25. This means: Second Kings (implying the existence of First Kings), chapter 2, verses 23 through 25. Here's the text: "Elisha went up from there to Bethel and while he was going up on the way, some small boys came out of the city and jeered at him, saying, 'Go away, baldhead! Go away, baldhead!' When Elisha turned around and saw them, he cursed them in the name of the LORD. Then two she-bears came out of the woods and mauled forty-two of the boys." And you thought the Bible would be boring! So what's the divine message? Perhaps it is nothing more—or less!—than a mother's advice: "Do not be rude to prophets or strangers. If you mock them, something bad will happen." We'll talk more later about biblical interpretation, so, for now, I'm happy if you can decipher scriptural references.

Even if you've never read Genesis 2–3 (Book of Genesis, chapters 2 through 3), you've probably *heard* of Adam and Eve. A recap. God creates the earth and heavens and, out of the earth, forms the first human ('*adam* is Hebrew for "humanity"). God gives Adam a tour of Paradise and warns him not to eat of the Tree of the Knowledge of Good and Evil. Then it occurs to God: this guy is going to be lonely. So God makes more creatures, though none of them turns out to be a suitable partner for Adam. Thus, God causes the man to fall asleep, takes one of his ribs, and creates the first woman. Later, the woman has an unfortunate encounter with a snake who tempts her into eating the forbidden fruit (note: it says *fruit*. Artists often depict it as an apple, but it could have been a kiwi). The woman shares the fruit with the man. And boom: their eyes are opened, and they realize, to their dismay, that they are naked. It goes downhill from there.

You may say, "Father Ryan, do you expect me to buy this *myth*?" Well, biblical "myths" are not fairy tales. Myths are better seen as "structuring stories," narratives that may not be factually true but are, nevertheless, bearers of truth. They convey truth in a way meant to inspire belief, with all the consequences beliefs demand and not merely the assent or rejection that facts typically entail. Consequently, Catholics read the Creation accounts found in Genesis as symbolic stories and not science (yes, there are *two* narratives describing how God created the world. Read them yourself: Genesis 1:1–2:3 and Genesis 2:4–25). These stories reveal the way God lovingly creates the world, deems it good, and has a special role for humans to play within it. It is not, for Catholics, a textbook. In fact, in 2014, Pope Francis said the following:

When we read about Creation in Genesis, we run the risk of imagining God was a magician, with a magic wand able to do everything.
But that is not so . . . He created human beings and let them develop
according to the internal laws that he gave to each one so they would
reach their fulfillment. . . . Evolution in nature is not opposed to the
notion of Creation, because evolution presupposes the creation of
beings that evolve.[1]

Contrary to widespread belief, science is not the enemy of faith. In fact,
Catholics believe the two are compatible (Gregor Mendel, the father of
modern genetics, was a priest; so was Georges Lemaître, the father of
the Big Bang theory). This is where, I think, an Ignatian imagination can
help readers to appreciate how God speaks to us through the Bible. Using
our imaginations, Ignatius saw, permits us to enter the Bible's narratives
not to learn about DNA or physics but, rather, to encounter God because
of whom DNA and physics exist in the first place.

So, what do I mean by "Ignatian imagination"? Well, I think the
best way to get at this is by watching kindergartners play. My niece
Emma imagined herself as Dora the Explorer. With her brother Quinn
(Swiper), they went on adventures. These days, my nephew Con occu-
pies himself for hours pretending to be Spiderman. He inhabits these
stories in way that makes them real. He's not watching Spiderman but
enacting the hero's role, and I hope he's learning to be heroic by imagining himself doing heroic things. When we approach the scriptures
with an Ignatian imagination, when we risk putting ourselves into
these stories, we find that the stories become *our* stories. Ignatius
called this the "composition of place," meaning that we "compose" or
put ourselves into the stories that we read. We allow ourselves to play a
role in the narrative and open ourselves to the ways the Bible speaks to
our reality. Ignatius often achieved this by inviting the reader of scripture to engage their five senses, imagining the sights, sounds, smells,
tastes, and sensations within a scene as though they were there
themselves.

Let's exercise our imaginations by putting ourselves into Genesis 3.
Adam and Eve hear God walking through the garden and hide. They

are ashamed of being naked. Perhaps they, like us, are suddenly self-conscious. *Before* they ate the fruit, they were comfortable as they were. *Now* they know themselves as vulnerable and exposed. We all can recall times when we were embarrassed or ashamed. Maybe it was getting caught in a lie, giving a wrong answer, or losing a game. We might have said, "I want to disappear," meaning that we, like Adam and Eve, wanted to hide.

Aware of their nakedness, they make loincloths for themselves (Genesis 3:7). Just in time, too, because soon, "They heard the sound of the LORD God walking in the garden at the time of the evening breeze, and the man and his wife hid themselves from the presence of the LORD God among the trees of the garden. But the LORD God called to the man, and said, to him, 'Where are you?'" (Genesis 3:8–9). It never ceases to amaze me that this is God's first question in the Bible. God does not say, "What were you thinking?" or "Are you serious? I *just* told you. . . ." God's first question to Eve and Adam reflects tenderness, concern, and love: *Where are you?* If we use our imaginations and put ourselves into this scene, if we cower behind a tree and hope for God to walk past us without noticing, how do *we* hear the question raised to each of us: *Where are you?*

Sit with this for a moment: where are *you* right now in your life? How did *you* get here? What choices—good and bad—have brought you here? Of what are you proud? Of what are you ashamed and afraid? God, as revealed in this passage, is not angry or vengeful. This is a God who cares about creation and is willing to go out in search of it. Who is God? God is the Holy One who creates and cares enough to seek us out. Who are *you*? From the biblical standpoint, you are a precious creation, and you are so beloved by God that God will seek you out *even in* those moments when you are ashamed and afraid.

This is the stuff of discernment. As we practice it, discernment begins when we dare to say, "But what if. . . ." Here, the "But" invites us to risk looking at how we got to where we are, how our choices have formed (or deformed) us, and to question how the God who creates-and-cares might have been with us all along, loving us and calling out to us as individuals. The reality, for many of us, is that we simply don't reflect much on these matters. We remember things that happened to us, but do we take time to think about how our choices have led us to where we are now? How well do we really know ourselves? We get so caught up in living toward the future that we forget how we arrived at the present. In times when we are ashamed and afraid, we can be tempted to think that we have been abandoned by God. Yet Genesis 3:9 challenges us to discern— that is, to pause, to reflect, and to reexamine our lives and experiences. We can step back and say, "But what if God has been with me, searching for me, calling out to me, this whole time?"

As God's first biblical question shows, when we discern, we look *back* at our history to discover how God has been moving our hearts and guiding our lives, so that we can start writing our *future* story in a way that allows us to be integrated, flourishing, and—dare we say—holy persons. This is an ongoing task, one requiring a deepening self-knowledge and the acceptance that there are places where we still need to grow and mature. As we read the scriptures, we hear in God's question, *Where are you?*, an invitation to self-reflection. When we put ourselves into the text using our Ignatian imaginations, we discover that the entire Bible—from Genesis to Revelation—is a resource for discerning and coming to know who God is and who God invites us to become.

Please, do not flee this question. Ponder God's *Where are you?* Consider: Who are you that God cares for *you*? Take a moment to peer into the depths of your heart and ask what it would mean to be called by God in so intimate a way? God, as depicted in Genesis 3:9, is not aloof or indifferent to us. God wants to be *with* us, and when we have strayed or fallen or tried to hide . . . God *seeks* us out and calls us by name. At the heart of any and every discernment process is *becoming aware*, *understanding*, and *taking action* in response to the God who creates-and-cares calling us, as individuals and communities, by name. Throughout this book, you will have many chances to ask yourself *Who are you* and to consider *Who* God is calling you to become.

As much as God's question opens us up to new discoveries about ourselves, it also reveals a great deal about God. Today, God gets depicted as peevish and vengeful, an accountant who tallies up naughty things so we can be punished for eternity. Of course, there are depictions of a violent God in the Bible. We need to take these narratives seriously, too. But at this stage, I find it heartening that God's first question to humans reflects a God who searches for those who are hidden. Let's look at Jesus's first question in the Gospel of John. Two guys are following Jesus, trying to figure out *who* this guy is. Jesus notices: "What are you looking for?" (John 1:38). He then invites them to learn by walking with him. Moreover, Jesus's stories regularly depict God as feverishly searching for what has been lost (read Luke 15). For Christians, this is important because we do not believe in a God who is detached and cold but, rather, in one who is keenly interested in each of us. We believe in a God who notices us and seeks us even when we're hiding. Sure, we can know about this God through academic study (theology). But we also believe that we can know this God through prayer because this God continues to call us into relationship. When we discern, we risk hearing Jesus's invitation directed to each of us: "Come and see" (John 1:39).

Imaginatively put yourself in the Garden again. Hear the branches swishing and footsteps booming. Panic. "Oh, God! It's . . . God!" Duck behind a tree and control your breathing. What are you afraid of? Whatever it is, name it. When people come to me for spiritual advice, I start the same way: *Think of something you will never, ever, tell me. I will never ask what this is.* But I do ask, *Why?* The answer is always the same: fear. Fear of being ashamed, of being judged, of being rejected. Fear leads us to hide ourselves and keeps us skulking behind trees. But hear the gentle words of the God who created you: *Where are you?* Step out from the tree and imagine seeing yourself as your Creator sees you. Allow God's assessment of creation—"It is good"—to fall on you. Wherever and however you are now, this is your launch point. Owning this, saying boldly, *Here I am*, is the first step along discernment's transformative pilgrimage.

So far, we have done two things. First, we learned to decipher biblical references and began to get a sense for how Catholics understand the Bible. There's more to be said about this. At this point, I'm glad (1) if you're still reading and (2) if you're warming to the idea that the Bible has something to say to us today. Second, using the idea of the Ignatian imagination, I suggested how one might enter into the biblical texts. Catholics regard the Bible as divine Revelation, which means it is simultaneously *informative* (we learn about God) and *formative* (God speaks to us through the Word). Imaginatively dwelling in Genesis 3:9 permits us to hear God's question—*Where are you?*—with our own ears. Entering into this text begins to introduce us to a God who is interested in and intimately involved with our lives. Through the prayerful use of imagination, we encounter a God who creates (Genesis 1:1), who searches (Genesis 3:9), and who, in Jesus, invites (John 1:39).

Still, you may be skeptical. "OK, Duns, we get it. You're a priest and you believe in God. But where's your proof? Why should I believe in *your* God and not in Zeus or Cthulhu?" Alas, I do not have a knock-down proof for God. If I did, I'd be rich and famous. Nevertheless, if you permit me another story, I may suggest how we can use God's question, "Where are you?" in a way that leads us back to God.

Searching by the Seashore: *Where Are You?*

In a book entitled *The Varieties of Religious Experience*, American philosopher and psychologist William James distinguishes between "once-born" and "twice-born" souls. The "once-born" seems to make one's way through life with few struggles or spiritual dilemmas. This is one for whom all is right with the world and faith is easy and assumed. I don't know many people like this and, to be frank, those I do know are really annoying because they're always chipper. I'm more familiar with James's "sick souls" who cannot turn away from the world's pain and suffering, who cannot avoid asking questions about life's purpose. These are people who stare into the abyss and refuse to blink at the nothingness. Yet a shift can occur within the sick soul, a healing that delivers one from despair to a feeling of unity and wholeness within oneself and the world. This "twice-born" person is one in whom spiritual dissonance has given way to harmony. I find this type of person compelling because they have insight into our struggles and, if they have religious faith, they have it because they feel as though they have been "saved" from the darkness by a healing and redeeming source.

I reckon most of us are of the "sick soul" variety. From a young age we're told to excel, to compete, to score. We get involved in clubs, cram for tests, lose sleep over exams, and work hard to burnish our resumes. But then . . . the bottom drops out. We don't get into the college we wanted, or we're not good at our major, or we don't get the internship or job we want. A parent or relative dies, a divorce breaks up a family, a trauma interrupts life. Plunged into darkness, it's like the world's color drains and we're left cold and alone. It is fitting, then, that God's question to us becomes, when we are disoriented and confused, our question to God. From the turmoil and chaos, we cry out: *Where are you?* What we are asking for with this question is not a logical proof or an explanation. When we raise this question, we are calling . . . praying . . . for nothing less than an experience of the divine for whom we search. Authentic prayer is rare and difficult because it arises from the most vulnerable part of the heart, the part that knows itself threatened by doubt and that exposes itself when it cries out for help.

To get a sense of how this questioning or praying can play out, let me invite you on a family vacation. In 2018, I joined my family at a rented beach house. One balcony overlooked the ocean, and each morning I sat there as I drank coffee and watched the sunrise. My nephew Hugh was not quite three months old and required lots of attention. One evening, his parents wanted a "night out" and I agreed to stay back with Hugh and his brother Con. By 10:00 P.M., everyone but me and Hugh were asleep on the couch. He was fussy, so I took him out to the balcony.

The sky was a black blanket covered in glimmering diamonds; the ocean's waves softly lapped the shore. The air was calm, heavy, and smelled of salt. In my arms Hughie grew quiet. I stood there for what seemed an eternity.

I do not have children. But here in my arms I held a new life. I was thirty-eight years old and it struck me, "When you are my age, Hugh, I'll be 76. To you I'll be an old man, but I'll remember this moment. I'll remember my mom and dad in the house with your brother, your parents out for the evening. I'll remember that in all the world I couldn't imagine loving anyone more than I love you right now." For a moment, everything seemed absolutely perfect.

Suddenly, my mind lurched in a different and darker direction. It was as if cold water had been poured over my heart. Was this too good to be true? In a moment, I saw everything—life, my family, the cosmos—as small and insignificant and . . . well, pointless. Under the night sky, baby in arms, I began to wrestle with a one-word question: *Why?*

I looked down. A question stirred in my mind: *Why Hughie?* I studied chemistry as an undergraduate, and I can answer this question on a lot of levels. I know his parents and I know where babies come from. I know biology, biochemistry, and genetics. I knew *what* he was—a bundle of tissue and bone and chromosomes . . . but was there a purpose or meaning? *Why* was he in existence at all? I shifted Hugh from one arm to another, leaned my hip against the balcony, and wrestled with my thoughts. *Why? Why does anything even exist at all?*

My mind turned to my family. Like all parents, my parents are getting older, and I know they have more yesterdays than tomorrows. My siblings, my friends, my family: many of them were successful and happy and healthy . . . but for what purpose? Does life have any meaning? War and famine, hunger and violence, injustice and oppression, poverty and disease: we are surrounded by signs of mortality. The more I unleashed my imagination and let it roam over the cosmos, the more I felt nauseous because it seemed pointless. The beauty of this baby, the glory of the night sky, the awesomeness of nature . . . was it all just random? My head swooned as I looked for reasons. A cry erupted from my innermost depths: *Where are You, God, in all of this?* No answer forthcoming, I rested in the silent night, surrounded by salty air, the sound of waves retreating on the beach, and felt Hugh's heartbeat against my chest.

Oh God, where are you? My heart cracked. Is it all for nothing? Is life's purpose only what *we* give it? On one level, this seemed satisfying. I don't *need* God to explain physics or chemistry, I don't *need* God to work for justice. Was there proof of God? "You were a good chemistry student," I whispered so as not to wake Hughie, "Would you have accepted lab results without evidence? Are your religious beliefs just wish-fulfillments, a way of coping with fear and doing away with doubt?" This is a question that keeps me up at night: Is asking about God a waste of time? Should we expend precious time on asking "big questions"? Should we accept the pointlessness of existence and move on with our careers? Should I trade my PhD for an MBA?

I suspect I'm not alone in this struggle. In college I sometimes pondered life's meaning but, busy with video games and lab reports, I didn't dwell on these questions. I went to Mass on Sundays out of habit but, when my lab partner teased me for bowing before an "old man in the sky," I really couldn't answer him. I knew that whatever "God" was, it wasn't an old man. Over the years, I studied "proofs" and arguments for God, and in college, I had the opportunity to study philosophy and theology. Over the years, I fought, wrestled, doubted, and after a decade of study and experience eventually was ordained a Catholic priest. Even after so many years of thought and reflection, I must admit that I was totally terrified as I stood holding my nephew and questioning whether I'd wasted my life! Beneath the vastness of the sky, I felt small and worthless. Inwardly, I was plummeting and no matter how hard I tried, I couldn't grasp anything. My hands were filled with Hughie; my heart seemed to be drained of everything. I didn't know whether to hide or to vomit.

What William James called the "sick soul" is hardly a new phenomenon. Fifteen hundred years ago, Saint Augustine of Hippo, in his *Confessions*, confronted his own soul sickness. He, too, asked of God: *Where are you?* In Book X, he recounts how he ranged all over the world asking creatures about God. At one point, he begs creation: "'Tell me about my God—the God who you are not—tell me something about him.' And they cried out with a loud voice, 'He is the one who made us.' My scrutiny of them posed the question; their beauty answered it."[2] The lesson to be learned from Augustine: if there is a God, whatever God is, will not be one more *thing* found on the map of creation. God, in other words, is not a thing amid other things. As Augustine knew, "God" is the word used to name the source and origin of everything that exists. Put otherwise, God is the reason there is something rather than nothing.

If you say, "Well, that's a mysterious way of putting it," I'd agree. "Mysterious," in this sense, is a compliment. You see, when we try to demonstrate God's existence through logical proofs, we risk turning God into a variable—solve for x in terms of y. The risk is that we start to think of God as a thing or an object within the equation. My approach (like that of Saints Augustine and Thomas Aquinas) is to ask the question *Why?* We can ask *why* of everything: from quarks to quasars, aardvarks to zebras, hydrogen to oganesson. We can follow the chains of causes and effects on and on and *never ever* have to invoke "God" to answer any question about *this* or *that* thing. Until, of course, you're standing by the ocean, holding a baby, questioning life's meaning, and you ask the radical question: *Why anything?* Herbert McCabe calls this "the God-question" because whatever answers the question "Why is there anything rather than nothing?" is what we call God.[3] If we put the cosmos into question, if we stand in awe before the whole map of creation and marvel at its fragility and non-necessity, we can be struck by the mystery *that it is at all*. The theologian does not say, "Oh, creation? It's a mystery," and walk away. The opposite is the case. The theologian spends a lot of time musing the mystery of existence because this mystery—the reason there is *anything* at all—is known to theologians as *God*, and discerning how God is present and at work within every created being *is the lifeblood of discernment*.

The more we open our minds and hearts to the whole universe, the more we face the mystery, the more we can ease into seeing creation as given. As I looked at Hugh by the moon's light, I didn't see a living lump. I saw potential, a life about to begin an adventure. I beheld Hugh as a total and gratuitous gift. This isn't me trying to *prove* anything. I'm just sharing that in a moment, something within me dislodged, and I felt a surge of joy and gratitude and awe. The world was not beige or gray but shot through with a sense of a God who creates out of love. Hughie was a sacrament—a tangible sign of God's activity in the world—making God known to me. As I look back on my life, I now see other similar experiences that likewise "make sense" in light of this experience. Do not read me as rejecting all "proofs." But there at the shore, as I probed the deep question of life's meaning and opened myself up, it wasn't proof but prayer. I opened my heart and cried out *Where are you?* The answer wasn't an equation or a concept but an experience of love. To ears attuned through theological study, love itself spoke: *Here I am.*

Enough sharing . . . for now. I do not expect many readers have a Hughie to hold. I think, however, that imaginative readers could put themselves in my place, not to repeat *my* experience but to imaginatively experience it for themselves. Perhaps this approach will launch a reader on their own imaginative journey of asking *Why?* In fact, I encourage the reader to do this. We are so often caught up in life's busyness that we become numb to the mystery of existence. We take our gifts and talents, friends and family, *for granted.* If we step back and meditate on them, we begin to see them as *granted.* A theologian, one steeped in the Bible and formed through prayer and liturgy, interprets these as gifts and signs of a Creator and Giver—"God"—who creates out of love and who desires communion with us. When we risk raising the *Why?* question and pose it to the world, when we open our hearts and minds to ask *Where are you?* of God, we embark on a spiritual quest bringing us face-to-face with the mystery of existence. Discernment neither settles nor solves the mystery. Instead, it plunges us head-long into its depths and gives us an opportunity to reflect and respond to where this creative force, where this call of divine Love, is leading us.

The *Examen*

A skeptic retorts: "Well, you're a priest, *so of course* you'll interpret this as an indication of God. I've had similar feelings, but I wouldn't call this God. It might have been a moment of 'flow,' an 'oceanic feeling,' a sense of nature's beauty . . . but why call it God?"

I grant the point. It's certainly not a drop-the-mic "proof" of God. To be sure, it'd be a pretty small God who could fit into a logical demonstration! Think about it: could the finite mind of a creature possibly hope to capture and make sense of the infinite Creator who, for some reason, wills everything that is *to be* in the first place? No, I'm not offering a proof. Think of it, instead, as an experience that points beyond the finite world toward something infinite. Even today, when I think about this experience within a context of philosophical and theological reflection, when I compare it to experiences of personal and liturgical prayer, when I read it in light of scripture . . . I can't help but to see this experience as "fitting in" with the Christian story. I feel no need to pressure the reader to *be* a Christian or a Catholic. I can only share why I find the Christian life—with its stories and traditions, its beliefs and practices—making sense of what I've undergone. So, take this not as an argument but as an invitation to try out a theological way of reflecting to see if it helps provide a good, or better, account of your life and experience. You may be a theist, an agnostic, or an atheist: wherever you are, it's where you are, and I'm glad you're reading along. I ask nothing more than that you open your mind, that you exercise your Ignatian imagination, and try this practice yourself.

Ignatius understood the importance of pausing to take stock of our experiences and to see what was going on within them. Whereas Socrates once said (as mentioned in the introduction), "The unexamined life is not worth living," Ignatius might say, "The undiscerned life is not fully lived." To help us live a full and flourishing life, Ignatius insisted that we need to examine the heart's innermost movements. He called this practice the *Examen*, and when we practice it, we gain clarity in where we are and where God is at work in our lives. Think of the *Examen* as a way of calibrating our GPS: our God Positioning System. It's a way of discovering where in our lives God's signal is strong and daring to go where it leads us.

Let me suggest why and how a student might make use of this spiritual exercise to calibrate the GPS. Students regularly feel stress, anxiety, and uncertainty about the future. Strange as it may sound, the *Examen* is a way of looking at the past in a manner that brings clarity about how to move forward. It might be useful, before you undertake this exercise, to make a grid like the one below.

	Monday	Tuesday	Wednesday	Thursday	Friday	Saturday	Sunday
Distraction							
Attention							
Intention							

You'll notice three rows. As you practice the *Examen*, you'll have opportunities to write down whatever it is that distracts you, attracts you, and inspires you to take action. By writing these things down, you'll notice patterns forming, things that attract you and things that repel you, ideas that motivate you and some that scare you. A theological eye will notice in these patterns the way God moves the heart in particular ways. And this is what this book is about: learning to notice and interpret these movements. Consider this the practice of *becoming aware* and growing *attentive* to how God is present in your deepest desires and is at work in your life.

Think of the *Examen* as something like the Pensieve from *Harry Potter*. A magical artifact, the Pensieve is a basin into which one pours extracted thoughts and memories. "One simply siphons the excess thoughts from one's mind," Dumbledore says, "pours them into a basin, and examines them at one's leisure. It becomes easier to spot patterns and links ... when they are in this form."[4] The Pensieve allows users to look at events from the past in order to learn how to negotiate within the present. The great thing the about the *Examen* is that you have only to open your mind and your heart and let your desires, the power source of your GPS, chart your life's adventure. Here is how it works.

Meditation: Becoming Aware

1. Pick a regular time for this practice. Before bed might be a good time. Begin by taking three deep breaths. In through the nose for four counts, out through the mouth for six.

2. Start from an attitude of gratitude. Bring to mind one or two
    things you feel grateful for. Big or small, it doesn't matter.
    Open your heart in thanksgiving.
3. Now, use your imagination to walk through the past
    twenty-four hours. Can you identify a time when you felt
    not fully present? A time when you felt divided or jaded or
    hopeless? Can you name a time when you were distracted
    and not living in the moment? Bring this experience to
    mind and ponder it. Then, write down a word or phrase to
    capture this (in the "distraction" box if you are using the
    chart).
4. Continue to imagine your day. Was there a moment when
    you were fully present? A moment when you were firing on
    all cylinders, when you were totally attentive to reality?
    What was it that gave you such focus and energy? Bring this
    experience to mind and then, in a word or phrase, write it
    down (in the "attention" box).
5. Finally, as you look ahead to the rest of the day, can you
    anticipate a choice that you will have to make that will call
    for your total attention? Comparing those times when you
    felt disintegrated with those times when you were whole
    and integrated, how can you make the better choice? Once
    again, use your imagination to meditate on this choice and
    then write down what you intend to do (this is the
    "intention" box).

If at first you feel or notice very little: don't fret! It'll take time and
practice, but if you give it a week, I promise you that you'll start to notice
things you had never sensed before going on in your life. Take this as a
practice of plumbing your depths. Be cautious! Entering your deepest
depths may confront you with desires and hopes you never knew you
had. It is in these desires, the theologian believes, that God speaks most
clearly to you. So, with this kind of practice in place as a basic foundation, we can move further into the process of discernment.

Key Terms and Ideas

- Biblical citations: Each citation is in the format of "Book Name followed by Chapter: Verse."
- The Bible is a compilation of books revealing the nature of God and God's desires for creation, including human beings. Catholic Bibles have forty-six books in the Old Testament and twenty-seven books in the New Testament.
- Ignatian imagination: using the creative force of your mind to put your whole self into a biblical story or narrative. Like a little kid play acting, we enter the scene to experience for ourselves what the story describes.
- Using the Ignatian imagination, one can "dwell" in a biblical text and experience it in a new way. One can even take God's first question in Genesis—*Where are you?*—and meditate on it. If we turn this question back to God, we do not find "God" in this or that spot. Instead of dispelling mystery, the search for God leads us to the deepest of mysteries: *Why is there anything at all?* God, according to theists, creates and sustains the whole of creation as an act and expression of love.
- *Examen*: a meditative practice allowing us to notice patterns within our desires, which is where, theologians believe, God speaks most clearly to us. This is a spiritual exercise we must practice regularly for it to be effective. Through the *Examen*, we discover how God is working through our lives and empowering us to become who we are called to be.

Recommended Resources

Genesis 1–2

The two creation accounts in Genesis provide the fundamental Christian (and Jewish) answer to McCabe's question, "Why is there anything rather than nothing?" Particularly when read in contrast with other ancient creation accounts (see Enuma Elish below), the selfless love of God explains the existence of all creation, creating the conditions for discernment as a theological task.

Enuma Elish—Summary and full text available at *World History Encyclopedia* (https://www.worldhistory.org/article/225/enuma-elish—the-babylonian -epic-of-creation—fu/).

Abridged, animated version available through *Extra Credits* (https://youtu.be /U74xXGRaBiM).

This Babylonian epic, which predates Genesis, shows an alternative answer to the "God-question" and thus reveals, by way of contrast, the distinctive claims found in the Bible's creation accounts. Stressing violence and divine competition, the Enuma Elish suggests the gods created all that exists to serve their own desires, not for the sake of creation itself.

Gerard Manley Hopkins, SJ, "God's Grandeur."

A poem by the famous Jesuit poet who lived and wrote during the Victorian era. Hopkins's words evoke the same spirit of awe discussed in the second section of this chapter, revealing a particularly Ignatian way of reacting to the beauty of creation.

Rowan Williams, "Bible," in *Being Christian: Baptism, Bible, Eucharist, Prayer* (Grand Rapids, MI: William B. Eerdmans, 2014), 21–39.

A short essay introducing the Bible as a text that is meant to be heard, not simply read, thus inviting a response from those who encounter it. Outlines key issues for biblical interpretation and explains what it means to engage the Bible as a theological text.

"The Ignatian Examen" at https://www.jesuits.org/spirituality/the-ignatian -examen/.

Online resources, including walk-through video, assembled by the Jesuit Conference of Canada and the United States to explain Ignatius's *Examen*. Includes links to multiple "applied" examens to encourage reflection on various aspects of ordinary life.

Notes

1. Pope Francis, "Plenary Session of the Pontifical Academy of Sciences," Vatican website, October 27, 2014, http://www.vatican.va/content/francesco /en/speeches/2014/october/documents/papa-francesco_20141027 _plenaria-accademia-scienze.html.

2. Augustine, *Confessions*, trans. Thomas Williams (Indianapolis, IN: Hackett, 2019), X.6.9.

3. Herbert McCabe, OP, *God Matters* (New York: Continuum, 2004), 5.

4. J. K. Rowling, *Harry Potter and the Goblet of Fire* (New York: Scholastic, 2000), 518–19.

2

Who Will You Become?

Once we have established where we are and begun to notice where God has been active, the next step in discerning well is to get a sense of where we are headed. We must, in a phrase, identify who we desire to become.

Of course, given everything we have said in the introduction and chapter 1, there should be no illusion that any of us can completely answer this question in an abstract fashion. If life is indeed a series of choices, all of which shape us, then we will ultimately answer this question little by little with each choice we make. This does not mean, however, that we have no agency in the process. On the contrary, to recapture the GPS imagery from the last chapter, we exercise free will when we set the course for who we will become and then, again, as we work to realize that vision through our individual choices. By seizing this opportunity, we can make our choices with a consistent vision in mind, and we can ensure that we are happy with the person we become through all those decisions. Conversely, if we fail to take the time to establish our end goal, we abdicate control over the construction of our identity, focusing too much on *what* we are doing and not enough on *who* we are becoming.

For me, the moral agent who best exemplifies the importance of using our freedom to define who we want to become with clarity and intentionality is Batman.

Recall Batman's origin story. Bruce Wayne, while still a child, witnesses the tragic death of his parents at the hands of a criminal. Determined to prevent others from similarly losing their loved ones, Bruce invests his time, energy, and considerable wealth into training his mind and body to become a crime fighter. At the end of this process, he reappears in Gotham City as the Batman, a caped crusader dedicated to reclaiming civic life from nefarious actors like the Joker.

Christopher Nolan's 2005 film *Batman Begins* takes these standard plot points and mines them for dramatic depth, detailing Bruce Wayne's careful transformation into Batman in a way that highlights the character's personal development. In a pivotal scene early in the movie, Bruce confronts a choice that will define his mission as a champion of justice, and he stands firm in his commitments because he has a strong sense of the person he wants to—and, in fact, needs to—become to halt the growing influence of criminal powers in Gotham. While training with the League of Shadows and mastering ninja skills, Bruce is told that he must prove his dedication to the cause of justice by punishing a captured thief. Refusing to kill the man and rejecting the League of Shadows' plans to sow destruction so that civilization can start over, Bruce defends the importance of compassion and baldly declares, "I will not become an executioner."

At this point in the film, Bruce Wayne has not created his superhero alter ego, so it is not as though he knows he will be Batman and tries to act like Batman should. Instead, he relies on his deepest commitments (his ultimate concern?) to keep an image of the *type* of person he wants to become at the forefront of his mind as he decides how he needs to respond to the demands of the League of Shadows. This vision sets critical boundaries, allowing him to rule out certain courses of action that are antithetical to the goal he has set for himself. As the rest of the movie highlights, Bruce does not have it all figured out, but because he has taken the time to identify who he wants to become as a human being, he has no trouble making the choices that will lead him to the future that he is finally proud to call his own.

Obviously, none of us is going to become Batman. For one thing, Bruce Wayne has already done it; for another, it would supposedly cost $682 million to do it in real life. Nevertheless, we all tread a similar path insofar as we too change ourselves over time through the choices we make. It does not take much imagination—Ignatian or otherwise—to recognize that we also need to make the same fundamental decision that allowed Bruce Wayne to eventually turn into the Dark Knight. We need to determine what kind of life will make us truly fulfilled, so that we can rule out the paths that resign us to our worst impulses (like the League's attempt to turn Bruce into an executioner) and instead select the roads that bring out the best in who we are. The only way to get to that destination, though, is to have an end goal in mind. This is why we must discern, in broad strokes, who we want to become.

Who We Can Become

In theological terms, the question of who we want to become is crucial because it is at the heart of humankind's free will. St. Thomas Aquinas, a thirteenth-century Dominican priest (the Dominicans are a religious order, like the Jesuits) who became one of the most influential Catholic theologians, insisted that the thing that makes human actions authentically *human* actions and not just the instinctual responses of some animal nature is that they are done for an intended end.[1] He, like the ancient Greek philosopher Aristotle, constructed an entire ethical system on this notion, arguing that one could identify good and bad actions according to the ends they were designed to achieve. More specifically, he maintained that everything that exists has a proper end for which it has been made, and he argued that it was good for things to move toward their end and bad to move away from it.

This approach to ethics is teleological (*telos* is the Greek word for "end") because it asks about the ends at which an act is aimed and, by extension, the end toward which the acting person is moving. Significantly, a teleological approach requires a clear sense of what the most appropriate end should be. To cite an example, think about a basketball. A basketball is made for a very specific end: playing basketball. Its rough exterior helps players grip the ball when taking shots, and its firm pressure when inflated allows dribbling and bounce passes. A basketball flourishes (so to speak) on the basketball court because this is where it was meant to be. Great basketball players, like LeBron James or Caitlin Clark, can take this ball and bring it to its fullest potential with acrobatic dunks and artful drives. When we see this kind of perfection in the game, we can appreciate the goodness involved. It is good to use a basketball this way.

Contrast this with a different image. Take the same basketball but put it on a soccer field and imagine Megan Rapinoe charging toward the ball, preparing to deliver a surefooted kick for a game-winning goal. If there were a soccer ball at the end of her toe, we would watch with rapt attention at another startling display of sporting prowess. When we think of the basketball in its place, however, we can only wince because this juxtaposition denies both Rapinoe and the basketball their chance to flourish. The reason for our changed reaction is the claim at the heart of Aquinas's teleological approach to ethics: it is good for things to fulfill the ends for which they were made.

Now, the point of this discussion of teleology is to put the question of who we want to become in its proper perspective. Unquestionably, this is a decision that allows us to assert our free will, and the options for who we might become are virtually infinite. But not all choices are equally defensible because human beings also have a proper end. Granted, the telos of a human being is more complex than that of a recreational plaything, which is why it has been the object of discussion from ancient times until today. Nonetheless, to the extent that we accept there is such a thing as "the good life"—which is to say, the good human life that is worth living—we also accept that human persons have a proper end that accords with their distinctly human nature. This is a big claim because it is supposed to capture something of our shared humanity, setting an end that applies equally to all. Consequently, this common telos must set some parameters for the type of people we should become.

To make a good choice when facing the decision of who we will become, we therefore need to think about our telos as human beings. Sometimes, the best way to think about an end, though, is to think about a beginning. A telos, after all, answers the question, "What is this *for*?" It is the end someone or something was designed to serve from the start. The telos is the reason this person or thing exists, so taking stock of its origin story and answering what it is *for* helps to reveal what it should become.

On a personal level, this sort of backward review is precisely what the Ignatian *Examen*, introduced at the end of the last chapter, allows us to do. We look back not as a pointless exercise in navel gazing but to understand who we really are on a deeper level. Equipped with this knowledge, we are then in a position to make better choices about the type of person that we most genuinely want to become if we are to lead an authentically happy life.

Based on his experiences with the *Examen*, Ignatius crafted a comprehensive vision for the good human life based on his Christian convictions and placed it at the start of the *Spiritual Exercises*. Defined as the "First Principle and Foundation," this vision serves as one of the earliest meditations in the Ignatian retreat (the *Spiritual Exercises* are really a guide for a retreat of prayer and reflection, originally envisioned for participants to undertake over thirty days), providing a metaphorical cornerstone for both the *Exercises* and the spiritual life itself. Given the priority we place on an Ignatian approach to discernment, this Principle and Foundation is worth quoting in full:

> *Human beings are created to praise, reverence, and serve God our*
> *   Lord, and by means of this to save their souls.*
> *The other things on the face of the earth are created for human*
> *   beings, to help them in working toward the end for which they*
> *   are created.*
> *From this it follows that I should use these things to the extent that*
> *   they help me toward my end, and rid myself of them to the*
> *   extent that they hinder me.*
> *To do this, I must make myself indifferent to all created things, in*
> *   regard to everything which is left to my freedom of will and is*
> *   not forbidden. Consequently, on my own part I ought not to seek*
> *   health rather than sickness, wealth rather than poverty, honor*
> *   rather than dishonor, a long life rather than a short one, and so*
> *   on in all other matters.*
> *I ought to desire and elect only the thing which is more conducive to*
> *   the end for which I am created.*[2]

Ignatius packs a lot into this, and some of the language can be confusing, but we can discuss two important features right now. First, Ignatius's Principle and Foundation is a decidedly teleological text. The point of the *Exercises*, according to this Foundation, is to help people achieve "the end for which they are created." Ignatius devised a whole system for discernment and spiritual growth that moved toward this one goal: helping humans reach their true telos.

Second, the Principle and Foundation is also a work of theological anthropology, which is a particular kind of theological claim. Like any anthropology, theological anthropology is an account of the nature and purpose of a human being, but it is based on claims about the relationship between God and humanity, looking to establish the significance of human existence in deeper terms. For Christians, the starting point for theological anthropology is found in Genesis 1:27, which proclaims that "God created humankind in his image, in the image of God he created them; male and female he created them." This indicates that human beings were designed for a close relationship with God, in whose image we have been made. Following this vision and the rest of the creation accounts in Genesis, Ignatius proclaims, "Human beings are created to praise, reverence, and serve God our Lord."

The teleological elements of the First Principle and Foundation are thus grounded in a specific vision for the kind of life humans are supposed to lead. This vision is theological, rooted in scripture, and based on the assumption that humans exist because God made them so. For Ignatius, the type of person every human being is ultimately called to become is the type of person who praises, reverences, and serves the God who brought them into existence.

If this all sounds high and mighty and maybe even a little abstract, it is. But please do not dismiss it out of hand for either its grandiosity or its religiosity. Although this is not the language we commonly use today, these words were not arbitrary ideas for Ignatius. On the contrary, praising, reverencing, and serving God represented Ignatius's summation of the larger Christian vision for how to live a good life. It reflected a kind of hopefulness for the height of human potential that can resonate with today's audience, both Christian and non-Christian alike.

A good way to think about what Ignatius had in mind with his teleological vision is to remember that he started with an understanding of God as the Father of Jesus and, by extension, of all human beings. When he described the universal call to praise, reverence, and serve God, he essentially highlighted the importance of honoring one's place in a grand parent–child relationship. He was talking about how to make one's parent proud. Given the imperfections of human parenting, this image may not immediately strike a chord for everyone, but recall that Ignatius envisioned God as the perfect parent, one who is all-loving and deeply committed to the well-being of every single child. In this sense, God is like the parent who always wants what is best for us and who actually knows what that would be! If we can imagine being the child of this parent, we can see why we would want to live the kind of life that would make this parent proud. We would want to honor this parent by the way we live our lives, becoming a testament to the values our loving mother or father instilled in us.

When Ignatius describes praising, reverencing, and serving God, he is really saying that humans are made to live a life that would make God proud. This is not a platitude about the importance of being a "good person" in some generic sense. The God Ignatius professed is a God who is all powerful and all good, a God who takes the side of the oppressed in the fight for justice (see the book of Exodus in the Bible), and a God who came into the world as a lowly child (more on this later) and died the painful death of a convicted criminal for the sake of others (ditto). To make this God proud, one must embody these values, and that asks for a very specific type of life, one that Christians today still champion as the pinnacle of human existence. This life is, in its simplest description, a life of self-gift. A life generously lived at the service of others.

Christians say this life leads to our fullest flourishing as human beings because this is the life that God lived when God became a human being. Central to the Christian faith is belief in the mystery of the Incarnation, the conviction that God came into this world in human form as Jesus of Nazareth more than 2,000 years ago. The earliest followers of Jesus were amazed by what they witnessed: miraculous healings, powerful sermons, and victory over death itself. As they shared this good news with others, a religious movement was born, and this new community of believers worked hard to explain the transformative experiences life with Jesus provided. After centuries of reflection, the Christian community eventually settled on a succinct pronouncement of their faith in Jesus Christ as God incarnate. He is fully God and fully human.

We will explore the significance and implications of this central Christian tenet in subsequent chapters, but for the moment it will be sufficient to focus on the "*fully*" aspects of the claim. Part of what Christians assert when they say that Jesus is fully human is not only that he experienced every element of the human condition but also that he is perfectly human. He reveals the fullness of our humanity. He shows us what we, at our best, always had the potential to become.

For a Christian looking to determine the proper telos of the human person, there is no better example than Jesus Christ. The message of his life is that selflessness is the point of it all, for not only was Jesus's entire preaching about the various ways in which "the last will be first" (Matthew 20:16), but the culmination of Jesus's life itself was the selfless act of accepting a death sentence he did not deserve. In dying the death of a criminal on the cross, Jesus revealed that genuine human flourishing is not in fame or riches but in selfless acts of love.

Christians, convinced that Jesus is fully human and fully divine, insist that this type of self-gift represents the key to a life well lived. While they base this understanding on religious convictions, it is not exclusively a religious claim. After all, the main assertion is that Jesus reveals a fully *human* life, so the argument is fundamentally about what it means to be human. To return to categories presented in the introduction, this is a matter of belief, not opinion, and it is therefore accountable to the facts. Accordingly, each of us can (and should) judge this vision for ourselves, but I believe that it holds up pretty well under broader human scrutiny. One would be hard-pressed to find a more consistent theme across our human stories—both fiction and nonfiction—than the value of self-sacrifice for the benefit of others. In history, we lionize our ancestors who valiantly gave their lives for the well-being of the nation, "the cause," or the family. In books, plays, movies, and more, we see dynamic characters becoming heroes and fulfilling their destinies in selfless acts that involve sacrificing love, life, limb, or all three. Why are we so moved by these representations of human selflessness? Because deep down we recognize the truth about ourselves that these acts underscore: there is nothing greater than to use our human lives so completely for someone or something that there is literally nothing left of us to give when we are done.

This self-gift, according to Christianity, is the fullness of human potential that Jesus reveals. It is the way humans can make God proud with a life that imitates Christ's own so perfectly. This self-gift, in Ignatius's terms, is to praise, reverence, and serve God our Lord. It is the end for which we are created. Whether one takes this idea on Christian terms or ratifies it on strictly human ones, whoever is willing to accept that there is in fact no greater human act than to lay down one's life for the benefit of others would be foolish not to account for this teleological vision when answering the question, *Who will you become?*

Who We Want to Become

The challenge, of course, is to figure out how to translate this grand vision for human flourishing into a practical answer to the question of who you want to become. The solution to this puzzle lies in two pieces: one found in the First Principle and Foundation and another found in the insights of the *New York Times* columnist David Brooks.

To begin with Ignatius, a vital feature of the First Principle and Foundation is the notion of indifference. After identifying humanity's proper telos, Ignatius asserts that everything that exists on earth has been given as a gift by God to help us achieve our ultimate end. We ought to properly order those things so that they are not distractions but instead become tools allowing us to arrive at our telos. This is why he says, "I should use these things to the extent that they help me toward my end, and rid myself of them to the extent that they hinder me."

To achieve this clarity in our priorities, Ignatius maintains, "I must make myself indifferent to all created things." This type of indifference is not apathy, like the dismissive eye-rolling of a teenager who resigns herself to her parents' plans with a "whatever." On the contrary, Ignatian indifference is about a laser-like focus on what matters most. It is about a rejection of needless anxieties—like those about health, wealth, fame, or longevity, all of which are all ultimately beyond our control—so that we can instead direct our undivided attention to the commitments that carry us through. Rather than apathy, Ignatian indifference stems from a deep and abiding passion for something in particular, reflecting our conviction that this thing is so important that we will find a way to pursue it regardless of the circumstances in which we find ourselves. It is the stance that makes a total response of self possible.

For me, Conor, the clearest experience of Ignatian indifference and my deepest appreciation of its power came during a turbulent house-hunting period. For complicated reasons, my wife and I were looking for a house with her parents, intending to create a multigenerational home. As any married couple can tell you, house hunting is complicated because two different people always bring two different sets of interests to the search. For most couples, the best-case scenario is a house in a location that checks at least a few boxes for both parties. Once the search party moves from two adults to four, however, the challenges increase exponentially. At times it seemed like we were embarking on a fool's errand, with so many competing hopes involved that we all began to wonder if any house would ever suffice.

Eventually, our exhausting process led us to two houses, and we had to make a choice. Between the two options, I had a clear favorite because it was located in a community where my wife and I already had established roots and gave us the opportunity to walk to parks, stores, and the library. My mother-in-law preferred the other house because it was still under construction and could therefore be customized to suit our particular multigenerational needs. We would have been completely car-bound, however, and this thought weighed on me heavily.

The decision belonged to my in-laws, but they absolutely wanted our input. My wife and I did not want to foist our preferences upon them, although we did have a preference (at least I did). For a period in the midst of our collective indecision, stress about the whole thing consumed me. One day, through the continual work of prayer, however, I came to a new-found peace. In a moment of Ignatian indifference, I realized that the whole point of our housing search was to find a place where we could all be together, and I knew that we could achieve that in either home. I got to a place where I was able to let go of my personal preference for a specific place so that I could imagine being happy with my extended family wherever we ended up. Instead of letting the choice of a house become a stumbling block to our relationships, I took a step back and accepted that, however it happened, our home could be a tool for strengthening our connections to each other and the community in which we settled. This indifference was a great gift in the moment, providing me with a profound sense of freedom—from anxiety and for relationality—that helped me discern well. It is a good thing, too, because neither house worked out. Through an unanticipated series of events, we moved into a place that none of us even knew about at the time we were debating those two options, and it allowed us to support one another in all the ways that we had intended.

Ignatian indifference, then, demands focus and freedom. It provides the ability to rediscover what matters and to free ourselves from the fears and anxieties that otherwise cloud our judgment. It is essential for discernment at all stages, but it is even more paramount when we tackle who we want to become. In this context, indifference empowers us to prioritize the life we want to lead, allowing us to sift through the noise of any particular decision to see how our identity is at stake. It also provides us with the freedom to pursue the goal we most deeply want to achieve because a spirit of Ignatian indifference reminds us that we can always find a way to seek our proper telos as human beings, regardless of the circumstances, as long as we take the time to find our way.

This vision, while positive, still leaves us with the obvious question of how to take the time to find our way and how to settle on the proper path when we do. This is where the second puzzle piece enters the equation.

In 2015, David Brooks published a book about the good life called *The Road to Character,* which emerged from his reflections about the good humans he encountered in the world around him and in the history books. He summarized its message in a Sunday *New York Times* column with the headline "The Moral Bucket List."[3] Distinguishing between "résumé virtues"—the skills that will get one a job—and "eulogy virtues"—the personal traits "that are talked about at your funeral"— Brooks underscored the importance of taking more time to develop the latter and suggested that we should all work our way through certain human experiences that can help us cultivate the best eulogy virtues. This was his moral bucket list, a set of six "specific moral and spiritual accomplishments" that everyone should pursue before they die to cultivate the strongest character traits.

Brooks's list is fascinating and well worth reviewing on its own terms. All the items on the list speak to the importance of self-gift as the pinnacle of a life well lived, and in various ways, each lays out tips for how to pursue this end. The one that has the most direct relevance to the question of who one wants to become, however, is called "the dependency leap." For Brooks, this spiritual accomplishment is about recognizing "life as a process of commitment making," wherein one dedicates oneself to relationships, ideas, and causes that transcend themselves.

When I think about what it means to move from the general vision of Christ-like selflessness as humanity's common telos to a specific answer to the question of who I want to become, this dependency leap captures the movement we must make. What (or who) is it that I care about enough to give my whole self over to it? What relationship, what mission, what vision will I doggedly pursue throughout my life? For some people, it may be a religious tradition (or a religious order); for others, it may be a social concern or a person such as a spouse or a child. Whatever it is, it can become the specific way in which we can give ourselves away for the benefit of others. It becomes our path to flourishing, our way of realizing our true telos.

Once we identify this goal, we establish a viable vision for the type of person we want to become. More specifically, we set our sights on slowly becoming the person who prioritizes this particular person, this special pursuit, or this ambitious ideal no matter what. Realizing this kind of end is a lifetime project. To achieve this long-term goal, we will need the focus and freedom that Ignatian indifference provides, so that we can stay the course even when the seas are rough.

But how do we identify this goal? How do we set our sights on the person we truly want to become? This calls for discernment, which means that our deepest commitments (our ultimate concern) need to enter the conversation. Yet this is a concrete question that demands some concrete advice. In this case, we can find just such advice in a curious connection between Ignatius and Brooks. Remember what Brooks called the traits developed through the moral bucket list? Eulogy virtues. These traits are the building blocks of character, and he designated them eulogy virtues to highlight the fact that they are the ones that endure after we are gone. On some deep level, Brooks argues, we recognize the importance of these traits, but in practice we often put more work into the things that bring external, worldly measures of success. The thing that puts the eulogy virtues back into perspective, though, is death. When we think about the end of our lives and imagine the kind of eulogy we hope someone will share at our funeral, we know we value inner goodness more than external appearances.

Ignatius, too, understood death's power to sharpen our vision. At the heart of the *Spiritual Exercises*, when discussing discernment most explicitly, he introduced the "Deathbed Meditation" as a tool to help exercitants arrive at the decision that reflected their deepest desires and their truest self. Since these are precisely the elements that are supposed to be at stake in the question of who we want to become, this chapter closes with a guided reflection based on this famous meditation, so that you can move from understanding the importance of this question to actually answering it for yourself.

Meditation: An Exercise in Discernment

1. Take a moment to focus. Close your eyes and take three deep breaths. In through the nose, counting slowly to four. Out through the mouth, counting slowly to six.

2. Now imagine yourself at the end of your life, looking down at a group of people gathered for your funeral. Who do you hope to see there? What sort of relational connections do you want to have established by the end of your life: A big family? A network of people from different walks of life? A collection of former students still moved by the memory of your inspiring classes? Some other group? Your answers here will reveal something about the types of relationships you want to prioritize in life.

3. Next, immerse yourself further in the scene and begin to listen to the conversations. What do you hope the people gathered to remember you will be saying? What sort of personality traits do you want them commemorating? These are your eulogy virtues. These are the contours of the person you want to become.

4. Finally, take a minute to muster some connections between these reflections. What sort of commitments do you feel called to make as a result of these insights? How can these relationships and these character traits help you identify a unique way to pursue the life of self-gift that represents the fullness of human flourishing?

Those who take the time to seriously work through this exercise often find inspiring results. While this can be motivating, it can just as easily be paralyzing. When we set big goals for ourselves, we often worry about how we might fail along the way. As the spiritual writer (and one-time presidential candidate) Marianne Williamson once opined, "It is our light, not our darkness, that most frightens us."[4] The last part of *becoming aware* (the B in the Ignatian B.U.T. framework) therefore involves tackling the stumbling blocks that often hold us back from our fullest potential. The next chapter addresses this task by taking an honest look at why, once we have settled on an optimistic vision of who we want to become, it is so hard to realize the ends we set for ourselves.

Key Terms and Ideas

- Teleological approach to ethics: an assessment of good and bad actions based on whether the ends they are intended to achieve match the end humans have been created to serve; in a Christian account, this human telos can be summarized in self-gift.
- First Principle and Foundation: a succinct summation of the Christian worldview at the start of Ignatius's *Spiritual Exercises*, laying out the vision for the type of person Christians are called to become
- Theological anthropology: an account of the nature and purpose of a human being based on theological claims about humanity's relationship to God.
- Indifference: an Ignatian concept highlighting the need to dismiss unnecessary attachments to anxieties so that we can focus more fully and more freely on the most important things in life.
- "Eulogy virtues": David Brooks's language for the character traits that truly define us as human beings and are therefore far more important than the "résumé virtues" that are typically key to social and economic success.
- "Dependency leap": the need to identify connections or commitments bigger than oneself to live a meaningful life.

Recommended Resources

Batman Begins, directed by Christopher Nolan, Warner Brothers, 2005.

The first half (roughly) depicts Bruce Wayne's transformation into Batman, illustrating how a clear teleological vision can drive a series of choices to help us become the person we long to be.

"Teleology w/ Fr. Dominic Legge, OP (Aquinas 101)," *Thomistic Institute* (available at https://youtu.be/uoPjFnqO7j4).

A Dominican priest explains Thomas Aquinas's understanding of teleology using everyday objects to help us understand how flourishing depends on realizing the end for which we were made.

David Cloutier, "Human Fulfillment," in *Gathered for the Journey: Moral Theology in Catholic Perspective*, ed. David Matzko McCarthy and M. Therese Lysaught (Grand Rapids, MI: William B. Eerdmans, 2007), 134–52.

Technical essay explaining how the proper understanding of who we are called to be, as a matter of teleology, helps us identify what will make us truly fulfilled. Much like this chapter, Cloutier connects this question with Christ's model of selfless love to insist that we are properly fulfilled when we give of ourselves for others.

"First Principle and Foundation Resources" via Xavier's *Jesuit Resource* website: https://www.xavier.edu/jesuitresource/resources-by-theme/first-principle-and-foundation-resources.

Webpage containing various translations of Ignatius's First Principle and Foundation, offering multiple ways of accessing and interpreting this influential text.

David Brooks, "Should You Live for Your Résumé or Your Eulogy?" TED Talk (available at https://www.ted.com/talks/david_brooks_should_you_live_for_your_resume_or_your_eulogy).

Brooks's short TED Talk explains the fundamental tensions between résumé and eulogy virtues and makes the case for prioritizing eulogy virtues in our lives.

Notes

1. Thomas Aquinas, OP, *Summa Theologiae*, 2nd ed., trans. Fathers of the English Dominican Province (Denver, CO: New Advent, 2017), www.newadvent.org/summa, I–II, q. 1, a. 1.
2. Ignatius of Loyola, SJ, *Spiritual Exercises and Selected Works*, ed. George Ganss (New York: Paulist Press, 1991), 130.
3. David Brooks, "The Moral Bucket List," *New York Times*, April 12, 2015, https://www.nytimes.com/2015/04/12/opinion/sunday/david-brooks-the-moral-bucket-list.html.
4. Marianne Williamson, *A Return to Love: Reflections on the Principles of a Course in Miracles* (New York: HarperCollins, 1992), 190.

3

Why Is Discernment Difficult?

Even under ideal circumstances, discernment is difficult. Each fall, students arrive on campus and face a smorgasbord of choices. From picking courses to settling on a major, signing up for clubs and sports, and trying to establish a new friend group, there are so many choices and so much pressure to choose. Rightly, students often turn to parents and guardians for guidance. When I (Ryan) left for college, my dad and I went for a walk, and he gave me this advice: *I don't care what you study. Just love it enough that you'd be willing to teach it.* He always wanted to be a teacher and knew that whether business or biology, chemistry or computers, theater or theology, "to love" anything, even our college majors, means wanting to share it with others. For Dad, the life worth living is not about "getting" but about "giving" to others. Our choices either contribute to or take away from our freedom to *become aware* of how we are called to give.

Conor and I are privileged to work with students, and we are sensitive to the fact that they rarely find themselves in ideal circumstances. Many of them struggle with anxiety and depression and addiction. Racial, gender, and economic inequality create rifts within college campuses and divide our nation. Hardly a day goes by that we do not hear of pandemics, ecological crises, acts of violence, and senseless deaths. Our world is a mess. The skeptic groans: "Why would anyone commit themselves to a God who permits such chaos?" To build a compelling case for the importance of discernment, especially during troubled times, we must face the reality of evil and confront the challenges it poses to believers. Why, if there is a good and loving God, is there so much evil in the world?

This chapter has two sections. First, I distinguish *natural evil* from *moral evil* and situate both within a theological framework. My goal is to show that belief in God's goodness *is* reasonable despite the reality of evil. In fact, theological reflection on evil can even be an opportunity to rethink our understanding of God and ourselves. In the second section, Conor examines the way evil manifests itself in our lives and the way it deforms our lives. If this appears dark and heavy, it is! But we need courage to probe the painful cracks in history and society. After all, it is through these cracks the light gets in.

Disentangling Evil

Not long ago, I found myself wedged between my nephews' car seats on a lengthy trip. To pass the time, we watched Disney's *The Lion King*. Three times. And then we sang the soundtrack. For variety's sake, we listened to Elton John's recording of "The Circle of Life." The opening verse contains a stanza *not* included on the movie soundtrack. Sir Elton croons:

> *Some say, "Eat or be eaten"*
> *Some say, "Live and let live"*
> *But all are agreed as they join the stampede*
> *You should never take more than you give*

As we sang, it dawned on me that *The Lion King* offers a vivid way for us to reflect on the question of evil. As Mufasa and Simba survey the savannah, Mufasa admonishes his son to respect every living thing "from the crawling ant to the leaping antelope." Simba replies, "But dad, don't we eat the antelope?" Mufasa does not deny that their flourishing comes at the antelope's expense. Antelope (and zebra and hippos) die so lions may live. Nevertheless, *all* of creation—everything the light touches—is caught up in the "Circle of Life," and when the lions die, their bodies return to the earth and eventually become the grass the antelope eat. In the great scheme of existence, lion and antelope eat and are eaten, each providing sustenance to the other. Even though it is bloody and painful, there is a savage beauty and harmony as creatures take their places in life's circle.

Given the death and destruction we observe in nature and society, can someone *actually* believe a good God to be behind it all? As a theologian, I do . . . but it's not easy. For all Christians, the path to claiming that God is indeed good in the face of pain and suffering requires a willingness to look at the evidence and to make a choice to hold on to this optimistic conviction. It is a matter of belief that emerges from an honest grappling with the facts of brokenness in the world and that simultaneously chooses to interpret these facts in a certain way. To explain this, I use *The Lion King* to distinguish *natural evil* (found in the "Circle of Life") from *moral evil* (evident in Mufasa's brother, Scar). I do not deny that evil poses a challenge to belief, nor do I want to minimize pain or suffering. I seek only to disentangle two types of evil and show how theology offers resources for recognizing its manifestations. Learning to distinguish between two types of evil equips us with the skills necessary to discern God's life-giving presence and call even amid the messiness, darkness, and ambiguity of our lives.

First things first. When we talk about evil, we are not talking about a shadowy entity that creeps about and inflicts harm. Rather, evil is an absence or a lack of something that should be present but isn't. In the Christian theological tradition, this claim coexists with the conviction that it is nevertheless possible to speak about evil influences in more concrete terms—Catholics, for example, are asked to reject Satan (a.k.a., the devil) in the Rite of Baptism, showing that there is a real force to evil in the Christian understanding. On one hand, these two claims about evil as the absence of what should have been and also the presence of what should not be are not irreconcilable. One can talk about the devil as an evil creature without ascribing substance to evil itself. On the other hand, there remains a real tension between these two ideas, which helpfully serves as a reminder that the problem of evil is not one that yields a simple solution. It is a mystery that demands at least some degree of humility as we acknowledge that finite humans cannot fully grasp its intricacies. We will say more about the mystery dimension toward the end of the chapter, so for now, we just want to clarify that we are exploring the problem of evil by adopting the classic Christian theological claim that evil is best understood as a kind of absence, even as there are other ways Christians think about evil too.

To continue with our point about evil and absence, you can impress your friends by telling them that evil is a *privatio boni* or a "privation of goodness." Evil is parasitic; it takes away or deprives a being of what makes it good. A maxim: *God creates, evil negates.* Evil detracts from a being's goodness by making it less than it is created to be. It is a subtraction that works against and prevents a being from being what it should be. No matter how you slice it, evil always involves some sort of loss. To make this clearer, let's take a trip to the Serengeti.

Evil, Thomas Aquinas thought, comes in two varieties: natural and moral. Natural evil (*malum poenae*) is what the theologian Brian Davies, in his own analysis of Aquinas's work, calls "evil suffered."[1] This sort of evil happens as a consequence of being finite. When Simba asks about lions eating antelope, he is asking about natural evil. What's *evil* about the food chain? Well, the lion's action is bad for the antelope. Indeed, it's so bad that the antelope ceases to be an antelope and becomes a meal. Relative to the antelope, this is evil. At the same time, it is good for the lion, because lions flourish (reach their telos) by eating antelope. Herbert McCabe observes that when a lion eats a lamb, "From anybody's point of view what happens is bad for the lamb, and this is not just because the lamb dislikes it (perhaps it is a masochistic lamb and enjoys it), but because eventually it dies. I should maintain that any evil suffered by one thing is always a good achieved by something else. The meal which is bad for the lamb is always good for the lion."[2] One creature's flourishing often comes at the expense of another creature. The lamb suffers real evil when the lion bites into it, but this is good for the lion. Striving to be a *good lion* requires, given what lions are, that the lamb and the antelope suffer evil. But note McCabe's observation: the "evil suffered" by one being (lamb) is a "good achieved" by something else (lion). How?

"The Circle of Life" refers to the cycle of life and death. Mufasa tried to impart this insight to Simba. McCabe appreciates this wisdom, too, and wants to acknowledge that when the lion eats the lamb, *some good* comes of it. The "good" is the lion being a lion and achieving its telos by doing what lions do. We'd judge a vegan lion a *bad* lion not because of any moral defect but because we expect lions to be carnivorous. As far as we know, a good lion is one that effectively and efficiently hunts for and secures prey. A good lion has a negative effect on what it captures, but this does not make the lion evil. On the contrary, the lion's *being a good lion* renders the antelope *a bad antelope* or, once it's dead, dinner. "The lion is being fulfilled, indeed he is being filled, precisely by what damages the lamb and renders it defective."[3] Evil suffered by one creature contributes to another's good. Natural evil, in a way, contributes to the ongoing act of creation and pushes "The Circle of Life" forward.

There also exists what Aquinas calls moral evil (*malum culpae*), which Davies calls "evil done."[4] Theologians call it *sin*. Unlike natural evil, where evil is a consequence of a creature achieving its good at the expense of another, moral evil is of no benefit. With sin, *no one flourishes*, and any good is *accidental*. Imagine: It's Christmas time and my nephew Declan wants a toy, but they're sold out. I walk to my car and see a woman with the toy and her back is to me. I swipe it. It's easy to see evil suffered: I stole it from her. What makes it *morally* wrong, however, is not just the act of taking what doesn't belong to me. What makes it moral evil, sin, is that by acting unjustly, I fail to be fully human. The moral defect is in *me*, and I am lessened as a human because of it. That's why it's a total loss: the woman is hurt (bad) *and* I am less of a human (bad). I have succeeded not only in injuring another but also in lessening myself. McCabe describes this sort of sin as an evil "I inflict precisely on myself. The inflicter, the one who ought to be getting good out of it, is precisely the one who suffers evil. So evil done is a dead loss, nobody gets anything out of it, except accidentally."[5] Sin negates what we are created for; it's a self-imposed obstacle to reaching our telos. What makes sin *sinful* is not that we do naughty things but that sin is our freely chosen failure to be what we are meant to be: human. Sin is self-sabotage.

If you are not tempted to steal toys from children, perhaps you could think of something more proximate to your experience. In the era of ChatGPT and AI, it is incredibly easy to pass off someone—or something—else's work as your own. Who gets hurt when one plagiarizes? The original author does not experience any ill effects, and the student gets a good grade. A win! Perhaps not. Plagiarism is an act of dishonesty, of fraud, because it misrepresents the student by taking credit for work someone else did. Plagiarism reflects a failure to be honest, to be a person of integrity, to be a student and a learner. As a teacher, I find plagiarism heartbreaking because it has such dire consequences: an F on the assignment, a total loss of trust, and a note in one's file that could have long-lasting consequences. Plagiarism is an instance of academic sin, of failing to be a student. It is an act of self-sabotage, subverting the learning process and, if caught, potentially destroying one's prospects for graduation, graduate school, or employment. Think about it. If you were an employer, would you want to hire an accountant who cheated his way through Accounting and Finance? If you are looking for a lawyer, do you want to hire someone who cheated her way through Contract Law? My free and pragmatic advice: be the kind of student *you* would want to hire!

Whether it is stealing a toy, cheating on a test, or plagiarizing a paper, these self-sabotaging moral failures result in a dead loss of good. The person injured by my evil act suffers and—this is key—I, too, suffer. By acting dishonestly or unlovingly, I diminish my humanity. No denying: sin can have good effects. Declan gets a new toy. The plagiarist gets an A on the assignment. But this good is accidental, a good fruit from a rotting human tree. But whether I am caught and convicted or my crime goes undetected, I am a thief. And this, I think, is why theologians take sin so seriously. For sin involves two tragic negations: the evil inflicted on another and the self-inflicted evil that diminishes humanity. Sinners do bad things, but what's equally problematic is what sin does to us; it makes us defective humans. Moral evil deludes us into thinking we are free when, to theological eyes, genuine freedom is embodied not in doing whatever we want but only by being what God calls us to be: human. This call to human fullness, for the Christian, is the "First Principle and Foundation" revealed by Jesus.

Hughie, even at the age of two, intuits this. He throws Cheerios at the screen when Scar appears. He sees Scar embodying the diminishment of self from "evil done." Sly and sinister, gaunt and emaciated, Scar has a penchant for lurking in the shadows. He pledges loyalty to Mufasa while scheming to supplant Simba by forming a murderous coalition with the hyenas. After Scar betrays Mufasa by allowing him to fall to his death, he seizes control of the Pride Lands. As McCabe would observe, this is but an accidental good. Scar continues to diminish as a lion and grows more haggard as the land is overhunted. The balance Mufasa counseled Simba to maintain is ruined, and everyone suffers because of it. You'd think the movie's producers were reading Aquinas because they vividly convey that "moral evil" is a total failure. Scar's "evil done" is *his* failure to flourish—he's a bad relative and a terrible ruler—and his evil corrupts his environment. Scar willingly negates the created order, he deliberately chooses to sound a discordant note in creation's melody, and the effects are catastrophic.

The distinction between natural and moral evil boils down to this: in natural evil, there is *some* good gained, but in evil done, there is no true good achieved. In fact, moral evil is an undoing of the good because the agent willingly acts against one's telos. Sin is self-destructive, it's self-sabotage, because it's a deliberate and voluntary failure *to be* what one is meant to be. Evil done or sin is actively willing to be less than fully human.

Before concluding, I must admit that our discussion is incomplete. Due to space, our discussion of evil has been limited to living beings within the food chain. But we can find instances of natural evil within our bodies. Bacteria flourish at my expense; achieving their telos—a good for them—is dangerous for me. Cancer is the result of a cell that is *really* good at self-replication. The trouble is that the cell's flourishing spreads into surrounding tissues, disrupts bodily functions, and damages the whole. I am out for a run, trip, and break my ankle. A grandfather is diagnosed with dementia. Parents learn their child has leukemia. We would be monstrous to say, "Ah, in this case of natural evil, there is *some* good." There is no good achieved by a child's suffering from cancer. It is an evil, a privation of a good that should be there, namely, health. Still, given the type of creatures we are—finite and contingent beings—we can at least understand why we are susceptible to natural evils. As complex and marvelous as the body is, we do not live in a friction-free universe. Bones are liable to breakage at a certain point (we are not, after all, Wolverine with an adamantium skeleton). With trillions of cells multiplying and dividing in the body, there is always the possibility that something can go awry, leading to cancer. Given the nature of our brains and biology, we can understand the way organs and systems function and malfunction. These breakdowns do not explain away pain and suffering, but they do situate them within a framework that allows us to understand them. As finite and fragile creatures, our vulnerability to external forces is a mark of our contingency. Make no mistake: by no means am I dismissing the pain caused by cancer or dementia. Nevertheless, I can understand them on a scientific level, and I do pray fervently that we find a cure for both of them. But although I can "understand" cancer, bone breaks, and dementia, I simply cannot rationalize moral evil because it is self-destructive. Unlike the natural evil of cancer or dementia, the moral evil of sin will not be healed through pills or potions but only through the conversion of the heart.

We have also failed to probe instances of nonliving natural evil: earthquakes, tsunamis, hurricanes, and so on. It's easy to see how these cause "evil suffered" but harder to see much, if any, "good" coming from them. I see the effect of such natural disasters as being a mixture of both types of evil. For instance, an earthquake is a geological event that often causes destruction. As a physics event, the shifting of tectonic plates is not evil, although the creatures living atop those plates might experience the jarring movement as calamitous. On its own, an earthquake is part of the natural law of geology, and I can understand the disruption it causes as a natural evil. To balance pressure and maintain homeostasis, the plates of earth's crust shift . . . although this shifting does have a consequence for other creatures. Geologically, understandable. But when buildings are not built to code or when substandard materials are used in construction, a terrible toll is inflicted on humans. Can we blame the Creator, though, when shoddy buildings made with inferior materials and poor planning fare far worse than better-built (and more expensive) structures? This is, after all, often the reason that poorer neighborhoods suffer greater damage than wealthier enclaves during natural disasters. Is this because God punishes the poor? Or might it be that moral evil—cost cutting, unequal distribution of goods, neglect of the poor—has an important role to play? Human sinfulness or moral evil exacerbates the scope of natural evil. If we had more time, we would have to look deeper at "structural sin" (a concept we explore later in a different context) and try to parse out how human society can also be guilty of "evil done" both by what it does (perpetuate inequality) and what it fails to do (commit itself to promoting and preserving the common good).

We also need to add a crucial caveat to these analyses. As much as the distinction between evil suffered and evil done can help us make *some* sense of these calamities, we must not get too haughty and assume that we have perfectly explained how the world works and why suffering exists. After all, the theological claim that evil is the privation, or absence, of goodness means that evil is precisely that which is not supposed to exist at all. If we develop an explanation that completely resolves the "problem" of evil, we have failed to treat it as a privation at all and have instead given it the same status as any other thing that exists in the world. Or, as the systematic theologian Michael Himes puts it, "If ever we think we have answered [the problem of evil], then we have made evil less than evil."[6] Perhaps, then, it would be best to accept that there are times when a clear distinction between evil suffered and evil done will not satisfactorily account for all the pains we suffer in our lives. At those times, we can instead take solace in the fundamental conviction that evil is not supposed to be at all and thereby appreciate that as part of the pain of evil in the first place.

With these limitations acknowledged, let me conclude by raising a theological question: Given the reality of evil, can we still believe in a good God? Is God responsible for evil? Let's return to *The Lion King*.

Recall Simba's first meal with Timon and Pumba. Their "rustling up some grub" is a massacre as they feast at the expense of "slimy, yet satisfying" insects. That's just *one* meal! Even if we don't fancy eating grubs, it is undeniable that each day, millions of them lose their lives to predators. Can God *really* allow such carnage? Our maxim—*God creates, evil negates*—proves helpful. No doubt, this is an instance of "evil suffered." Bad for bugs, good for heroes. Although there is a negation, this negation contributes to creation by allowing Simba to thrive. We may not *like* that God creates a world such as ours where flourishing requires taking in nourishment from external sources, but the harmony of "The Circle of Life" is not incompatible with a Creator. And we may even speculate about how a God could have created our world otherwise, a world without death or suffering . . . but it would be a world quite different from ours. Personally, I do not *like* death, but as a science aficionado and lover of nature, I do not see "evil suffered" as a definitive refutation of God's existence because I can discern how these negations contribute to creation's good. If God sets in motion and sustains "The Circle of Life," I as a believer can at least try to find my place within it.

But if we can attribute "evil suffered" to God because of the way God created the cosmos, we cannot blame God for evil done. Why not? Because evil done does not contribute any good at all to creation. Moral evil is de-creative because the perpetrator is lessened as a result. Sure, crime may result in wealth; lies may secure power. To the theological eye, the tragedy of moral evil is that no good results: Scar grows more haggard and embittered, the Pride Lands are denuded. In cases of evil done or sin, the agent's negation is a rejection of God's creative activity. Rather than taking one's place in the chorus and achieving one's telos, one defiantly sings out of key and wreaks havoc overall. The theological eye can, I think, discern God's creative presence within evil suffered; the same cannot be said of *evil done* where, in an attempt to "box God out," one fails at being what one is created to be: human.

Pondering evil and distinguishing its two types requires the theologian to look at reality's dark side. No matter how you slice it, the reality of evil touches every created being. Everything within "The Circle of Life" achieves its telos by somehow depriving another being of its good. We may question *why* a good God would create a world that required this life cycle, but "evil suffered" need not discount belief in God. Even if God is responsible for a world that operates according to natural law, if the created order involves evil suffered, we cannot attribute evil done to God. In no way does moral evil contribute to creation. It is a negation that prevents perpetrators from attaining their end. Moral evil is a self-inflicted wound that diminishes the self and one's victims. Although we don't often talk about sin, if you listen to the news, you'll hear its echo. We describe upstanding citizens as *humanitarians*, as persons whose work contributes to the flourishing of the human species. And we decry others as *inhumane* for committing deeds—abuse, murder, racism, sexism—that negate creation and work against human flourishing.

I have not "solved" the problem of evil. But by disentangling natural and moral evil and putting them into a theological framework, I hope readers better appreciate the way theology gives us a "lens" through which to look at our lives and to help make sense of our experiences. I turn this over to Conor, who will lead us further down the dark path to look more intensively at the nature of moral evil and its corruptive effects.

Discernment in the Face of Evil

As Ryan explained, disentangling natural and moral evil helps to address a major wrinkle that evil adds to the fabric of discernment. Our personal experience with evil can easily challenge our willingness to discern anything in conversation with God, a problem Ryan framed around the question, "Why would anyone commit themselves to a God who permits such chaos?" The contrasts between evil suffered and evil done offer a response to this challenge, revealing that God's goodness need not be indicted by the existence of evil and suggesting that the identification of the Christian God as one's ultimate concern (and thus a starting point for discernment) is not as hopeless as it might first appear. The very distinction that reclaims the goodness of God, however, introduces a second problem for discernment. The reason moral evil is not imputed to God is that it represents *our* failure to flourish; it is a departure from the way God intended *us* to be. This becomes a challenge for discernment because, as we discussed in the last chapter, discernment is supposed to help us pursue our proper human telos. By frustrating this telos, moral evil moves us farther away from the goal we are trying to achieve when we discern well.

Anyone wishing to discern effectively must therefore have a keen understanding of moral evil. As one of the key obstacles to human flourishing, moral evil—which theologians typically refer to as sin—emerges as a diversion from the path we intend to walk when we identify our eulogy virtues and set our sights on the person we want to become. By understanding the nature of evil done more fully, we can recognize the deceptive allure of sin more clearly and resist its pull more successfully. We can, in other words, stay the course so that we actually end up where we are called to be as we form ourselves through the decisions we make.

The first thing to recognize about moral evil is that it undercuts a person's proper telos in a particular way. Recall how Scar exemplifies moral evil. He makes choices that harm not only others but also himself, causing him to become a bad brother (who kills his sibling), a bad ruler (who abuses his subjects in order to enrich his cronies), and a bad lion (who does not live up to his place in the circle of life). When humans sin, they certainly undermine their relationships and their roles, but at the end of the day, they invariably mar their humanity. In effect, they reject their true potential as human beings. Given the teleological vision of the fullness of human flourishing discussed in the last chapter, this rejection amounts to a movement away from self-gift.

Two theological definitions for sin help to highlight the denial of human potential inherent in moral evil. First, the twentieth-century theologian Walter Rauschenbusch, famous for connecting Christianity with social responsibility as part of the "Social Gospel" movement that rose to prominence in the United States at the start of the twentieth century, argued that sin "is essentially selfishness."[7] This description, of course, reflects the denial of self-gift involved in sin, emphasizing the fact that moral evil turns us in upon ourselves in a way that makes us less aware of others and their needs. The second definition, from the Jesuit moral theologian James Keenan, describes sin as "a failure to bother to love."[8] What he means is that in every sin, we close ourselves off to some human connection, choosing to ignore a relationship that would allow us to grow in self-gift. Whether it is a decision to pretend that we do not see the homeless person who asks for change on the sidewalk, the choice to break a promise to a friend, or the refusal to take the time to care for ourselves, sin involves a denial of relationship and a disregard for a person's human needs. By considering sin as a failure to bother to love, we can better recognize the way that moral evil inflicts harm on the agent who acts and not just on the person who is hurt by the action, for nothing is more human than love, and nothing is more devastating to our own humanity than a selfish indifference to the ways we could be using our lives to help undo some of the suffering in the world—including our own.

While these two definitions of sin are quite helpful, they also introduce a new challenge for the notion that moral evil is a danger to discernment. If sin is so inimical to human nature, one might reasonably ask, then why would anyone choose to sin in the first place? Can we not expect that humans would want to be good humans and, therefore, that they would readily reject temptations to selfishness that move them away from their proper end? In the abstract, these are logical assumptions, but in practice, moral evil rarely reveals all its damaging consequences to us at the outset. On the contrary, sin tends to appear more attractive than it actually is, through both its own deception and our confusion. Aquinas, for instance, argued that sin unfailingly appears under the guise of the good, enticing us with the prospect of positive benefits that either fail to materialize or only yield a short-lived benefit at the cost of long-term destructiveness. Thus, a child lies about the source of a broken vase for the immediate benefit of avoiding punishment but reaps the consequences of a lack of parental trust for the next two months. We are always seeking some good, but we do not always accurately perceive what is genuinely good for us, and when we get it wrong, we are often the cause of some degree of evil done.

The real challenge for discernment, then, is not only that moral evil prevents us from reaching our proper telos but also that it clouds our vision so much that it is difficult to notice when we are on the wrong path. One way to overcome this problem is to be more reflective about our decisions, subjecting them to greater scrutiny so that we can identify the false moves more quickly. Ignatius's approach to discernment provides good tools for this process because he recognized the deceptive nature of moral evil. We will talk in more detail about Ignatius's rules for discernment throughout part III, but for now, suffice it to say that he described "two spirits" at work in our discernment process, one good and one evil. Good spirits, he argued, lead to integration, allowing us to become that person we most deeply long to be. Evil spirits, meanwhile, prompt disintegration, turning us away from the eulogy virtues we want to leave as our legacy. By attending to these competing movements and keeping our eyes fixed on the end we are ultimately trying to achieve, we can better distinguish between the good choices that will honestly lead us to our true telos and the sinful indulgences that deceive us into thinking we are still headed where we want to go.

Of course, recognizing the existence of these two contradictory movements is one thing, but if we want to discern well and avoid the pull of those evil spirits that lead to our disintegration, we need to be able to nip them in the bud. For this task, I find the work of the twentieth-century Protestant theologian Reinhold Niebuhr helpful. In one of his more prominent books, *The Nature and Destiny of Man*, Niebuhr explored how humans first succumbed to sin. (Despite the gender-exclusive language in the title—a product of the period when it was written—Niebuhr intended his analysis to cover the experience of *humanity* as a whole; as we shall see below, however, criticisms suggest he may not have been as comprehensive as he imagined.) The question of how sin emerged has vexed Christian theologians for centuries because, according to the creation accounts in Genesis, God created humans not only good but "very good" (Genesis 1:31). Yet with the passage of just one more chapter, these same humans are next seen disobeying God, doing the *one thing* they were told not to do. This narrative begs the question: how could the ostensibly good God have added a creature so obviously prone to mischief to this earth? Niebuhr tackles this question directly, offering insight into how the evil spirits can work their way into our lives and deceive us into choosing sin under the guise of the good.

Niebuhr accepts that God is good and therefore assumes that humans must be the cause of their own sinful transgressions. This is a delicate solution, however, because God created humans, and if we had the power to sin built into our nature at the beginning, this would seem to call into question the very goodness of God. Niebuhr explains that sin is not part of God's design but an effect of humanity's precarious position as a creature (and, thus, not God) made in God's very image (and, thus, like God). Together, these two aspects of our nature mean that humans are inherently finite, because we are creatures, but also uniquely capable of imagining the infinite, because we have something of God's nature within us. We therefore live a complicated life, caught between the infinite hopes we can establish for ourselves and the finite outcomes we can realistically achieve. The result, in Niebuhr's terms, is an existential anxiety that is fundamental to the human condition. This existential anxiety, which is an unavoidable consequence of humanity's peculiar placement in the larger schema of creation, lays the foundation for sin to emerge because, as anyone who has experienced persistent anxiety can explain, anxiety cannot be ignored. Invariably, it festers until we decide to do something (anything!) to disarm its uncomfortable hold on our psyche. Often, that something is not our best choice because it is aimed at addressing the discomfort we feel when we are anxious rather than the source of our anxiety itself. We seek short-term solace at the expense of long-term pain, with an action that typically includes a failure to bother to love someone in our lives—perhaps, most commonly, ourselves.

Niebuhr understood that humanity's struggles to overcome the existential anxiety of being caught between the finite and the infinite would lead to sin. More precisely, he maintained that humans would inevitably gravitate toward one end of their nature at the expense of the other, undercutting their proper telos by denying the tension that makes humans human in the first place. At one end, he explained, some will embrace the infinite possibilities of human freedom and ignore the limitations of creaturely finitude. These people will sin with pride, elevating themselves above their nature and failing to attend to the shortcomings in themselves and in the world around them. At the other end, some will find the prospect of freedom too overwhelming, so they will turn their energies toward their creatureliness, indulging in the pleasures of earthly life so that they never have to deal with the prospect of deciding how they actually want to live their lives and thus never have to face the consequences of failing to achieve their goals. These people will sin through "sensuality," abdicating their freedom and rejecting their responsibility to choose wisely. Significantly, both extremes match the definitions of sin relayed above. Pride (at a vicious extreme) is selfish, but sensuality is also selfish too because it involves us ignoring our responsibilities so we can do something that seems pleasant to us. Both pride and sensuality, meanwhile, represent a failure to bother to love insofar as they undercut our true nature, harm our relationship with God, and leave us less equipped to respond to the needs of others in our lives.

I realize Niebuhr's diagnosis can be a bit heady, though, so let me give a quick example to capture how anxiety leads to sin in his account. Employ a bit of Ignatian imagination and return with me, for a moment, to the college days of my coauthor, Ryan. As he mentioned obliquely before, he started as a pre-med major, studying chemistry. If you can, imagine that he is told by one of his chemistry professors that he has an amazing science talent. He is so skilled at chemistry that he could one day win a Nobel prize. If he takes this vision seriously and says, "Yes! I can do this!" he embraces his freedom. But, the road to Stockholm is not an easy one, and maybe Ryan approaches his first Organic Chemistry exam with trepidation. "I might fail!" he bemoans, coming face to face with his finitude. What is he going to do the day before his exam?

Feeling the pressure of the possibility of a 4.0 alongside the possibility of an F minus, Ryan will be in a state of anxiety, and if he resolves this anxiety by choosing only his freedom or his finitude, he will make some serious mistakes. For instance, he might turn toward freedom and become puffed up with pride, thinking that he can do anything he wants with his God-given chemistry talents. Refusing to study, he marches into the lab expecting to discover the drug that cures cancer . . . but, because he is totally unprepared, he sets the lab on fire instead. Alternatively, Ryan could acquiesce to his finitude, wasting his college days binge watching reality TV shows on Netflix so that he never has to deal with the situation where he tries to earn the Nobel prize and fails. Rather, he can console himself by lying, "I could be on that stage in Stockholm if I wanted to. I just don't want to!" In this case, he has not killed anyone with a freak chemistry accident. He has only left everyone who could have been saved by his miracle cancer drug uncured because he refused to apply himself.

Granted, there is an element of the extreme in this illustration, but I think it demonstrates Niebuhr's point. Temptations take advantage of

our anxieties, offering us quick and easy solutions to the kinds of problems that never go away quickly or easily, if at all. What this means for
discernment, then, is that we need to confront our anxieties if we are to
avoid the roadblocks that moral evil introduces on our path to becoming the person we want to be. We need to understand those anxieties so
that we will not be hoodwinked by the false promise of a short-term fix.
We also need to be ready to live with some tensions in our lives, for none
of us is perfect and the road to the life we want to live will not be simple. If it seems too easy, it probably is!

At this point, I want to highlight something that has been mostly
implicit in this section. The language of sin as selfishness and its associations with pride can make it seem like the antidote to sin is pure selflessness. Such an interpretation fails to appreciate all the ways we can
go astray and undermine our humanity, narrowing sin too quickly and
defining it too neatly. I mentioned earlier that there have been criticisms
of Niebuhr's account of the origin of human sinfulness for not being
comprehensive enough to account for all human experiences. Those criticisms, most famously presented by the feminist theologian Valerie
Saiving (Goldstein), hinged on precisely the relationship between sin,
selfishness, and selflessness. As Saiving outlined in a landmark academic
article that helped give rise to an entire branch of theology now known
as feminist theology (which has numerous iterations, even within the
Catholic tradition, but is broadly defined by its commitment to gender
equality and its insistence that women's experience must be a central
source for theological reflection), there are gendered differences in how
men and women experience the temptation to sin as a result of the distinct social pressures each face. In Saiving's account, selfishness and
pride may be primordial sins for men, who are culturally conditioned to
establish their masculinity by demonstrating their power over others,
but self-abnegation is a much greater source of temptation for women,
who are more regularly conditioned to accept subordinate roles.[9]

There are likely some today who would bristle at Saiving's description of these culturally assigned gender roles, but before dismissing her
too quickly, think about two things. First, she wrote in 1960, when strict
assumptions about masculinity and femininity were decidedly part of

the cultural ethos. Second, despite our efforts toward greater equality, we still see these influences on men and women today. In fact, one could read the *Barbie* movie as a manifestation of these two impulses through the different trajectories of Barbie and Ken. More important, Saiving's larger point stands: if we think about sin in just a narrow sense of selfishness, we will not cover the totality of temptation in our human experience. This is why Niebuhr's combination of pride *and* sensuality is so valuable because it helps us recognize that the corrective to sin is not some simplistic form of self-rejection but rather a much more honest recognition of one's place in the world as a finite creature who, while not God, is still very much an important part of the cosmos all the same. Turning away from sin therefore requires rejecting the type of selfishness that closes us off to relationship, but we move the pendulum too far if we forget that one of the relationships we need to honor is the relationship we have with ourselves. Tellingly, Fr. Keenan, who proposed the definition of sin as a failure to bother to love, has also asserted that "self-care" is one of the four essential virtues—or positive character traits—humans need to cultivate in order to flourish.[10] Yes, self-gift may be the highest form of flourishing for us as human beings, but there needs to be a self there to give away, and that means we cannot ignore the duties we have to ourselves. Or, put another way, we sin whenever we fail to bother to love that which God loves, and this absolutely includes each one of us.

So far, I have only discussed how moral evil affects discernment by affecting us—how it obstructs our pursuit of the eulogy virtues that represent our way of giving selflessly (again, defined appropriately) to others in our lives. The last piece of our "discerning in the face of evil" puzzle has to do with how both evil suffered and evil done should affect our discernment process, not just how moral evil alone can throw a wrench in our plans. This piece emerges from the fact that evil, in all its forms, is a negation. Evil is, again, that which ought not to be. Consequently, for those who discern in conversation with a God who is good, the presence of evil introduces another dimension to the decisions we make, setting the expectation that part of our calling is to respond to the effects of evil in the world. In other words, because Christians say evil should not be, they must assume that part of how God wants people to live in the world is to confront the evil they see. Part of discernment, then, is not simply identifying who we want to be in general, by setting our sights on our telos using our eulogy virtues, but also establishing how we can counteract the impact of evil as we pursue that end.

This task will require a slightly different approach depending on the type of evil we see. Evil suffered serves some good, so it is not something we can ever remove entirely. Instead, we should look for ways to address the negative effects natural evil inflicts on others in pursuit of its positive results. Thus, we might think about how to provide aid in the face of a natural disaster or how to design buildings to better withstand the inevitable earthquake. Evil done, meanwhile, is harmful to all, so we ought to think about ways to avoid it in ourselves and also ways to assist others in choosing a path that moves them away from sin. Ultimately, this is a complicated process, and frankly, the rest of the book is necessary to wrestle with this question fully. To prime the pump at this point, however, we would like to close with a meditation to lay the groundwork for what it might mean to respond to evil in a fruitful way consistent with the vision of human flourishing that shaped Ignatius's First Principle and Foundation.

Meditation: How the Light Gets In

Saint Ignatius of Loyola was no stranger to history's darkness. He knew well how sin diminishes humans and how its effects ravage the world. And, in this reflection, based on Ignatius's "Meditation on the Incarnation," we ask you to consider the scope of human history from a God's-eye view to get a sense of how Christians insist God does respond to real-world suffering but in a very particular way.

A Crack in Everything

1. Sit upright. Take a few deep breaths and relax. Let the day's cares slip away. Open your mind and give your imagination permission to explore.

2. Look down at the earth. Behold the vast array of earth's population. Take in the world's diversity. People of all shapes and sizes. Different races and sexes and professions. See villagers trading their goods, laughing. Watch distracted mall-shoppers rush from store to store to buy the latest goods. Let your mind visit wedding receptions and funerals, football games and poker nights, a hospital's delivery room and a hospice. Dwell on the "The Circle of Life" in all of its savage beauty.

3. Now, open your ears. Hear the laughter and singing. Hear, too, the cries of anguish as a mother laments the murder of her son. Note the tear-streaked face of a man watching his partner of many years slip away into dementia. Do not flinch from the angry words and accusations flung between neighbors, citizens, and nations. With your Ignatian imagination, use your senses to *feel* what it is to be among the people. Be fully present to the joy and hope, the grief and sorrow; do not turn away from the pain. War and pestilence, famine and genocide, oppression and violence. The rich grow richer; the poor grow poorer. Anxiety and depression. Suicide and addiction. The innocent suffer and their tears go unheeded. The world is cracked and broken, and no matter where you turn, the shadow of evil is not far off.

4. From your perch in the heavens, how do you regard this world? Are you satisfied? Or does this vision somehow move your heart and call you into action? You see such potential, such goodness . . . but you cannot deny the darkness or ignore the sinful mess they have created. You see and know the chaos.

5. How would you respond? Do you turn away and let them work things out for themselves? Or do you resolve to make their reality *your* reality to show them the better path? Will you risk pain and suffering, indignity and death, to show them another way of life?

If your heart aches as you scan the globe and meditate on our history, consider how God's heart aches at what we have done to our world and one another. Christian theology refuses to deny or cover over the messiness of our lives. We must look unflinchingly at the wretchedness of history and summon the courage to act. At the core of Christianity and its theology is a belief that God has seen all of history, has heard the cry of the people, and has entered our chaos and made our reality God's reality. Christians believe that Jesus Christ, God's Word made flesh, is the light that pierces history's darkness and illuminates for those who have faith in him a new way of life. What Jesus offers is not a self-improvement plan but a radical new way of being a people. If we wish to *understand* before we *take action*, as the Ignatian B.U.T. framework demands, then it is to this claim that we must now turn.

Key Terms and Ideas

- Evil suffered: also known as "natural evil," this is the type of suffering that is an inevitable part of the flourishing of creation as a whole—the antelope dies so that the lion can live. In cases of natural evil, *some* good is achieved, albeit at the expense of another.
- Evil done: also known as "moral evil," this is the type of suffering that is bad for all parties involved, directly harming the victim of an evil action while also undermining the humanity of the agent who commits the act—stealing candy leaves the victim sad and hungry and makes the taker less appealing as a person. In these cases, no true or lasting good is achieved.
- Sin as a "failure to bother to love": Fr. James Keenan's definition of sin (a.k.a. evil done/moral evil), which highlights the fact that sin always undermines the telos of the sinner by preventing them from giving themselves lovingly to others.
- Freedom and finitude: Reinhold Niebuhr's description of humanity's contradictory impulses that are always in tension, opening the door to sin. Freedom refers to the human person's ability to imagine all they can achieve with free will, while finitude defines the limits of creaturely existence. When humans gravitate toward one pole or the other, they tend toward the sin of pride (freedom without finitude) or sensuality (finitude at the expense of freedom), failing to bother to love as they ought.

Recommended Resources

Genesis 3

This classic scriptural text on sin describes "the Fall," or humanity's descent into sinfulness when Adam and Eve, the humans God created "very good" in the first chapter of Genesis, decide to disobey God. Read the text carefully to analyze potential explanations for why they may have chosen this problematic path. (We explore some implications of the Genesis 3 story in the next chapter.)

Brian Davies, OP, *The Thought of Thomas Aquinas* (New York: Clarendon Press, 1993).

Chapter 5 provides a clear, if still technical, treatment of Aquinas's understanding of evil.

Lisa Sowle Cahill, "Catholic Feminists and Traditions: Renewal, Reinvention, Replacement," *Journal of the Society of Christian Ethics* 34, no. 2 (Fall/Winter 2014): 27–51.

This academic article, written by one of the world's leading Catholic feminist theologians, provides a typology of different Catholic approaches to feminist theology, demonstrating both the breadth of this branch of theology in the Catholic tradition and its common elements.

Ursula K. LeGuin, "The Ones Who Walk Away from Omelas."

This short story puts the painful consequences of evil in stark relief. Read theologically, the story invites one to analyze whether evil suffered or evil done is on display, something readers can determine by asking whether the people of Omelas actually gain from the arrangement or instead frustrate their telos by failing to bother to love.

The Lion King, directed by Roger Allers and Rob Minkoff, Disney, 1994.

As the first section of this chapter notes, Disney's *The Lion King* demonstrates the distinction between evil suffered and evil done. The film's emphasis on the balance of the "Circle of Life" depicts the ways evil suffered can ultimately contribute to flourishing, while Scar's descent illustrates the self-destructive nature of evil done.

Herbert McCabe, OP, "Evil," *New Blackfriars* vol. 62, no. 727 (January 1981): 4–17. https://www.jstor.org/stable/43247228.

McCabe frames this article as a legal proceeding intended to demonstrate that belief in God is compatible with the existence of evil.

Frankenstein, directed by James Whale, Universal Pictures, 1931; and *I Am Legend*, directed by Francis Lawrence, Warner Brothers, 2007.

These two films—one a classic "monster" film and the other a postapocalyptic movie—can support a deeper appreciation of Niebuhr's insight into the tension between freedom and finitude. In both films, viewers watch as humankind rejects its finitude and attempts to "play God," with disastrous results.

Barbie, directed by Greta Gerwig, Warner Brothers, 2023.

This cultural phenomenon was, by Gerwig's own account, intentionally crafted to wrestle with theological themes, including those that emerge from the story of creation. The characters display both of Niebuhr's paradigmatic sins at different points in the film, with some seeking freedom at the expense of finitude and others seeking finitude at the expense of freedom. The conclusion, in fact, gives some indication of what it means to keep both these poles in tension.

Notes

1. Brian Davies, OP, *The Thought of Thomas Aquinas* (Oxford: Clarendon Press, 1993), 89–97.
2. Herbert McCabe, OP, *Faith within Reason* (New York: Continuum, 2007), 83.
3. Herbert McCabe, OP, *God Matters* (New York: Continuum, 2004), 31.
4. Davies, *The Thought of Thomas Aquinas*, 94.
5. McCabe, *Faith within Reason*, 83.
6. Michael J. Himes et al., *Doing the Truth in Love: Conversations about God, Relationships, and Service* (Mahwah, NJ: Paulist Press, 1995), 70.
7. Walter Rauschenbusch, *A Theology for the Social Gospel* (Nashville, TN: Abingdon, 1960), 47.
8. James F. Keenan, SJ, *Moral Wisdom: Lessons and Texts from the Catholic Tradition*, 2nd ed. (Lanham, MD: Rowman and Littlefield, 2010), 57.
9. Valerie Saiving Goldstein, "The Human Situation: A Feminine View," *Journal of Religion* 40, no. 2 (April 1960): 100–12.
10. James F. Keenan, SJ, "Proposing Cardinal Virtues," *Theological Studies* 56, no. 4 (December 1995): 709–29.

PART II

Understanding

4

The Light Side of a Dark Story

For as long as I can remember, one of my "guilty pleasures" has been watching horror movies. I have a soft spot for zombie films, ranging from George Romero's shambling classic *Night of the Living Dead* to the fast-paced *28 Days Later* to the South Korean gem *Train to Busan*. On a Thursday night, after I've prepped for class and before I go to bed, I might watch a slasher flick (*Scream*, *Texas Chainsaw Massacre*), something about demonic possession (*The Exorcist*), a movie about nature run amok (*The Nest*, *Squirm*), or whatever I find on Netflix or Amazon. I love the subject enough that I teach a course called "The Theology of Horror," where we spend the first seven weeks analyzing the metaphysics and theology of Netflix's 2021 hit *Midnight Mass*. During my sabbatical in 2023, I wrote an entire book entitled *The Theology of Horror: The Hidden Depths of Popular Films*. As odd as it may sound, I think my love for horror movies has made me a better theologian and has helped me to understand discernment better.

Using examples from the horror genre, this chapter explores how stories work. I do this for two reasons. First, as far as we know, humans are the only creatures who tell stories. A kid comes home from school and the parent asks, "What did you do today?" If the kid is not being moody, the parent gets a story about the day's events. That same kid, a few years later, may face a college recruiter who asks, "Why do you want to come to this college? What do you want to study? Why do you want to study this?" If the interview is going to go well, the question will elicit not one-word answers but—you guessed it—some sort of story. When we meet new people, we are often invited to tell our stories; when we include others in our peer group, we invite them to take part in the group's ongoing narrative. Advertisers try to convince consumers that by buying Product X, attending School Y, or wearing Brand Z clothes, one will share in this bigger, flashier story. There are family stories, national stories, ethnic stories, and religious stories. Some stories we celebrate, others we regret, yet no matter how hard we try, we cannot escape them. We use stories to explain who we are, to understand where we have been, and to share with others where we hope to go. Stories, and learning to tell our stories, are essential to developing and deepening the spiritual life.

There's a second reason for drawing on the horror genre. As I hope to show, the Bible and horror stories have a lot in common. But where humans respond to scary and horrific events by running away, Christians believe that God does the opposite. At the end of the last chapter, we invited you to contemplate that Christians believe in a God who sees the messiness of human history yet lovingly chooses to enter it. In Jesus Christ, God makes the horror story of human history God's own story and begins to rewrite it. Instead of watching passively, God gets in on the action and reveals how we, too, can respond to the world's evil. So let's take a plunge into horror's darkness to see how it might illuminate the Bible and bring us to understand why believers choose to make the Christian story their own.

Plot I: The Overreacher

In *The Philosophy of Horror*, philosopher Noël Carroll identifies two types of plots we tend to find in horror fiction. The first type, "overreacher," is evident in Mary Shelley's *Frankenstein* and in movies like *Hellraiser* or *Candyman*. The gist of this plot is that some knowledge is dangerous to possess. An ambitious scientist, or a too-curious investigator, makes some discovery that unleashes a terrible force into the world. If you've ever tried to conjure up "Bloody Mary" in your darkened bathroom (repeating "Bloody Mary" five times into a mirror in the hope of glimpsing her ghost), you've tinkered with this plot.

Carroll identifies four moments in this plot. Let me list and describe them:

1. Preparation: character assembles items and ingredients
    (body parts in *Frankenstein*, puzzle box in *Hellraiser*).
    Author/director reveals—in a story—character's motives.
2. Experiment: on the first attempt or after several, character
    achieves what they set out to do. Body is reanimated, demon
    conjured, portal to the supernatural realm opened.
3. Negative consequences: experiment unleashes an
    uncontrollable and dangerous force (*Candyman, Frankenstein*).
    Or, in other versions, the malevolent being may have been
    deliberately freed and is under the control of a villain
    (*Sleepy Hollow*).
4. Confrontation: the overreacher wises up and tries to destroy
    the creation or undo the deed. An all-or-nothing battle
    ensues, a conflict pitting good against evil.[1]

Overreacher is an apt description of such plots because they unfold stories of agents whose "will to knowledge" leads them into dark territory. The scientist, magician, or curious teenager seeks some secret knowledge only to discover, often too late, that some things are not worth knowing.

Sound familiar? Yes, there are hints of Genesis 3, that story once again of Adam and Eve. So let's look at the text with the overreacher plot in mind. My wager: reading Genesis 3 through this lens reveals how the Bible can speak *to* human life because it speaks *from* human life. What Christian theologians understand is that this isn't just a story. It's our story. Let's see why.

If you read Genesis 2, you know God created a beautiful paradise filled with good things to eat. One rule: don't touch the tree in the middle of the garden. All else is open. One day, Eve, out and about, meets a serpent. Here's Genesis 3:1–7:

"Did God say, 'You shall not eat from any tree in the garden'?" The woman said to the serpent, "We may eat of the fruit of the trees in the garden; but God said, 'You shall not eat of the fruit of the tree that is in the middle of the garden, nor shall you touch it, or you shall die.'" But the serpent said to the woman, "You will not die; for God knows that when you eat of it your eyes will be opened, and you will be like God, knowing good and evil." So when the woman saw that the tree was good for food, and that it was a delight to the eyes, and that the tree was to be desired to make one wise, she took of its fruit and ate; and she also gave some to her husband, who was with her, and he ate. Then the eyes of both were opened, and they knew that they were naked; and they sewed fig leaves together and made loincloths for themselves.

Overreacher theme: despite divine prohibition, the desire for forbidden knowledge is too great to be resisted. The serpent's words enkindle Eve's desire and endow the fruit with an aura that makes it irresistible. Indeed, notice how the author portrays Eve justifying her action: *it looks tasty, it's beautiful, it'll make me wise.* Prepared by the serpent who awakens desire, Eve takes and eats, and ever since, we have had to negotiate the consequences of a world broken by sin.

Now, Genesis 3 is no eyewitness account of events. It's a story (not a fairy tale) that tries to reveal a truth about what it means to be human. What it reflects is the theological insight that humans have an uncanny knack for abusing their freedom and failing to achieve their telos, just as Niebuhr acknowledged and we explored in chapter 3. Indeed, the author of Genesis seems to be saying that from human history's beginning, we have actively and willingly chosen against being in harmony with God's plan. The story speaks not only of an event way-back-when but also of an ongoing struggle we all deal with. For this temptation is one we face today, a whisper that woos: *Go ahead. You're special and can handle it. Do it. It's forbidden because others are afraid.* So we reach out . . . and discover that what we thought would deliver us from temptation betrays us and begins our downfall. The age-old lesson often repeated yet seldom learned: turning away from our telos is self-destructive, and it diminishes our humanity and severs our relationship with creation. The plot may have been made frightfully famous by *Frankenstein* and *Candyman*, but the lesson about freedom's potential for abuse is one that theologians have long considered.

One takeaway from Genesis 3 and horror stories with overreacher plots is that events seldom, if ever, unfold according to expectation. Eve did not expect to discover herself naked and certainly did not want to fall out with God; Helen, in *Candyman*, did not expect a hook-handed ghost to wreak havoc on her life. Even if this can be dark, there's something profoundly realistic about Genesis's story. Instead of downplaying history's messiness, the author told a story to make sense of it, one that speaks to readers because it reflects our experiences of temptation, sin, and turning away from God. Or, as it is said in Ecclesiastes, "There is nothing new under the sun" (1:9). But there is another horror plot that lets sunlight into even darker places.

Plot II: Complex Discovery

Overreacher plots generally focus on a single character. A mad scientist, curious teen, rogue magician. You could probably include in these plots stories of explorers or researchers who go too far in the quest for knowledge (the *Alien* franchise). And if these narratives speak *to* us, perhaps it is because they speak *of* us and reveal parts of us to ourselves. The Greek philosopher Aristotle began his *Metaphysics* with a general claim about humans: All humans have a deep desire to know. And like any desire, one must *become aware* of it and discern the best practices for acting on it. Failure to use our intellectual gifts and talents well, as these movies remind us, can have catastrophic consequences . . . like opening portals to demonic realms.

If overreacher plots focus on individuals who push their desire to know too far, what Carroll calls "complex discovery" plots explore how dark and mysterious forces reveal themselves to us. The babysitter hears a noise at the window; teenagers ignore a "Do Not Swim" sign and go for a moonlight dip; a possessed artifact—doll, car, jewel—acts as a doorway for an evil power to enter our world. In each case, there is an element of discovery as characters discover something unknown and, often, unnoticed by others. Carroll notes four movements:

1. Onset: monster's presence made known to the audience and—too late—the victim. *Jaws* is a good example as it opens with the shark attack. Sometimes the audience sees the monster right away (*Night of the Living Dead, A Nightmare on Elm Street*), and other times the nature of the villain takes time to be revealed (*Friday the 13th*). Importantly, the reader/audience has information—that an evil force exists—others do not possess.

2. Discovery: eventually, someone survives an encounter with the monster *or* pieces the evidence together to establish the monster's existence. But when the person presents the evidence to others or the authorities, they are not believed. Despite evidence of the shark's presence, the mayor in *Jaws* refuses to close the beaches; no one believes Andy when he tells them "Chucky did it" in *Child's Play*. And while those "in the know" try to convince others to believe them, the body count mounts.

3. Confirmation: finally, something convinces others of the monster's existence. In *Jaws*, it's a really bad beach day. Eyewitnesses see the creature (*Jeepers Creepers*). At this point, a reliable authority may emerge to reveal the villain's story, as Dr. Loomis does in *Halloween*. Often enough, some theory about the creature will give a hint about how to overcome it.

4. Confrontation: characters take a stand against evil. This may involve several failed attempts before good triumphs. To be sure, good's victory is not certain (*The Omen*). And when good wins, evil still endures . . . otherwise, we wouldn't have sequels! So, even though humans win *this time*, a monstrous shadow still falls and leaves open the possibility of the horror's return.[2]

Good horror stories work by drawing the audience into their dramatic unfolding as they create tension and suspense. Even if one doesn't believe in poltergeists or demonic dolls, a good horror story gets the audience to second-guess their assumptions about the world. As Carroll puts it, horror plots show "that there are more things in heaven and earth than are acknowledged to exist in our standing conceptual frameworks."[3] If you give this insight a twist, you'll see why theologians have a reason to embrace the horror genre. Let me explain.

As the complex discovery plot indicates, the horror genre revolves around some type of evil breaking into and threatening human life. Its monstrous arrival interrupts the characters' accepted status quo. Freddy disrupts life on Elm Street; Jason ravages Camp Crystal Lake; the zombie horde sows death and terror. Ghost or ghoul, djinn or mutant worm, horror stories narrate the way a monstrous and usually disgusting force breaches the boundaries of what we consider "normal" and poses an existential threat to humanity. Even when they are utterly fantastic, a good horror story casts a shadow over reason and makes us wonder *What if?* What if the Ouija board's planchette actually *did* move on its own? What if my nocturnal neighbor *really is* a vampire? What if the tapping at my window, the chill feeling I get when I approach the cemetery, the faint footsteps following me . . . *What if* there's more to reality than meets the eye?

Religious believers are convinced that there is, in fact, more to reality than what we see. In this way, they accept the premise of the complex discovery plot. But there's a twist: If horror involves a malevolent force entering history to destroy humanity, the Bible recounts the long narrative of the way the benevolent Creator enters history to rescue it. The Christian, to put it into horror-speak, believes that God has entered the horror story of human history to redeem and save it. Recall the meditation at the end of the last chapter where you imagined God beholding the whole of human history and seeing the deep wounds caused by sin. Christian belief holds that God's response is not to eradicate humans, or to hit the reset button on history, but to enter our chaos to show us another way. The Gospel of John puts it this way: "The Word became flesh and lived among us" (1:14). This is the Incarnation: the act whereby God, through the Word "becoming flesh" in Jesus Christ, takes a role in our horror story to save us from it.

Plot Movement	Horror	Bible
Onset	In-breaking of evil; rift created in sense of "normalcy." This evil presence should not be there and is dangerous to humans.	Genesis 3: Evil recorded as humans choose against their telos. Sin interrupts and corrupts human history. The presence of sin dehumanizes and diminishes. New Testament: *Annunciation* of Jesus's birth (Luke 1:26–38). God enters human history, not to destroy but to save it. The Incarnation as God's in-breaking into history to heal our horror story.
Discovery	Presence of evil made known, but its presence rejected by those in authority and power.	Old Testament prophets cry out against sin and try to call people back to right relationship with God. New Testament: Jesus's life and ministry testify to God's saving presence within history as the Kingdom is revealed. In deed and word, he shows and tells how God is trying to redeem creation. Meets resistance from those in power.
Confirmation	Authorities convinced of evil's threat. A way of combatting evil is discovered.	Jesus begins to gather followers, who believe that he reveals how God intends for humans to live. He reveals a new way of life others can make their own to counteract the evil (sin) that should not be.
Confrontation	Good squares off against evil.	Jesus threatens the order of sin that rules our world. This leads Jesus to the Cross, the paradoxical sign of God's victory over death. Resurrection manifests this victory over evil and becomes the sign of evil's undoing for those who preach the Good News.

It might be helpful to provide a diagram (see page 90) to show how the complex discovery plot we find in horror fiction can be found within the Bible. We will make this clearer as we go.

Studying a new subject requires learning new ideas and concepts, so don't fret if you've never heard of "Annunciation," "Redemption," "The Cross," or "Resurrection." Right now, just focus on "Onset." This is what we have been studying when talking about sin and moral evil. Genesis 3 tells the beginning of the horror story that sin causes in human history. It's a story that reflects that we humans have a history not only of failing to live up to our telos but—far more horrifically—of actively choosing against it. It's a tragic story that touches and tarnishes every aspect of our lives. Nevertheless, Christians believe in a loving God who sees and hears the plight of those who suffer in history and resolves to do something about it. We believe in a God who takes the side of the victim (Genesis 4), who liberates the chosen people from bondage (Exodus), who summons prophets to call the people back to their senses and to accept their God-given telos (Isaiah, Ezekiel, Jeremiah). Yet the story that Christians tell about Jesus Christ does not begin with a God who violently invades history. Rather than a violent and bloody home invasion (*The Strangers*), Christianity's story begins with gracious persuasion when a faithful young Jewish woman says "yes" to a mysterious invitation to transform human history from the inside out. It is her story, Mary's story, that Christians believe begins a new chapter in human history.

The Incarnation: Discovery for Discernment

For all the ways the Bible parallels the conventions found in horror stories, there is also a dramatic departure that arguably tells us the most about how we should react to the horror of sin as we discern our response to the effects of evil (both suffered and done) in the world. In a discovery plot, we watch the teenage babysitter slowly opening the door to investigate the thump from the basement and want to scream at the screen, "Run away!" because that is exactly what we would do in her situation. It is only natural. God's response to the horror story that we have used our freedom to create is rather different, however. Instead of running away, the celestial horror movie viewer uses the unique powers of the divine to become a character in the very plot that we would do everything in our power to avoid. The way God does this is by becoming a human being, in the person of Jesus of Nazareth. Christians call this action the "Incarnation" because it is the way God came into the world in human flesh (*carnis* is Latin for "flesh").

The Incarnation is *the* central belief distinguishing Christianity from other religions, so it unsurprisingly yields numerous implications for Christian theology. In fact, theologians tend to refer to belief in the Incarnation as a "mystery" because it is so deep and multifaceted that no one expects to sort out all its implications. Nevertheless, Christian thinkers have been able to establish the essential elements of this mystery, which boil down to two claims: (1) Jesus was indeed God, and (2) Jesus shared every aspect of humanity except our sin (which, as chapter 3 explained, was never part of our humanity in the first place). With these two claims, the mystery of the Incarnation has much to teach anyone seeking to discern well because the Incarnation represents God's decision about how to act in the face of sin, creating a model for how we can reach our telos in a world haunted by the effects of evil. We only discover these insights, however, if we take the time to examine the mystery of the Incarnation with the scrutiny that comes from questioning the significance of its claims.

The first question to consider in this process is why God bothered with the Incarnation at all. Why did God become human? In a sense, the parallels with horror's discovery plot provide a basic answer to this question, suggesting that God became human to interrupt the conventional path of sin's horror story, facilitating the discovery of evil's true nature and offering the confirmation necessary to convince people in authority to take the dangers of sin seriously. Yet, surely this was not the only way for God to assist with discovery and confirmation. An allpowerful being could literally have chosen any other method to achieve this end, so why did God choose *this* interruption?

The answer can be found in the particulars of the Incarnation. If we think about God as the horror movie viewer, and if we read the Incarnation as an active entry into the plot to assist the characters who have been seemingly abandoned to their own fate, then we would expect God to appear on the scene as a seasoned warrior, but that is not the way the gospel unfolds. Luke introduces Jesus by introducing his mom, Mary, and recounting the Annunciation—the moment when an angel announced to Mary that God wanted her to bring Jesus, the Son of God, into the world. She used her freedom to accept this invitation, and through her body, God came into this world in a way familiar to every human being: as a baby.

This is not a point to gloss over lightly. On the contrary, this is perhaps the most profound piece of the mystery of the Incarnation because it conveys the depth of the human experience encompassed in the Incarnation. Babies are completely dependent on others for their survival and lead what might be called an unseemly life, at least during those initial years when there is not yet even control over bodily functions. That God would choose to share in this stage of human development showcases God's interest in joining our humanity to its fullest extent, messiness and all. It reveals that the significance of the Incarnation lies in the fact that God literally became one of us in such a complete way that we cannot ignore or dismiss that presence.

For the fourth-century theologian Athanasius of Alexandria, this was in fact the point of the Incarnation: God took on human flesh because it was the best way to get our attention. God created the world to show us the beauty and love of the Creator, but after introducing sin into the world, we forgot to read creation as a sign of something deeper. Instead, we treated creation as though it were an end in itself. Recognizing the problem, God decided to meet us in the flesh, using the very thing that had captured our attention to send us a message about where our priorities ought to be. The image this calls to mind for me is an adolescent boy so captivated by his smartphone that he fails to hear his parents calling him for dinner. Instead of getting angry at the child, though, the parents realize that the boy is not ignoring them but that their voices cannot get through. So, they (crafty parents) change the code of his favorite game so that they can appear in a pop-up ad on his screen, interrupting the game and telling him to come downstairs to eat. They use the object that has taken his focus away to reclaim that focus so that they can deliver a message. In essence, then, the Incarnation is one giant pop-up ad, interrupting our game to deliver a serious message.

The next question, naturally, is what that message might be. A detailed response to this question gets us more into the confirmation elements of the plot, which is really the focus of the next chapter, but I can still provide a general answer to this question here. In broad strokes, the basic message is that God is with us in the quagmire of sin. By sharing in our humanity, with all its finitude, God experiences the effects of evil suffered and evil done just as we experience them and thereby ensures that we are not alone in this broken world. Indeed, God offers the hope of a friend who walks along the same path so that we do not have to face the darkness alone.

Ultimately, this message of radical, fleshy accompaniment should effect some change in us. If we take the time to think about what Christians are really saying in their belief in the Incarnation, we have to acknowledge the absurdity of it all. God, the creator, has become a creature? The infinite has decided to limit itself to the finite? And not just any type of finite creature, mind you, but the very finite creature that has rebelled against God and caused the devastation of this horror story. These claims are downright scandalous, and yet Christians profess them—we (Ryan and Conor) profess them—because they are powerful claims. They are claims that yield a twofold lesson for human action, preaching the importance of humility and stressing the strength of compassion. Notably, however, this is not some lesson we can solve and leave behind, like a lesson in a calculus textbook. It is a lesson that we need to sit with and mull over, like the lessons we learn about the people we love, which continue to unfold over time. We need to meditate on this scandalous claim to unpack and interiorize its deeper message, that God has entered our mess as a companion.

One of the best resources for unpacking the twofold lesson of the Incarnation, so that we can appreciate its implications for action, is the short story "Parker's Back," by Flannery O'Connor. (The text, like many of O'Connor's stories, presents a realistic picture of its setting—the US South in the early twentieth century—including characters uncritically accepting their culture's assumed racial hierarchies and expressing these beliefs with derogatory language. Thematically, "Parker's Back" challenges these sins and is valuable both for its indictment of them and its broader theological substance, but it is notable that O'Connor's own story is not so neatly on the side of progress toward racial equality, and all readers of her stories must contend with this aspect of her history.)[4] The story relates the tale of Obadiah Elihue Parker, a contrarian young man married to a devout Christian wife named Sarah Ruth. Obadiah Elihue has tattoos all over his body, representing various experiences and ideas from his life. He does not get along well with his wife. One day, he pays his tattoo artist to ink his back with a giant icon of Christ, most likely a version of the famous Christ Pantocrator ("Almighty Christ") from St. Catherine's Monastery at Sinai. Although he tries to continue his debauched ways after getting the tattoo, he quickly realizes "the eyes that were now forever on his back were eyes to be obeyed" and decides that he would rather amend his ways.[5] He returns to Sarah Ruth to reveal his newfound faith and announce his plans to be a much kinder husband, but he does not receive the welcome he expects. Enraged at the new tattoo, confessing, "It ain't anybody I know," Sarah Ruth berates Obadiah Elihue and literally beats the face of God drawn on her husband's back as a punishment for his "idolatry."[6]

In typical O'Connor fashion, this is a weird story (a horrific story if not a horror story), but it is fundamentally about the mystery of the Incarnation and its effects. Through the tattoo, God is incarnated on O. E. Parker's back, and because his flesh knows God, his life begins to change. Sarah Ruth, however, believes she knows God better than her husband, and so she refuses to recognize the positive prospects this religious experience has brought and rejects the face of God before her. Although she is the more outwardly religious of the two characters and ostensibly acts in defense of the divine by trying to punish what she sees as an act of idolatry, Sarah Ruth is the one who gets the message wrong. As O'Connor explained in a letter to a friend, "Sarah Ruth was the heretic—the notion that you can worship in pure spirit."[7] She ignored the impact of the Incarnation, putting her pride and self-assurance above the invitation Parker's tattoo represented and thereby failing to see the face of the God she purportedly served in the husband she was supposed to love. By recognizing Sarah Ruth's response as a failure to appreciate the significance of the

Incarnation, we can see the twofold lesson more clearly, establishing the real importance of saying that God is not made known in theory but in the broken, and breakable, flesh of human existence.

First, Sarah Ruth's pride juxtaposes with the humility of the Incarnation, resulting in a form of hypocrisy that undermines her relationship with Obadiah Elihue and with God. She is so preoccupied with her personal piety and so convinced of her righteousness that she believes it is her job to defend the honor of God against idolatrous images. She then acts violently, in direct opposition to the love of neighbor (to say nothing of the love of one's spouse) that Christianity promotes. If she had appreciated the Incarnation, O'Connor suggests, and understood that God is not just an abstract spirit but humbly took on human flesh (with all its finitude and needs), Sarah Ruth would not have given in to this kind of pride and become a walking hypocrite who uses her words to affirm Christian teachings while violating them with her actions. By highlighting our finitude, the Incarnation reminds us that we must be humble, particularly when we deal with things related to God—a list that includes discernment!

Second, Sarah Ruth's mistake is amplified by the fact that she not simply whacked her husband on the back but also beat him until "large welts had formed on the face of the tattooed Christ."[8] She literally scars the face of God while scarring her husband. As a result of their faith in the Incarnation, Christians say the same thing happens whenever humans harm one another, whether Jesus is visibly tattooed on their flesh or not. The idea is that God took on the entirety of human flesh in the person of Christ, meaning that God can be found in every person with human flesh now. The call to recognize God in the flesh is therefore not just about identifying God in the person of Christ. It is also a summons to embrace a newfound compassion for all of humanity. The viral statues of *Homeless Jesus*, which show Jesus (recognized by the nail wounds on his hands and feed) as a homeless man sleeping on a bench, illustrate this conviction, taken straight out of Matthew 25, where Jesus insists that anyone who cares for the hungry, the thirsty, the naked, the sick, or the imprisoned cares for him directly. The message of the Incarnation is that we cannot worship God in spirit alone but must also serve God by caring for the wounded flesh we find around us.

Between this twofold lesson and the larger message of accompaniment, the discovery of discernment that lies latent within the mystery of the Incarnation begins to emerge. Put these pieces together and notice how the Incarnation works as a reaction to the reality of sin. In chapter 3, we discussed Niebuhr's idea that sin grows out of the existential anxiety humans experience in the tension between freedom and finitude, resulting in pride and sensuality as humanity's primordial sins. The Incarnation responds directly to both of these temptations. As a pop-up ad, it refutes sensuality, calling us out of our infatuation with creaturely goods so that we can recognize our potential. Meanwhile, as a form of accompaniment that stresses humility and compassion, it dismantles pride, reminding us that our freedom also has its limits. The Incarnation delivers both these messages powerfully but never in a scolding fashion. Instead, the messages are shared in love, with the very same compassion that the Incarnation demands of us.

When we consider how we can discern a path that allows us to make a difference in a world marked by sin, we should attempt to cultivate a similar disposition. That is, we should look for ways to counter the effects of evil suffered and evil done with love rather than condemnation. We should start with the assumption that we can have the most dramatic effect on the pain and suffering wrought by the horror story of sin when we accompany others caught in this darkness, running into the nightmare when the most natural inclination is to run out, for this is precisely how God reacts. When we set our sights on this goal, we can discern a wise way forward to a meaningful life that leads us to our proper telos while helping others along the way.

Meditation: Strength for the Journey

Although the accompaniment God offers us in the Incarnation should soothe our anxieties about the delicate balance between freedom and finitude, its implications for discernment can still be overwhelming. To say that we are empowered to counteract the effects of evil in a meaningful way through our own accompaniment of others is very freeing. At the same time, our knowledge of the depth of evil's effects still presents a serious reminder of our finitude. The vastness of the suffering that continues to confront us can be paralyzing, even when we want so badly to be doing something about it. Fortunately, the mystery of the Incarnation offers a solution to this problem too, for God's response to evil succeeded in ways ours can never hope to imitate, even as it started in a state far more precarious (i.e., infancy) than the one we bring to our discernment now. As a response to those moments when we feel overwhelmed by what accompaniment might mean or skeptical about our abilities to handle all that this journey might entail, we close this chapter with another meditation adapted from Ignatius's *Spiritual Exercises*, this one stressing the way Christians insist God's journey through our horror plot began.

1. Sit upright. Concentrate on your breathing as you take a few deep breaths. Slow your thoughts and prepare yourself to focus on the reflection at hand. If you have a Bible handy, you can prime your imagination's pump by reading Matthew 1:18–25 and Luke 1:26–2:7. The narratives here are both trying to reflect on and share the mystery of the Incarnation.

2. You will reflect on the birth of Jesus, so take a moment to set the scene in your head. Mary, still a young woman, is nine months pregnant and traveling by donkey to a small town she has likely never seen before. Her husband, a carpenter, has walked the whole journey with her and cannot find even a room to rent for the night. The couple must settle for a cave on the outskirts of town usually reserved for animals.

3. Imagine yourself as an observer on this night. You sit in the cave and watch as this couple arrives. Use your senses to enter the scene. Is it damp in the cave? Hot or cold? Can you feel the hay or smell the wool on a lamb? When you are there, focus on Mary and Joseph. How do they talk with one another? What emotions pass between them?

4. Allow yourself to imagine the cave after Jesus has been born. Do cries, from mother or baby, break the night? Is there peaceful rest? How do the animals react? Can you feel what Mary, or Joseph, or someone else in the scene is feeling?

5. What would it be like to hold this child in the scene? Imagine looking down at this infant face. What would you want to say to the baby? What do you realize about the child's dependence and innocence? How does this compare to your own abilities now? How can it instill confidence in you going forward? How do you respond to the mystery of these events? Is this *just another child,* or is there something special about *this* child? Christians believe that the God who creates and sustains the cosmos has been made flesh here . . . and this fleshy baby will soon need a diaper change. What does that tell you about God? About humans? About yourself?

Key Terms and Ideas

- Incarnation: the distinctive Christian belief that God became human (took on human flesh) in the person of Jesus of Nazareth, freely choosing to experience all aspects of human existence so that humans might not be left completely alone with the negative consequences of sin.
- Overreacher plot: one of two horror story plots identified by Noël Carroll, the overreacher plot centers on a character who reaches for some form of forbidden knowledge. Upon accessing the knowledge, dark things happen until a final confrontation between good and evil is required. The overreacher plot has notable parallels with the story of humanity's fall into sin in Genesis 3.
- Complex discovery plot: the second of Carroll's two horror story plots, the complex discovery plot introduces some kind of evil influence whose presence is only slowly acknowledged by those caught in its terrifying wake. This plot too ends with a confrontation between good and evil. The complex discovery plot has notable parallels with the theology of the Incarnation as God's response to sin.
- "Parker's Back": short story by Flannery O'Connor exploring the consequences of Christian faith in the Incarnation, highlighting the need to see God in the flesh of others.
- Two lessons of the Incarnation: the way the Incarnation teaches humility—as an illustration of God's own humble willingness to adopt human finitude—and compassion—as an act of God that seeks to give humans genuine comfort in the face of sin and its consequences.

Recommended Resources

Denise Levertov, "On the Mystery of the Incarnation," in *The Collected Poems of Denise Levertov* (New York: A New Directions Book, 2013), 818.

Levertov's poetry calls attention to the theological significance of the Incarnation as a response to human sinfulness. With a vision akin to Ignatius's meditation on the Incarnation we introduced in chapter 3, Levertov stresses the generosity and love of a God who would freely enter into the horror story humans have created through our sinfulness, presenting a poignant illustration of themes from the first half of this chapter.

Mary Karr, "The Nativity," *Poetry* (December 2001): 14. https://www .poetryfoundation.org/poetrymagazine/issue/71377/december-2001.

Karr's poem focuses on the humanity of the Incarnation, emphasizing the messiness of human birth and highlighting the depth of God's entry into human existence through Jesus. Together, "The Nativity" and Levertov's "On the Incarnation" offer a comprehensive vision of Christianity's two crucial claims about the Incarnation: this one person (Jesus of Nazareth) is truly God and truly human.

Athanasius, "On the Incarnation."

This Christian text from the fourth century offers a classic explanation of why God would have chosen to become human. Athanasius's emphasis is on the ways the Incarnation invites and empowers a change in humanity, especially through a turning away from sin and back toward God.

Flannery O'Connor, "Parker's Back," in *Everything That Rises Must Converge* (New York: Farrar, Straus and Giroux, 1965).

The short story analyzed in this chapter presents a visceral account of the impact of the Incarnation. Readers should be forewarned that the story contains harsh language, including a character using a racial epithet. As noted above, the theological lessons of the text challenge this language and combat racist assumptions (especially as critics note the ambiguity of Parker's own racial identity), but every reader is forced to grapple with the racism of the story's setting in plain view.

The Day the Earth Stood Still, directed by Robert Wise, 20th Century Fox, 1951.

This classic film has a curious "incarnational" theology. An alien comes to earth to deliver an important message, but humanity is afraid of what it does not know and refuses to listen. As a result, the alien tries to use a human form to learn more about humanity—learning about pain and death as a result—so that humans might be more likely to listen to the message. Although an imperfect parallel to Christian theology of the Incarnation, there are nonetheless valuable points of comparison, especially with Athanasius's interpretation.

"Bloody Mary," short film written and directed by Alexander Rönnberg Bloody Mary | Horror Shorts | IRIS.

This is a great short film illustrating the fundamental movements of the overreacher plot.

Notes

1. Noël Carroll, *The Philosophy of Horror or Paradoxes of the Heart* (New York: Routledge, 1990), 118–25.
2. Carroll, *The Philosophy of Horror*, 97–108.
3. Carroll, *The Philosophy of Horror*, 102.
4. Paul Elie, "Everything That Rises: How Racist Was Flannery O'Connor?" *The New Yorker* 96, no. 17 (June 22, 2020): 82–85.
5. Flannery O'Connor, "Parker's Back," in *Everything That Rises Must Converge* (New York: Farrar, Straus and Giroux, 1965), 241.
6. O'Connor, "Parker's Back," 243, 244.
7. Flannery O'Connor, *The Habit of Being: Letters of Flannery O'Connor*, ed. Sally Fitzgerald (New York: Farrar, Straus and Giroux, 1979), 594.
8. O'Connor, "Parker's Back," 244.

5

A New Vision

As chapter 4 explained, the mystery of the Incarnation describes the way God acts to subvert or undo the horror story of sin. Christians believe that God entered *our* story to reveal to us a new way of life. This claim asks us to pause, to ponder, and to ask: *But what does this mean for my life?* When we think in terms of the discernment process outlined with the Ignatian B.U.T., the Incarnation helps us to *understand Who* God is and *How* God desires our world to be. Indeed, the entirety of Jesus's life, including his death, contributes to our ability to *understand* what God desires for creation. Ignatius stressed the value of these parts of Jesus's story for precisely this reason, dedicating two of the four weeks in his *Spiritual Exercises* to Jesus's ministry, Passion, and death. We will discuss the significance of Jesus's death in chapter 6. In this chapter, we explore how Jesus's ministry speaks to the question of how we can use our lives to achieve our full telos, spelling out the values we should prioritize in our efforts to craft lives worth living. To achieve this level of *understanding*, we consider two components of Jesus's ministry: what he taught people with his words and what he showed people with his deeds. Before addressing either of these elements, however, we need to establish some context for what Jesus was trying to do.

The Upside Down

There are so many ways to characterize Jesus's ministry that it is hard to know where to begin. If we think about where we left off with the Incarnation, we should approach the ministry of Jesus looking for a message. After all, we explained in the last chapter that the Incarnation represents

God's intervention into the horror story of human sin, providing an interruption that fits with the initial discovery phase in a horror plot. We also described how God became flesh to get our attention, much like a pop-up ad we cannot ignore. Most of the chapter, however, dealt with the question of why God would use a pop-up ad. We left the content of the ad itself largely unexplored. As we move from the Incarnation to Jesus's ministry, we need to reflect on just what Jesus was trying to communicate.

The traditional answer to this question is that Jesus came to spread a message about the reign of God. (Sometimes this is called the "Kingdom of God" because the Greek word, *basileia*, can be translated either way, but in English, we tend to think of a kingdom as a place, and Jesus's message is less about a place and more about the way God rules, so reign is a more fitting translation, but we will use both throughout this chapter and book.) I completely embrace this traditional answer. In fact, most of my former students will tell you that I am rather heavy-handed on this point, insisting that they know the reign of God is the central message of Jesus's life. Nevertheless, I do not think the traditional answer stands on its own because our contemporary experience of kingly reigns is too limited to generate a sufficient appreciation of the layers in the original imagery. I therefore prefer to introduce the central message of Jesus's ministry with a different analogy, drawn from Netflix's *Stranger Things*.

If you have seen *Stranger Things*, the image I want to use needs no explanation. In case you have not seen it, let me set the stage. The basic premise of *Stranger Things* involves an encounter with another dimension. The characters describe this new dimension as "the upside down" because it is essentially a perverted mirror image of this world where the air is toxic, darkness is omnipresent, and the environment seems intent on destroying itself. (If you want to get some sense of the juxtaposition, do a Google image search for "Hawkins Public Library Stranger Things" and you will find a photograph of the real building they used for the fictional town's library as well as a picture of the creepy version the characters encounter in the upside down.) *Stranger Things* builds its narrative around the interactions between the normal world and the upside down, following the contours of the complex discovery plot pretty consistently.

For the characters in *Stranger Things*, the contrast between our world and the upside down is self-evident. They know when they are in the upside down because they have to leave the normal world to get there. But what if there were a man who lived his whole life in the upside down? What if he had never encountered our nice, happy world? This man would still be living in a toxic waste dump that wants to eat him alive, but he would never know it. He would live his life in this nasty place thinking this was as good as it gets. He would have no hope of a better world because he would have absolutely no reason to imagine that another reality might be possible. He would need someone to show him the truth about his situation and to offer him a positive alternative before he would be willing to consider a different life.

The way to understand the central message of Jesus's ministry—the significance of his proclamation of the reign of God—is to think of him trying to tell his hearers that they are living in the upside down but have never realized it. Indeed, by describing a new way of existing under the reign of God (that is, in a realm where God is in charge and everything goes as God had planned), Jesus presents a contrast with our world, revealing that because of sin, we are very much living in the darkness and destructiveness of the upside down. It all seems obvious in retrospect, but without the counter-message of the reign of God, we would remain deceived, assuming this world, with all its evil and suffering, was as good as it could get. Jesus's ministry of the reign of God recalibrates these expectations, indicating that we have yet to achieve our real potential and insisting that it is so much greater than anything our limited imaginations have been able to conjure on their own.

Flipping to the Right Side Up: Three Reversals

Significantly, Jesus's message is not merely an indictment of our current state of affairs. More than just calling us to our senses, Jesus's ministry of the reign of God also offers us a way out to the happier, healthier world of the "right side up." By focusing on the specific teachings Jesus shared in his ministry, we can identify the pathway from the upside down of our sinful world to the right side up of the reign of God and strengthen our discernment process by adding new details to our personal plans to respond to the effects of sin in the world. Consistent with the idea that we are flipping from an upside-down world to a right-side-up existence, the best way to understand this pathway is to think of it as a journey built around three reversals: a reversal of expectations, a reversal of values, and a reversal of vision.

The first two reversals, of expectations and of values, appear most clearly in Jesus's Sermon on the Mount. This lengthy discourse, which makes up a considerable amount of the Gospel of Matthew (and also has a parallel in the Gospel of Luke), lays out how God wants people to act, identifying the rules people would live by if they were treating God like the ruler of their lives. What emerges from the Sermon on the Mount is a profoundly challenging vision that amounts to nothing short of a revolution in the way people live. Jesus expected his hearers to live out his teachings and to let his words become flesh in their lives.

First, the Sermon on the Mount calls for a dramatic reversal of one's expectations. In one section, known as the Six Antitheses, Jesus contrasts the things people normally expect of each other with the higher standards of the reign of God. For example, he explains how everyone knows they should not kill but insists that this is only a mark of success in the upside down. In the right side up of the reign of God, people go further to ensure that they do not even harbor anger toward someone else, cutting off the internal drive that might lead to killing long before it can ever escalate that far. Similarly, with sexual morality, Jesus says that *not* committing adultery is a low bar and explains that the true mark of moral success lies in refusing to entertain lustful thoughts in the first place. The other antitheses provide similar juxtapositions, culminating in Jesus's famous command to not only love one's neighbor (the traditional expectation) but also "love your enemies and pray for those who persecute you" (Matthew 5:44).

Scholars have proposed a variety of ways to interpret these antitheses, but they boil down to the idea that we need to change our expectations about how we are really called to live if we want to break free from the upside down and experience the reign of God. We can no longer be content with the bare minimum of human decency. Instead, we must prioritize our own moral development so that we become the kind of people who lead genuinely good lives and not just good enough ones. We need to expect more of ourselves so that we can do more for others.

Theologically, this interpretation makes sense for two reasons. First, theologians have stressed conversion as an essential component of Jesus's ministry of the reign of God. In fact, the first word of Jesus's preaching in the Gospel of Matthew is "Repent" (Matthew 4:17). The Greek term for conversion, *metanoia*, describes a turning around, carrying the connotation of a person walking down the wrong path and doing a complete 180 to move in the opposite direction. As a reversal of expectations, the antitheses serve as an invitation to this kind of personal transformation, explaining that the way out of the upside down must begin with an internal conversion that turns us away from the ho-hum aims of an ordinary existence and turns us toward the higher vision of an extraordinary moral life.

Second, if the fullness of human potential is only realized in self-gift—as Christian theological anthropology asserts—then shifting our expectations away from morality's lowest-hanging fruit is a logical prerequisite for authentic human flourishing. After all, when the goal is to give oneself away in love, the bare minimum does not cut it. I am not going to look at my son and say, "Congratulations! You didn't kill anyone today. You are an amazing human being. Actually, you're doing even better than that. You are living up to the entirety of your human potential!" No. I have higher standards than that for my kids, and the message of this first reversal is that God has higher standards for God's children as well. Unless we set our sights on these higher standards, we can never expect to live up to our full potential. The antitheses, as well as the reversal of expectations they represent, offer insights into how we might do this.

The second reversal adds to this *metanoia* by pushing us to reevaluate the things we prioritize and not just the standards we set for ourselves. The Beatitudes (Matthew 5:1–12, with parallels in Luke 6:20–22) offer the clearest example of this. Essentially a list of those who are "blessed" (*beatus* in Latin) or favored in the reign of God, the Beatitudes highlight character traits that are decidedly not the ones given highest billing in conventional accounts. Instead of the rich and powerful, for instance, the Beatitudes proclaim the blessings of the poor and the meek. In each case, the Beatitudes hold up a character trait usually denigrated by society and insist that it carries some kind of benefit in the reign of God—thus, those who are merciful now will be shown mercy.

The contrast of values involved in the Beatitudes provides a plan for flipping from the upside down to the right side up. By stressing that the lowly are the people most highly valued in the reign of God, the Beatitudes logically entail that those who want to follow Jesus's vision for the right side up should live like this now. They show that we need to prioritize meekness and mercy, that we should accept persecution for the sake of our ultimate concern, and that we should be lamenting the darkness of life in the upside down. When we embrace these values and turn away from the traditional priorities of riches, fame, and comfort, we can better pursue the ambitious life we identify in our discernment process, even when the realities of evil suffered and the pull of evil done get in our way.

Finally, the third reversal is the work of Jesus's parables. Based on the Greek word *paraballo*, meaning one thing set next to another, parables are analogies that use everyday objects and vivid stories to explain the unfamiliar with the familiar—like how I tried to explain the reign of God (the unfamiliar) with a comparison to *Stranger Things* (the familiar). These stories involve a reversal of vision because they function like metaphorical glasses, helping us to see something about the reign of God more clearly. When a person gets new glasses for the first time, the world looks remarkably different, but nothing about the world has changed. Rather, how that person views the world is transformed. So it is with Jesus's parables. They are designed to reverse our vision, reshaping the way we see the world around us so that we interact with it in a new way.

With so many parables, it would be impossible to work through each one to identify the reversal of vision involved in every instance. I will therefore trade breadth for depth and focus on one example. The parable of the Good Samaritan is an evocative story that recounts the fate of a man who gets beaten by robbers and left for dead on the side of a busy road. The reason Jesus tells this story in the first place is significant. The tale is occasioned by a lawyer's conversation with Jesus about how to get into heaven because, after being told to love God and neighbor, the lawyer follows up by asking, "Who is my neighbor?"

(Luke 10:29). In response, Jesus introduces this poor robbery victim and asks the crowd to imagine three passersby.

The first two are committed religious characters, not unlike the people in the audience to whom Jesus was speaking, and both are on their way to the temple to worship. Not wanting to lose their ritual purity by touching a dead body (presumably, they were unsure if the man was dead), they cross to the other side of the street when they approach the wounded fellow so that they can get to the temple on time. The third passerby is a Samaritan, a person from an ethnic group despised by most of Jesus's audience. Shockingly, the Samaritan does what the wounded man's ethnic brothers would not: he tends to the man's wounds and even takes him to a nearby inn, paying in advance for his room so that the wounded man can recuperate and promising to come back in case of additional expenses.

For Jesus's audience, this would have been an astonishing twist, not unlike the mind-blowing ending of *The Sixth Sense* or *Fight Club*. Samaritans and Jews hated each other at the time, so this person should never have stopped to help the wounded man. Recognizing the discomfort this parable would provoke, Jesus closes by flipping the lawyer's question and asks, "Which of these three, do you think, was a neighbor to the man who fell into the hands of the robbers" (Luke 10:36)? When the lawyer appropriately answers, "The one who showed him mercy" (perhaps because he cannot even bring himself to admit that it was a Samaritan), Jesus declares, "Go and do likewise" (Luke 10:37).

The reversal of vision could hardly be starker. Not only is Jesus dismantling traditional divisions that keep different ethnic groups apart, but he is also challenging the very notion of what it means to love one's neighbor. As the contemporary theologian Ian McFarland has noted, the lawyer's initial query presumes an exclusionary mindset. He wants to clarify who counts as his neighbor because he has just been told that his entrance into eternal life depends on his love for that person. This is not an unreasonable question in that context, but it is still designed to set some boundaries, with the thought that if he can identify people who are *not* his neighbor, he can stop worrying about how he has to treat them. At the end of the parable, however, Jesus upends the question, reversing the lawyer's vision by insisting that the issue is not *who* is a neighbor but *how* we can act as a neighbor.[1] The final exhortation, "Go and do likewise," hammers this reversal home, moving the conversation away from neighbor as a category used to separate others and toward a vision of action that implies a responsibility for all who want to flip from the upside down to the right side up. We must be neighborly to others rather than wasting our time trying to decide if they are a neighbor to us. The end result is a much broader vision not only of the idea of a "neighbor" but also of our own identity.

Significantly, the reversal of vision engendered in the parables is not a strictly intellectual exercise. There is a decidedly affective dimension to this reversal as well. In the story of the Good Samaritan, for example, Jesus invites his audience to *feel* merciful toward the wounded man, arguing that how one responds in the heart is the key to how one sees the world in their mind and thus determines whether they will act in accordance with God's reign or in opposition to it. As we will see in part III of this book, this affective dimension was especially prominent in Ignatius's vision for discernment too, adding further strength to relying on the Ignatian B.U.T. as we work to live the life that fulfills our human telos.

Ultimately, all three reversals function in this way, effecting a change in expectations, values, and vision that is supposed to lead to a new way of living in the world. The end goal is to influence action because the good news of the reign of God is that we do not have to settle for a life lived according to the conventions of the upside down. Admittedly, the analogy with *Stranger Things* breaks down a bit here, because the goal is not actually to move to a whole new world but to transform the one that we currently inhabit. By living with the expectations, values, and vision of the reign of God, we can make the right side up a reality here. For this reason, theologians talk about the "inbreaking" of the reign of God because the right side up breaks through the upside down and changes it from the inside out. This call to dramatic change should subsequently inform our understanding of discernment, helping us flesh out the message of the Incarnation by illustrating how God plans to address suffering and evil in the world through accompaniment. When we incorporate the reversals of Jesus's teachings into our own responses to these same problems, we have a stronger sense of what it means to effectively accompany others as a form of self-gift. We do not have to rely just on the words of Jesus in this process, however, because his preaching was not idle chatter. He walked the walk, using his actions to demonstrate the expectations, values, and vision of the reign of God. By evaluating his deeds, especially his miraculous ones, we can get an even clearer picture of what it means to work for the inbreaking of the reign of God through the life we decide to lead.

Miracles

I admit that "miracles" pose a challenge to the modern scientific mind. Claims about miraculous events fall outside the boundaries of everyday logic. In the Gospel of John, Jesus turned water into wine (2:1–12). Dream on! Yet the Gospels are filled with miraculous accounts of Jesus healing the sick, raising the dead, multiplying loaves, walking on water, and exorcising demons. But in a world ravaged by sickness and hunger, to hearts broken by grief, these miracles seem like fantasies. Still, I believe in miracles. In this section, I want to suggest why and how miracle stories "fit" into the Christian narrative.

Once again, horror, or what H. P. Lovecraft called "weird fiction," provides a suitable entry point. For Lovecraft, the test of a good horror story was to consider its effect on the reader. He writes, "The one test of the really weird is simply this—whether or not there be excited in the reader a profound sense of dread, and of contact with unknown spheres and powers; a subtle attitude of awed listening, as if for the beating of black wings or the scratching of outside shapes and entities on the known universe's utmost rim."[2] Horror stories and the gospels' miracle stories work in analogous ways. Both intend to unsettle readers and to provoke them into calling into question the way they understand the world in which they live. I know there is no monster in my closet, but a good horror story can make me wonder if maybe . . . *just maybe* . . . there is. Likewise, miracle stories push readers to consider that maybe, *just maybe*, an unseen and mysterious force may be breaking into and transforming our world—the inbreaking of God's reign.

Before we talk directly about miracles, let me say a word about worldviews. Each of us has a worldview or a "framework" in which our experiences make sense. Worldviews shape how we perceive and conceive reality. An example: In the West, we tend to expect our eggs to be prepared over-easy, hardboiled, or scrambled. Yet a treat in the Philippines is balut—a fertilized duck egg containing a partially developed embryo. A friend of mine, seeing this common street food, proclaimed, "That's disgusting. I can't imagine eating that!" It's an understandable reaction because balut is not a food that fits within an American's worldview . . . but it *could*, given a bit of courage on the taster's part.

Most of the time, we take our worldviews for granted. Every now and again, however, an event or experience causes us, or at least should cause us, to reexamine *how* we perceive the world. The British philosopher John Locke tells the story of an ambassador who visits the court of the king of Siam. The ambassador tells the king about Holland's geography, its culture, and its economy. Naturally, he also mentions the weather and, to shock his host, tells him that it can get so cold that the water becomes so hard that even an elephant could stand on it. Upon hearing this, the king guffaws: "Hitherto I believed the strange things you told me, because I look upon you as an honest man. But this is too far—you're lying!"[3]

The king's reaction is understandable. Having no experience of *cold*, he cannot begin to imagine what *ice* would be like (a problem we in Wisconsin do not have). His worldview is limited. We may snicker and say, "Ah, foolish king, you should trust the ambassador," but this is easier said than done. We are, all of us, limited by our worldviews, and it often takes significant effort to allow our vision of reality to be broadened. The ambassador's testimony, if I may refer to Lovecraft, was like a "scratching" at the edge of the king's worldview. Instead of having the humility to entertain the *possibility* of ice or the resolve to experience it for himself, he discounted the ambassador's testimony. The logic of this approach—a logic very much present in our world—may be stated: *If it can't be accounted within my framework, it can't count.* It is the function of miracles, like horror stories, to question the adequacy of our frameworks.

Historically speaking, there is little question *that* Jesus was a miracle worker. In his age, miracle workers were everywhere. But what set him apart from the other miracle workers was the way his words (teachings and parables) and his deeds (miracles) pointed away from himself and toward God's Kingdom. As Conor described, Jesus's parables are stories meant to transform listeners' imaginations. They are often disturbing because they reveal what God wants for us and show us how far short of God's desire we remain. In addition to teaching, Jesus was active, performing "deeds of power" that were "signs" of God's reign. Through Jesus's miracles, God's Kingdom touched and took flesh in history.

When we read the Gospels, we find four types of miracle stories. You can use the acronym H.E.N.D. to remember them: Healings, Exorcisms, Nature, and Death. Here is a miracle chart using Mark's gospel as a guiding text:

Miracle Type	Example	Symbolism and Meaning
Healing	Leper (1:40–45) Woman with hemorrhage (5:25–34) Blind man at Bethsaida (8:22–26)	In God's Kingdom, *the body matters.* Jesus restores bodily integrity and often invites those who have been healed to be part of his movement.
Exorcism	Possessed man at Gerasa (5:1–20) Possessed son (9:14–29)	As God's Reign unfolds, evil's power over humans is being diminished. There is no karma "balance" in God's Kingdom—evil, when confronted by God's Word and Deed, cannot stand against it.
Nature	Stilling the storm (4:35–41) Walking on lake (6:45–52) Feeding four thousand (8:1–10)	God's power is at work within creation itself. For those with eyes to see (*faith*), God's presence is detected in history. These are signs of how creation *ought* to be, a creation fulfilled where and when Jesus is present.
Death	Raising of Jairus's daughter (5:21–43)	A sign that death has no place in God's Kingdom. Life, not death, is the ruling principle of God's reign.

If you look at each miracle, you may appreciate how they *confirm* and give physical testimony to what Jesus preached in parables. But miracles are not *proofs* of Jesus's identity. Were that the case, everyone who saw a miracle might have said, "You're God Incarnate!" Many saw his miracles but did not believe that Jesus was anything more than a run-of-the-mill miracle worker. Yet others saw, believed, and followed. Why?

To answer this this, let me share my favorite Hebrew word: *dabar* (pronounced davar). *Dabar* is a word that accomplishes something; it is a speech act or a *word* that makes a difference in the world. When the umpire shouts, "You're out," his words affect reality: you're actually out. If your boss says, "You're fired," her words bring about a new reality called unemployment. Words have impact. Saying *Yes* when your beloved proposes turns you into a fiancée. The catch: for a word to have an effect, *all parties involved must be playing the same game*. You can't fire someone who doesn't work for you, and you can't (despite reality television) propose to someone you've never met. There must be some sort of *relationship*. In theology, we call this *faith*. Faith is a knowledge of another that trusts in and enables us to respond to what the other person shares with us. And it is faith, a knowledge that comes from knowing that we are loved by God, that expands our worldview to allow us to recognize and respond to God's *dabar* in history. Faith does not ask someone to see a different world. It is, rather, a gift that allows a person to see and live within the world differently.

If Jesus's parables reveal how we live in "the upside down," Jesus's miracles portray God's Kingdom as "the inside out" and "the outside in." According to a typical Western worldview, it is the powerful, rich, beautiful, and famous who are to be celebrated. Our political, social, and economic systems keep some on top and lock others away in the cellar. Women know how patriarchal structures make it hard for them to succeed professionally; minorities know how racist and classist systems put them at a disadvantage from birth. A glance at social media, websites, and television lets us know quite quickly who is *in* and who is *out*. We celebrate the lifestyles of the rich and famous while trying to minimize, if not ignore totally, the poor and broken. It is no wonder, then, that when Jesus proclaims Good News to the poor, so many find it incredible. Why would God's reign be preached first to history's margins and not the beautiful center? The answer, sadly, is that we have made a world where the "Good News" is hard to hear and, for the privileged, harder to accept.

Whenever we read about miracles, we are reading about experiences where God is revealing within our history what the Kingdom of God looks like. Where Jesus is present, it is as though all of creation is made new: the lame walk, the blind see, the deaf hear, and those who are oppressed breathe the air of freedom. Yet, as history makes clear, the way of the Kingdom is seldom how *we* have organized the world. *We* are quite happy defining who is in and who is out, and it is often distressing to realize that, in God's story, those who assume they are *on the inside* are, in fact, *on the outside*. This reversal irritated those who were in power, for God's new story required them to rethink *their* sense of right and wrong, good and bad. Jesus's teachings and actions challenged their worldview and called their logic into question. Like the king of Siam, they refused to rethink their positions . . . and did what we so often do. They silenced an inconvenient truth. For those who read and meditate on these texts, these narratives invite discernment: Can I see myself reflected in the Kingdom that Jesus proclaims, do I hear it as "Good News," or am I alienated and threatened by it? Do I want to be a part of this movement, or do I desire to oppose it because I have too much to lose?

Switch on your Ignatian imagination, and let's explore my favorite miracle story. I can't tell you medically *how* it happened . . . but, by dwelling in the text, I hope to suggest what it means. Here we see the speech act of Jesus's command making a difference in the world. Jesus's word *works* to transform and heal another person. Here's the story from Mark 3:1–6:

> Jesus entered the synagogue, and a man was there who had a withered hand. The religious authorities watched him to see whether he would cure him on the sabbath, so that they might accuse him. And Jesus said to man with the withered hand, "Come forward." Then Jesus said to the authorities, "Is it lawful to do good or to do harm on the sabbath, to save life or to kill?" But they were silent. He looked around at them with anger; he was grieved at their hardness of heart and said to the man, "Stretch out your hand." He stretched it out, and his hand was restored. The Pharisees went out and conspired with other leaders against Jesus.

Instead of reading this as a twenty-first-century Westerner, approach it imaginatively as an eyewitness. See the man lurking in the synagogue. He is drawn here—out of habit, out of hope—even though he is not welcome. *Everyone* knows of his deformity, and try as he might, he's never been able to conceal it from others. So he skulks in the shadows, his withered hand buried deep in his robe's folds. A few days back, he heard this preacher, someone named Jesus, in the streets and he has wanted to see him. He followed Jesus today with a hope of hearing more.

The man watches as Jesus gets hassled by some religious authorities. He grew up with a few of them and used to play with them until . . . well, until they grew old enough to know that one does not play with the infirm. Almost overnight, his hand had redefined their friendship, and they all grew apart. It wasn't proper, it "just wasn't good" to be seen with someone like him. *Everyone knows*, of course, that a "withered hand" is a sign of God's disfavor. It's a punishment, so steer clear. The man understood this way of thinking, for it was his worldview, but something told him that this preacher saw things differently.

Jesus's eyes lock on his. Jesus gestures and the man walks toward him and stands amid his former friends. Jesus addresses them and challenges their understanding of the sabbath and of God. Were God's rules meant to help humans or to burden them? Are they life-giving or life-taking? *Of course*, God's rules are life-giving, *so long as* you play by the rules. "The cripple," the authorities think to themselves, "obviously fell afoul of the rules. He has gotten his just desserts." Then Jesus does the unthinkable: "Friend, reach out your hand." Everyone knows the hand he is talking about, the hand that is such stigma and shame. Tired of living in the shadows, the man hears in his voice a faint hope and he does as invited. Somehow, he trusts and believes. He has faith. Freeing his hand from the fabric's fold, he extends it toward Jesus, who clasps it in his hands. "Stretch it out," he says, and the hand opens slowly. The authorities are enraged by this: Who is Jesus to challenge their social order? Who is he to call "the outsider" to the synagogue's center? The authorities have seen rabble rousers like this before, and they know the trouble they can cause to the well-balanced social order. So as the man walks out into the sunlight, throwing pebbles at the sky with his healed hand, they gather into a conspiratorial cluster to plot a way to rid themselves of this irritating preacher.

Each of us, I think, sees a part of ourselves in the man with the withered hand. We mutter fearfully to ourselves: *If they knew about . . . if they knew that . . . then could anyone love me?* We hide significant parts of ourselves, we hold back, and we take refuge on the margins. As a priest, it is my privilege to sit with people who have lived with a "withered hand" for a long, long time. Mistakes, addictions, patterns of behavior that need to be healed, and wounds inflicted by others are all exposed as people seek healing. No: I've never seen a severed arm regrow or an amputated leg regenerate. But I have watched as women and men who have been suffocating in an old framework break free from it and undergo a total transformation when they hear of God's unconditional love for them. It's a moment of watching the outsiders become insiders as God's grace heals and remakes those to whom it is offered.

What, then, do miracles stories do? They reveal a God who is present with us and who is concerned for us. Jesus's miracles challenge worldviews made hazy by sin and unsettle our sense of who is "in" and "out." Indeed, Jesus is the *dabar* of God, for his words enact and bring about God's Kingdom in our world; the miracles show us physically what it looks like when the outsider is made an insider and it turns our sinful upside down right side up. And for those who see with the eyes of faith, we can see glimmers of these miracles in our world. Wherever the lame are empowered to walk, wherever those enslaved by addiction are liberated, wherever those with "withered hands" are made whole, wherever hearts deadened by hate and prejudice are restored to life, wherever people are freed *from* fear and freed *for* love: there the Kingdom that Jesus preached is breaking into our world. By faith, we glimpse the Kingdom as it unfolds in history, and we discern an invitation to make its story our own. For, by faith, we continue Jesus's ministry as we take the Kingdom's values as the guiding values for our lives. In the messiness and chaos of human life, the miracles give us concrete examples and ways of identifying how God desires the world to be. In word and deed, through parables and miracles, Jesus exposes the "cracks" in our upside down and shows us a path, a way of life, that delivers us from sin to the new life promised in God's Kingdom. The Good News of the Kingdom is not that God wants us to live in a different world but, rather, that Jesus has shown us how to live in our world differently, and this new understanding should be our guide for discernment, giving us the faith to act differently now.

My granny was forever pushing us to taste new foods. Like most grandmas, she didn't begin by giving us recipes or telling us about ingredients. She invited us to taste new things, and often, we agreed to try because we knew she loved us and trusted her. We had *faith* in her because we knew that her love could be trusted. In Jesus's parables and miracles, we hear the testimony of Christians who believe that in Jesus, they encountered a love they trusted. So, they didn't believe in Jesus because of miracles but rather because they had faith they discerned in his words and deeds the Kingdom. Wherever he went, as he taught and interacted with people, those with faith could see God's reign taking shape on earth. We don't have faith because we see the Kingdom; we see the Kingdom because we have faith in the Jesus we have come to know in prayer, the scriptures, and in others. Faith, you might say, is necessary for believers to "taste" or participate in the Kingdom Jesus offers. A miracle, if you want something of a definition, is not an *exception* to the way the world works but is, rather, the *expression* of how God desires the world to be.

A skeptic might point to *this* or *that* miracle and say, "Yeah? This is impossible, so unbelievable." The Christian agrees: a miracle makes sense *only within* the context of Jesus's ministry. One needs the "whole" to appreciate its parts, so we evaluate miracles by considering how they disclose and reveal the "whole" that is God's reign. This is no cop-out. Consider: what else is basketball but players running back and forth as they try to throw a ball through a hoop. Without context, absurd. As part of a game, exciting. Thus, the believer looks at Jesus and muses on what he says and does. Is this a Kingdom *I* desire to live in? Given the horrors of this world, is this really *gospel* or "Good News?" If this is what God is up to, can I get on board with it? Is this love, put into word and deed by Jesus, a love I can trust? And, if I can trust it, where will I allow it to lead me? How will I allow this love to shape me into who I am to become?

Meditation: Reversing Our Vision

We close with a short exercise designed to help us appreciate the message Jesus preached in both word and deed about the reign of God. Based on one of Jesus's parables in Matthew's gospel, this meditation gives us a chance to explore our own reversal of vision.

1. Take a moment to compose yourself. Close your eyes and breathe in deeply, counting to five while you inhale, before exhaling completely. Repeat this two more times.

2. In one of Jesus's parables, Jesus likens the reign of God to a vineyard owner who goes out one morning to hire laborers to harvest grapes. Use your five senses to imagine yourself as one of these laborers. You stand in the town's dusty square waiting with other workers; worries about feeding your family weigh on you and you are hoping—praying—to get hired that day. What is it like to be there? Is it hot and sunny, or do you seek the shade of a building? Do you hear children playing, old women chatting, or the sounds of shops opening for the day? Can you smell the animals in the street?

3. Next, imagine that a vineyard owner approaches you and asks you to pick grapes for the day. Elated at the prospect of work, you agree to pick all day for a standard day's wages.

4. Imagine being out in the vineyard all day. Feel the oppressive heat; taste your sweat. Notice the pain in your back and the callouses developing on your hands. Consider your surprise when, a mere two hours before the day is done, one of the other laborers who stood with you in the square shows up and begins to work alongside you until the vineyard closes.

5. When the workday is done, the vineyard owner pays the laborer who worked two hours first, giving her a full day's wages. Surely you are giddy with excitement, expecting to get four times as much money as this late-arriving counterpart. When it is your turn, however, the vineyard

owner merely pays you the usual daily rate. When you protest, she replies, "I gave you what we agreed. Are you only envious because of my generosity?"

6. What is your reaction? Are you envious? Why? What does this tell you about our normal values in this world? What does it mean that this startling generosity is the typical way of proceeding in the reign of God? What does this reveal about the extent of the reversal that the reign of God demands?

7. How can this reversal of vision shape your actions in the world today? How might you better live with the conviction that "the last will be first, and the first will be last"?

Key Terms and Ideas

- Reign of God: the core message of Jesus's ministry, the "reign" or "kingdom" of God (translated from the Greek term *basileia*) describes the way the world would work if God were truly in charge and if everything therefore worked according to God's will.
- Three reversals: because of the disconnect sin has created between God's wishes for the world and the way we have built the world, Jesus's preaching asks humans to pursue three reversals of (1) expectations, (2) values, and (3) vision.
- Worldview: a framework in which our experiences make sense; everyone has a worldview that shapes how they perceive and conceive reality, defining what "makes sense" and what appears to be foreign or unintelligible. Jesus's ministry—in both word and deed—presents challenges to our contemporary worldview and invites us to consider a different framework altogether.
- Four types of miracles: Jesus's miracles of (1) healing, (2) exorcism, (3) nature, and (4) death showed God's power over the pains wrought by evil suffered and evil done, making the promises of the reign of God a reality for those who experienced his deeds firsthand.
- *Dabar*: Hebrew term describing a word that accomplishes what it represents. Jesus's miracles serve as a manifestation of his preaching, making the reign of God literally present and thus turning Jesus's proclamation of the reign of God into God's *dabar*, by turning his words into a concrete reality.

Recommended Resources

Stranger Things, created by Matt Duffer and Ross Duffer, 21 Laps Entertainment/Monkey Massacre Productions, 2016–2025.

The hit Netflix series *Stranger Things* offers a vivid presentation of the effects contrasting ways of life can have on the world around us. Read analogously as a contrast between the "kingdom" of earth and the reign of God, the dynamics between the "upside down" and the real world illustrate the extent of the reversals Jesus's ministry demanded.

The Chosen, directed by Dallas Jenkins, VidAngel/Angel Studios, 2017.

This television series depicts the life and ministry of Jesus, with an intentional focus on the ordinary people who encountered Jesus and the changes they experienced as a result of those interactions. The series shows numerous miracles as well as some of Jesus's most famous teachings, bringing gospel scenes to light. Throughout, the reversals of the reign of God are readily apparent.

Luke 4:14–44

A succinct display of the values at the heart of the reign of God, this short section from the Gospel of Luke shows Jesus at the start of his public ministry, when he proclaims a passage from the biblical book of Isaiah and insists that the long-awaited promises contained in the text—about liberation, God's concern for the marginalized, and the practical impact of conversion—are finally coming to fruition as a result of his presence.

N. T. Wright, "Jesus and the Coming of God's Kingdom," in *Simply Christian: Why Christianity Makes Sense* (New York: HarperOne, 2006), 91–103.

This chapter from the biblical theologian N. T. Wright's introduction to the foundational tenets of Christianity offers a detailed contextualization of the historical significance of Jesus's ministry and outlines the radical call at the heart of his message of the reign of God.

The Holiday, directed by Nancy Meyers, Sony Pictures, 2006.

Like many romantic comedies, this film demonstrates the way words and actions can break us out of hardened worldviews when we start to have faith in others. Although seldom cast as "miracles," the events shaping the dynamic characters and their relationships in the film provide a compelling account of the effects Jesus's miracles were meant to have on his audience.

Notes

1. For more on this reversal, see Ian A. McFarland, "Who Is My Neighbor? The Good Samaritan as a Source for Theological Anthropology," *Modern Theology* 17, no. 1 (January 2001): 57–66.
2. H. P. Lovecraft, *Supernatural Horror in Literature & Other Literary Essays* (Rockville, MD: Wildside Press, 2008), 20.
3. Adapted from John Locke, *An Essay Concerning Human Understanding*, ed. Kenneth Winkler (Indianapolis, IN: Hackett, 1996), 305.

6

Consequential Living

Just as Jesus's birth and life teach us about the best way to respond to the suffering of a broken world, Jesus's death can also contribute to our *understanding* of what it takes to discern well, helping us make the decisions that will lead us to become the people we were created to be. In fact, if we want to grasp the significance of the insights we have already gleaned from the Incarnation and the ministry of Jesus, we *must* look to the cross because there is a straight line from Jesus's birth, through his life, to his death that makes it impossible to interpret any one of these pieces without all the others. For discernment, the crucial lesson of the cross is that it is *consequential* in two important ways. First, Jesus's death was a direct consequence of the life he lived. His revolutionary message of the reign of God, a message dramatically enacted in his life and ministry, was perceived as a threat to the status quo, so those who sought to cling to their power did what came naturally: they eliminated the threat. Second, Jesus's death (and resurrection) has consequences in real life, effecting—according to Christian theology—the salvation of the world. By reflecting on and incorporating both these insights, we can begin to prioritize a similar kind of consequential living in our own discernment. Practically, this means pursuing the telos of self-gift in a way that will leave positive consequences for a broken, sinful world and preparing ourselves for the negative consequences that will inevitably accompany our efforts to live by the foreign values of the reign of God in an otherwise upside-down realm. We will begin by discussing the ways Jesus's death on the cross only occurred as a consequence of the ministry he prioritized while he was alive.

There Because of the Grace of God: Accepting the Consequences of the Cross

One morning, after reading a story about religion in *The New York Times* online, I read some of the comments. Life hack: *never* read comments on a newspaper article. One caught my eye, as it expressed a sentiment I have often heard: *Religion is just ancient storytelling (and mind control) that soothes people's fears, insecurities, anxiety and paranoia . . . often created by organized religion in the first place.* This is not a new critique of religion. Even if you've never read his work, you've likely heard Karl Marx's claim (in the nineteenth century) that religion "is the opium of the people."[1] Marx's concern was that religion could be misused to dull the pain of real-world suffering and that this numbing would keep people in oppressive conditions. Unlike the commenter who naively scapegoated religion for society's ills, Marx's critique hits the mark: religion *can* be used to dull believers to the world's suffering. Marx's worry, in a way, was that religious belief could be used to get people to accept societal oppression and injustice as the *status quo*, as the way things had to be, while they wait for a better outcome for themselves and others in the next life.

My Irish granny had a phrase that would have put Marx into fits. Whenever she saw something tragic, she would mutter quietly, *There but for the grace of God go I.* Whether we saw a traffic accident, heard about a sudden death, or learned about a dire medical diagnosis, she was apt to say it. What she meant, I think, goes something like this: God's grace *held her back* from the calamity that had befallen others. God's grace *kept her safe and secure.* Don't get me wrong, I do not doubt Granny's sincerity. Still, Marx would be right to worry as religion, in this saying, acts like a charm to ward off catastrophe. Yet, as Conor and I have been trying to stress, Christianity should have the opposite effect. Rather than preserving believers from the messiness of life, Christianity thrusts them into its midst. Instead of numbing them to the world's pain, it opens their eyes and ears to it. Let me, then, tweak Granny's saying. Instead of "There *but* for the grace of God go I" it should be "There *because of* the grace of

God, I go." Instead of anesthetizing believers to suffering, God's grace animates their courageous response to it.

The cross empowers this response not by glossing over the extent of humanity's suffering and glibly suggesting that a life lived in service to the values of the reign of God will insulate one from pain, but rather by baldly insisting that suffering will be an inevitable component of anyone's efforts to follow this path to human flourishing. This honest view of suffering is the unmistakable implication of the first consequential dimension of the cross, which again refers to the fact that Jesus's death on that tree only came about as a consequence of the life he led up to that point. This first consequential dimension becomes most apparent when we consider the cross as a symbol readily associated with Christianity.

The next time you're out walking, notice how often you see crosses. People wear crosses as jewelry, they hang crosses and rosary beads from their rearview mirrors, and some athletes make the "sign of the cross" before they step out onto the field or court. In the ancient world, the idea of wearing a little golden cross, or having a cross tattooed on your body, would have been regarded as absurd. Far from quaint and decorative, crucifixion was an act of state-sponsored torture and execution. It was a demeaning and agonizing method of sending a message about consequences: *If you stand in defiance against our power, this is what will happen to you.* Crucifixion was Rome's brutally efficient way of erasing opponents from history. We should note, then, that even the most beautiful cross—whether in a church, a necklace, or a tattoo—is a scandalous symbol. Writing to a new Christian community in Corinth, Saint Paul put it well: "The message of the cross is foolishness to those who are perishing, but to us who are being saved it is the power of God" (1 Corinthians 1:18).

The cross is a foolish and ridiculous symbol for a religion because, in its context, the cross is a brutal sign of the harsh consequences inflicted on those who have lost against an oppressive and powerful force. Objectively speaking, Jesus was a total loser. I mean, if I were to create a religion with a Messiah or Savior, my "hero" would not be a guy who gets tortured, thrown out of Jerusalem, and nailed to two pieces of wood like a criminal. Instead of the "Crucified Savior," my religion would have Jesus as a Rambo-like warlord who would lead his people to a decisive victory over the foe. I suspect this is a natural desire because this sort of hero would "make sense" within our worldview. Judged by our notions of success and failure—judged by our *logic*—Jesus is a loser. After all, our culture prizes dramatic action and celebrates victory, and so, by this standard, Jesus's death on Good Friday *should* be considered a failure.

Within another framework, however, an entirely different assessment emerges. According to this Christian worldview, which relies on the logic revealed in Jesus's parables and miracles—again, a logic that overturns and reverses our expectations—the cross is transformed into an astonishing sign of God's saving power. Indeed, for Christians, the cross redefines completely our understanding of what "power" really is. Yet to get to this transformative understanding of power, Christian theology—a way of reflecting on this scandalous logic—demands that we first face reality's darkness and consider whether, and how, the cross can in any way be a sign of "Good News."

One way the cross is "Good News" is that it expresses a universal reality: None of us is untouched by suffering. We are in this together. We all witness personal doubts and insecurities; trauma, grief, and addictions; racism, sexism, and economic inequality; ecological devastation; and genocide and health care crises. We all, as the saying goes, "have our crosses to bear." The pain of evil suffered and the shadow of evil done fall long over history. But the cross invites us to take courage, for just as Jesus faced the cross as a consequence of announcing God's reign, we too face the threat of the cross whenever we dare to challenge the status quo established by sin. If you live a life akin to Jesus, if you dare to resist the powers of darkness and live out the Good News, the consequence will be the cross.

Conor and I have focused on sin and suffering because we cannot deny the challenge they pose to belief. In this, we are following Ignatius, who anticipated Marx's critique of religion by asking people to meditate on sin's history in the world. We call this "Ignatian Realism" because Ignatius expected those doing the *Spiritual Exercises* to take a long, hard, painful look at how *we* are broken, how the *world* is broken, and to face the ways *we* have contributed to these ruptures. An Ignatian realist does not retreat into fantasy realms but, rather, dares to search within the world for what is true, good, and beautiful. Without a doubt, this quest for the good and the true often leads one to confront the horrors of history. Yet the Ignatian realist knows that this quest is part of the Christian story, because Christian faith is anchored in the belief that the Word of God became flesh (the Incarnation) and lived in solidarity with us. In word and deed, Jesus preached and enacted God's reign in history. By Baptism and through the gift of faith, Jesus continues to call his followers to embody this Good News today, even when threatened by the cross of resistance and rejection. Christian disciples thus struggle against the forces of darkness and oppression not because they want to suffer but because they desire to stand in solidarity with one another and with Jesus.

Ignatian Realism refuses to deny or downplay human suffering. It cannot do this because its gaze remains fixed on Jesus, who, due to his life and ministry, was crucified as a political insurgent. Make no mistake: Jesus was not crucified because he *preached* love or because he was a nice guy. He was crucified because, in word and deed, he put *into practice* a love that threatens to unsettle and revolutionize a sinful world. The cross was a consequence of the life he lived. If Conor and I are right, if sin diminishes us and makes us less human, then Jesus was crucified for being human and inviting others to be fully human as well. This realization is at the heart of a line Conor referenced in the introduction, a line I want to modify a bit: *A Christian spirituality without consequences is an inconsequential spirituality.* One cannot be a disciple or a friend of Jesus and an enemy of the cross. To live and love as Jesus did in our world means, one way or another, eventually colliding with the cross. Jesus's consequences are going to become our own.

Consider this the "dark grace" of Ignatian Realism. In a world allergic to authentic love and true humanity, anyone who lives as Jesus's disciple is assured of meeting resistance and rejection. These are the unavoidable consequences of embodying the right side up in the upside down. I consider it a dark grace because it propels those who accept it into the chaos of history, where they stand in loving solidarity with others who struggle beneath the cross. It is *because* of this dark grace that countless women and men have willingly and courageously faced opposition, persecution, and death, all in witness to the Good News. Rather than keeping its recipients on the sidelines, God's grace plunges believers into the full-contact reality that is discipleship. In the Incarnation, God held nothing back and gave us the Son, Jesus Christ. Accepting the dark grace of discipleship (think of *grace* as God's friend request, an offer God makes out of a loving desire to share God's own life with us) requires that we too hold nothing back. It means coming to terms with the fact that part of being a friend of God through grace is that we are asked to give ourselves entirely to serving and proclaiming the Kingdom as friends of Jesus.

This is a *dark* grace indeed because, in our world, real love is always threatened with real rejection; the cross is its inevitable consequence. While challenging, the reality of this dark grace should not be surprising. To live as a Christian means to live out the values of the reign of God in an upside-down world that would rather not change and that will, as a result of this inertia, respond to love with expulsive violence. Nevertheless, the dark grace of discipleship carries with it the assurance that, even when hatred and anger and violence attempt to rebuff our endeavors, we are never alone.

One might say, "If this dark grace promises to plunge me into chaos, why accept it? Wouldn't it be better to reject it and live apart from suffering?" Well, first, anyone who turns away from or refuses to respond to suffering does *exactly* what Marx thought bad religion does—although these days we say, "But if I get involved, my reputation will suffer/I'll lose my internship/people will talk about me." Like Marx's bad religion, these excuses "justify" or rationalize our inaction, turning us into passive spectators rather than activists. Second, to refuse to open one's eyes and ears to the reality of suffering is, to recall the definition of sin Conor described earlier, a failure to love. Saint Augustine called sin being *incurvatus in se* or "being turned in on oneself," like the roly-poly bugs that roll up into a ball when threatened. One must, then, discern: do I avoid all unfortunate consequences and live like a roly-poly bug concerned only with myself, *or* do I live a life of self-giving service in solidarity with my neighbor and accept the consequences courageously? The dark grace of following Jesus asks believers to put "skin in the game" and live out the values of the Kingdom. To accept this dark grace is to allow the theological reality Jesus proclaimed to take root in our political reality. It is this dark grace that makes theology not merely an academic discipline but, more radically, a consequential way of life.

Theology as a way of life? Many students only grudgingly take a theology class and want to get it out of the way. We are proposing that theology makes possible a credible and viable way of life. The political theologian Johann Baptist Metz coined the phrase "mysticism of open eyes" to describe the effect that accepting this dark grace has on disciples. A mystic is one who is acutely conscious of God's presence in one's life. For Metz, the mystic is not one who stares off into space or closes one's eyes in search of a vision. On the contrary, a "mysticism of open eyes" means opening oneself to the whole of reality. For Metz, it is "a God-mysticism with an increased readiness to perceive, a mysticism of open eyes that sees more and not less. It is a mysticism that especially makes visible all invisible and inconvenient suffering, and—convenient or not—pays attention to it and takes responsibility for it, for the sake of a God who is a friend to human beings."[2] Another way of putting it would be to say that this is the grace, the gift, of seeing who is missing within our society—those who are neglected and forgotten and unwanted—and struggling in solidarity with them. This is both personal and political: personal because grace opens *our* eyes to perceive what society so often misses, political because it dares to imagine and work for a society inspired by the vision of the reign of God that Jesus proclaimed and for which he died. The cross does not mean, "suck it up, things will be better in heaven." With grace-opened eyes, Christians see the cross as a symbol of oppression and violent subjugation and resolve to work against it. Ironically, the cross that Rome saw as *silencing* its enemies is, for Christians, the symbol they use to speak out and resist evil. The cross, for Christians, is a call to action.

Jesus's life and teachings, his parables and miracles, reveal what Christians believe is the shape and pattern of our telos or end as a society. It is a telos actively and strenuously resisted by those who want to cling to power. Whenever prophets arise and decry injustice, you can be assured that they will be opposed by those who are unwilling to change or convert their way of life. A sinful world reacts allergically and violently to expel anything that threatens its order. Old Testament prophets, Jesus and his apostles, and two millennia of martyrs testify to this grim reality. Jesus proclaimed God's reign on earth, and earthly powers responded by crucifying him. They unleashed the power of violence, and to all spectators on that Good Friday, it appeared that the wheel of torture had turned once more and claimed yet another victim. For believers, the graveyard silence of Good Friday would soon give way to an outrageous, scandalous, and, by our worldly standards, truly illogical claim: The cross was not a sign of Jesus's defeat but of his victory. Jesus's Passion, his terrible suffering and death, became the sign of God's totally unrestrained *compassion* for us. In Jesus Christ, God suffers with us as we are led beneath the shadow of the cross on the way toward Easter morning's celebration.

The Work of the Cross: A Consequential Mystery

Ryan's description of Ignatian Realism and the mysticism of open eyes helpfully highlights the first consequential dimension of Jesus's death on the cross. Christians have the grace to enter into rather than run away from suffering because they have been formed in a narrative that leaves no doubt about the inevitability of suffering. By saying that Jesus's pursuit of a fully human life is what led directly to his death— by affirming that the cross was indeed a consequence of Jesus's ministry of the reign of God—Christians know that they will face suffering and persecution too. This realism, this opening of our eyes to the truth of the world around us, allows us to persevere as we pursue our true telos as human beings made in the image and likeness of a loving God. The first consequential dimension of the cross thus assists us with discernment by giving us the strength and courage to follow through on the path we have identified as the road to becoming the people we most deeply long to be, even when that path turns out to be distressingly difficult.

Lest you think that the cross can only inform our discernment by telling us to "suck it up," however, I want to stress the second way in which the cross is a consequential mystery. This second way is less about the temporal meaning of consequential (i.e., that one thing follows another) and more about the notion that calling a decision or a thing "consequential" means that it has real significance; it will make a difference. To understand the cross as consequential in this sense is to appreciate that our discernment must also have a real impact. It too must make a difference, which is a goal we can achieve by modeling our efforts on Jesus's own consequential work.

Throughout history, Christians have been especially clear about this second consequential dimension of the cross. They have asserted emphatically and consistently that the cross is not a meaningless form of abuse but an event with major consequences, including, most profoundly, a transformed relationship between humans and God. The traditional way of summarizing these positive consequences is to say that the cross works our salvation. With this phrasing, Christians assert that Jesus's Passion (the technical term for his suffering, from the Latin word for suffering, *passio*) and death are essential features of the divine plan by which humanity is saved from sin and its effects. The cross thus epitomizes the divine response to the reality of evil initiated in the Incarnation, demonstrating that God's compassionate accompaniment of humanity is not an empty promise but an effective rejoinder that— through Jesus's subsequent resurrection—brings about the reversals presaged in Jesus's ministry of the reign of God.

For those who desire to discern well, Jesus's death combines with his life to establish a model of efficacy, revealing that our own efforts to lead fulfilling lives cannot be made up of vacuous assurances for those in need but must instead make a consequential difference in a world colored by evil suffered and evil done. By understanding the consequential nature of Jesus's Passion and death, we can develop a better sense of how we can use our lives to pursue similarly consequential goals.

To be clear, the point of studying the cross is not to get a better idea of exactly *what* we should be trying to do. Christians see the consequences of Jesus's Passion and death in the promise of salvation, which includes the forgiveness of sins, a restoration of humanity's desire for God, and a new hope for eternal life. We should not expect our discernment to lead us to take actions that achieve these ends because we cannot forgive sins, directly convert souls, and bring heaven to earth (nor do we have to, because Jesus already did). For the moment, then, we can focus less on *what* Jesus accomplishes on the cross and instead seek to understand *how* God could work through Jesus's Passion and death to bring about the newness of life enacted in the Resurrection. When we understand that process, we can more easily identify ways to use our own lives to generate real consequences for a damaged world. To help with this element of discernment, I want to explore the ways Christian theologians have reflected on the meaning of the cross to develop an explanation for how the gruesome death of one person could achieve all that salvation promises.

Significantly, Christians have not settled on one succinct answer to this question. Much like the Incarnation, the work of the cross is a theological mystery that no human can expect to comprehend completely. In fact, theologians refer to the matter of how the cross (combined with the resurrection) saves as the "Paschal Mystery," drawing on an allusion to the story of Passover found in the biblical book of Exodus (chapters 11–13), which similarly involved God's people being saved from the fate of death by the blood of a sacrificial party (a lamb, in the case of Exodus). As Christians have tried to reason through this mystery—with an appropriate level of humility about what they can determine with certainty—they have developed different theories to explain how Jesus's Passion and death can accomplish the work of salvation. Theologians call these "atonement theories" because they explain how the cross atones (makes up) for humanity's sinfulness and reunites humanity and God (bringing about an "at-*one*ment"). Collectively, these theories paint a picture of the consequential power of Jesus's Passion and death, providing a typology for thinking through our own efforts to use our lives to respond to the darkness of a sinful world in an impactful way.

As one might expect, there are numerous atonement theories, and some of them can get quite complicated. For the sake of thinking about the consequences of the cross in relation to discernment, I am only going to focus on three influential theories: the satisfaction theory, the moral influence theory, and the solidarity theory. Before I delve into any of the individual theories, however, I need to establish some context. The atonement theories all presume that humanity, through the original sin of Adam and Eve recounted in Genesis 3 and the continued sins of every individual (except Jesus and, for Catholics, Mary) since, has created a giant rift in the relationship between humans and God. The only way to restore this relationship is for some consequential act to intervene and bridge the gap.

At this point, the Christian account of atonement runs up against some of our modern sensibilities. We seldom think in the terms of sin and salvation that form the theoretical presuppositions of atonement theory. Moreover, if we ever do entertain these notions, we tend to appeal quickly to the mercy of a loving God who we assume must want to forgive us our trespasses, especially if we are truly sorry. Who needs a cross, or suffering, or even any kind of discomfort? God is all powerful and all good, so surely God could just say, "I forgive you," and make everything better.

While there is a certain beauty in the simplicity of this vision, it overlooks far too much about the depths and complexity of sin to be a persuasive explanation of how humanity and God can honestly become reunited again. For one thing, it completely obliterates the consequences of sin. Although contemporary readers may be quick to dismiss the severity of that first transgression in the Garden of Eden, if we remember that sin is first and foremost a relational rupture rather than an isolated action, the picture begins to shift. The issue is not so much that Adam and Eve ate some of God's precious fruit when it wasn't theirs (i.e., stealing). The problem is that Adam and Eve displayed a remarkable lack of concern for their friend's wishes and demonstrated quite clearly that they did not trust the God they had come to know personally and directly during walks in the Garden every day. The harm, therefore, was not in the action (after all, God had just created everything, including the fruit tree, so we have to imagine God could easily make another piece of fruit). The harm was in what the action signified: a rejection of relationship.

This is a pain that stings, and it does not go away just because we say, "I'm sorry."

Think about it in more personal terms. Imagine one of your closest friends betrays you by publicly sharing an embarrassing secret you had asked her to keep in confidence. If she were to return to say she was truly sorry, you might ultimately find it in your heart to forgive her. At the same time, you would not suddenly forget the betrayal. On the contrary, you would almost certainly think about the way she broke your confidence every time you were around her. You would likely watch yourself meticulously whenever you had future conversations so that you could carefully avoid any topics you wanted to keep private out of a fear that she would repeat her transgression. In this context, there is no sudden or easy restoration of relationship. When trust is violated, there is no factory reset that lets a friendship go back to the days before the violation occurred, wiping away any memory of the wrongdoing. From that point on, the relationship is unavoidably colored by the betrayal. You and your friend might still find some way through this challenge, but it will be a struggle because the relationship itself has suffered. It would take time for your friend to regain your trust, and no one would fault you for keeping her at arm's length while you asked her to prove her contrition in some tangible ways.

If we can see ourselves in this story, then we can better understand how Christians conceive of God's position after sin entered the world. However much we might want to imagine a merciful God who simply forgives humanity for its failures to bother to love, when we think about a friend betraying us, we quickly have to acknowledge that if we were in God's position, we would definitely want some concrete evidence of good faith before we would open the door to any relational restoration. Christianity's reflections on atonement have been shaped by the assumption that after the Fall, God likewise had every right to demand a gesture of goodwill from us and, more importantly, that we had every need to provide one. The catch, however, has always been twofold. First, it is hard to imagine how finite humans would ever come up with an appropriate gesture to undo the breach in our relationship with the infinite God.

Second, even if we could come up with the right action, the fact of our transgression would continue to haunt our relationship much like the pain of your friend's betrayal would always cast a shadow over your friendship even after you had accepted her apology. For Christians, the solution to these two shortcomings can be found in the cross, and the various atonement theories are simply ways to explain how this could be the case.

With this background in mind, I am now going to walk through three influential Christian theories of atonement, but to present each one in the most meaningful manner in our contemporary context, I want us to start with a slightly different account of the sin that needs forgiving. Instead of thinking about gardens and fruit, I would like us to focus on the one area of modern life where both the near impossibility of forgiveness and the absolute necessity of atonement are most acutely felt. I am, of course, talking about social media.

Imagine a young man (let's call him "Ryan," to pick a name entirely at random) who has just graduated from high school and has an athletics scholarship to attend a topflight university. In the summer before he starts college, he becomes embroiled in an internet controversy that involves an absolutely appalling post online. The specifics are not important for this thought experiment, so fill in whatever you think would generate the most uproar—the kind of shameful post that a person would want to delete the moment it goes viral. To make the experiment as relatable as possible, let's also assume that Ryan was not intentionally malicious when he crafted the post. Instead, think of it as an eighteen-year-old's ignorance and pride run amok, without the empathy necessary to recognize that hurtful words have consequences. Once the public furor shakes Ryan out of this ignorance and apathy, he quickly takes down his post, but screenshots were taken and widely shared. As a result, there remains a record of his transgression that will never disappear. No matter how much Ryan might apologize publicly, the world will always know what he said that summer after graduation. One quick Google search, and his name will forever be associated with this misdeed, and this is creating a real headache for Ryan because newspapers are pressuring his university to drop his scholarship and rescind his admission.

At this point, Ryan is desperately in need of atonement. If there were some kind of intervention that would blot out every memory (and every screenshot) of his terrible post, then he might just be able to save his future from serious jeopardy. As a result, Ryan's situation parallels humanity's position in our fallen, sinful state: we can say we are sorry, but we cannot remove the legacy of our shortcomings and act as though it never happened. There are plenty of "screenshots" in the memory of an omniscient God to underscore that we cannot be trusted. We can therefore make sense of the three classic Christian atonement theories by thinking through slight variations in Ryan's story.

In the first variation, we need to shift the context and imagine that Ryan was not caught up in this controversy by virtue of a post on his own personal social media account. Instead, pretend he is the marketing intern for a local athletic club team. The viral uproar has cast not just Ryan but all club members in his area in a bad light. The club, naturally, issues a quick and public apology, but the social media outrage machine is not satisfied. Ryan's club has a black mark, and everyone connected with it is guilty by association. Fearful that this negative publicity will vaporize his scholarship, Ryan approaches the founder of his club and admits to his misdeed in a weeping fit of remorse. Moved by Ryan's conversion, the founder reassures him that she can make it right. The next day, the club holds a press conference, and the founder's son announces that he is the culprit. He insists that he is deeply sorry and asks everyone to forgive him. More importantly, he insists that no one else at the club knew what he was going to do, and he therefore pleads that no other members should be punished for his misbehavior. Ryan goes on to keep his scholarship, pursuing an illustrious career, finally able to leave the sordid affair behind him because the crowd has someone else to blame. The founder's son, on the other hand, is permanently persona non grata.

In terms of atonement, this is a version of the satisfaction theory of St. Anselm of Canterbury, an eleventh-century monk and bishop who tried to make sense of the cross using the expectations of honor and dishonor baked into the feudal system with which he was familiar. From this perspective, Anselm was convinced that Adam and Eve's sin had so firmly tarnished humanity's reputation that God, who is all good, could not possibly associate with our wretched lot. Something had to be done to remove the stain of our offense before it would be acceptable for humans to be reunited with God, just as something had to be done in Ryan's case to remove the stigma of his post on the club's shared social media account before he could be seen on his new university's campus.

For Anselm, Jesus (the son of God) comes into the world and ultimately dies to atone for the reputational harm humans have caused through their repeated sins. This is known as the satisfaction theory because Jesus's death satisfies God's need to stand in opposition to sin and evil, in much the same way that the university's team needed someone to publicly take the blame for the wretched post so that it could satisfy the public that it truly rejected the venomous ideas that the post contained. If you can understand the need to undo reputational damage in the internet age, then you can understand the honor/shame assumptions built into Anselm's worldview and thus appreciate that his satisfaction theory not only gives a coherent explanation for why Jesus had to die but also shows that God will do whatever it takes to remove the legacy of our sin so that we can be reunited with God.

Anselm's account, however, is not the only way of explaining the positive consequences of the cross for our reconciliation with God. A second theory, the moral influence theory of Peter Abelard, explores how the cross can have a profound impact on us and not just on God or God's honor.

To understand the moral influence theory, modify the sordid tale of social media gone awry and assume again that Ryan posted the despicable message on his personal account. This time, however, when the post goes viral, Ryan is undisturbed. He argues that he has been misunderstood and maintains that any criticism is overblown. Instead of apologizing, he doubles down, issuing a "clarifying" post that amplifies the offensive content. A coach at Ryan's future university, who has become something of a close friend and mentor, is appalled but also compassionate. Confident that Ryan can come around if he only listens to reason, the coach sends his assistant to Ryan's house to talk some sense into him. Ryan, however, rejects the gesture and thinks the coach is out to get him too. He strategically stages a photo to make it look like the assistant coach agrees with Ryan's offensive positions and subsequently posts *that* online, resulting in a slew of bad publicity that ruins the assistant coach's life. Once he sees what this post has done, however, Ryan awakens to the depth of his wickedness. He never wanted to hurt anyone or destroy someone's career. Resolved to amend his ways, Ryan deletes his posts, admits that he faked the photo, and reaches out to the coach to express his contrition. Although Ryan is never going to make the team, the coach doesn't care because Ryan is finally trying to be a good person again and their friendship can be slowly restored.

In theological terms, this version of the story is closest to Abelard's moral influence theory, which similarly begins with the assumption that the obstacles to humanity's atonement are not on God's side but in the human heart. The cross does not need to do anything for God, like rebuilding God's reputation as it does in the satisfaction theory. Instead, the consequences of the cross are seen in its ability to convert human hearts, so that they will finally be in a place to accept the offer of forgiveness that God has presented all along. It provides a moral influence, helping humans recognize their sinful limitations and encouraging them to be better people. The cross atones, repairing the divine–human relationship, not because it changes God but because it changes us. The moral influence theory thus reveals that God's response to sin and suffering is truly all-encompassing, for it can address not just the external effects of sin but also the internal implications, re-creating a more righteous state of affairs by addressing the root causes of our shortcomings in the first place. The final atonement theory to be considered here underscores this conclusion, pointing to the deeply transformative nature of the divine reaction to the horror story of human sinfulness as Christians understand it.

To make sense of this third theory, the solidarity theory, start with the same basic facts from the last version: Ryan used his personal account and is refusing to admit that he did anything wrong. Now, tweak two things. First, assume that the post somehow cast his friend and mentor, the new coach, in a horrific light, leaving him feeling deeply wronged. Second, turn the intensity up to eleven and imagine that Ryan is becoming belligerent in his defense of the original post. He is in an all-out war with those who decry the post, and things are getting toxic as both sides ratchet up their rhetoric. In fact, the animosity has spilled over into real life, where people are picketing outside Ryan's house and Ryan is starting to fear for his safety after a string of threatening letters.

Amid this depressing turn of events, Ryan's coach is once again moved with pity for the misguided young man, even though the coach has been effectively rejected by his one-time recruit, and he decides to visit Ryan. His arrival is caught on camera, which is risky because he does not know if the picketers will hit him with a stray rock, and he is not sure if Ryan will lash out at him, but he does not care either way. He wants to be with Ryan while Ryan is in this dark place because the coach wants to send an important message: no one is left alone, and as soon as Ryan is ready to turn away from the cruelty he has been feeding for so long, his friend will be there to help him out of the hole. His presence alongside Ryan lays the foundation for a true atonement because Ryan can be moved by this act of compassion, reaching out to rekindle the relationship he broke (and, in the process, apologizing for his stupid posts and swearing off online feuds forever). This will not halt the animosity entirely—that only happens when everyone else sees the coach's generous act of solidarity and decides to let go of their anger—but it transforms the experience of those who are suffering from all this hatred and starts the process that will one day lead to the end of the feuding as more people try to act like this kind coach.

The solidarity theory of atonement argues that God reaches out to humanity through the cross in much the same way as this coach. Unlike the other theories, which give the violence of Jesus's Passion and death an essential role in the process, the solidarity theory rejects the idea that God *needed* Jesus to die in order to effect salvation. Instead, the solidarity theory says, God came into this world to show us that we were not alone in our sinful state. Then, when sinful people decided they wanted to kill the messenger, God let them do it to prove that point. In this way, the cross becomes God's rejoinder to the reality of evil in the world. God may not be the cause of evil done (because it involves humans using their free will to undermine their telos and frustrate God's plans), but God must at least *allow* it to persist or we would never sin at all. Without attempting to explain why God permits this situation, the solidarity theory presents the cross as an effective response to this unfortunate condition, sending the message that while God may not choose to stop all this evil right now (perhaps to preserve human freedom), God will join us in the darkness as long as sin endures. By meeting us in the very suffering that we have created, God shows the depth of the divine commitment to us and turns our current experiences of suffering into an opportunity for reunification with God. Now, every time humans are in pain, they can recognize Jesus on the cross alongside them. Suffering becomes the means by which a newfound atonement arises, but there is no sense in which God desired the suffering to achieve this end.

Obviously, these three different atonement theories tell three slightly different stories about how humanity's salvation comes about as a consequence of the cross. While one might be tempted to pit these theories against one another in hopes of finding the best, I want to caution against that approach. I think it is better to preserve the mystery and to keep the tensions among these three theories because they each offer us a piece of the puzzle. When we accept that there can be something of the truth in all these theories, we can look for the commonalities and, from those, develop a model for how we can build a similarly consequential life.

Connecting this all back to discernment, the atonement theories help us *understand* what it means to make consequential choices as we discern how to give our lives selflessly to a world marred by sin. The satisfaction theory indicates that we can make a meaningful response when we are able to help those who have been hurt by sin, providing some form of comfort and a type of restitution even when we ourselves are not the ones who caused the rift. Meanwhile, the moral influence theory suggests that we can make a difference when we help those who have erred find a new way, using our lives to provide hope for a new path out of the darkness. Finally, the solidarity theory confirms the mysticism of open eyes Ryan outlined, demonstrating that charging into the darkness to sit, and suffer, alongside those trapped by the forces of sin can be a powerful, life-giving response.

By better grasping how the cross saves, we can therefore add three new data points to our model of a life well lived, strengthening our discernment process by fleshing out our options for action more fully. We do not need to pursue all these paths at once, but by focusing on one, we can discern the life that will make us most fulfilled. None of these paths will be easy, however, for they all work through the pain of the cross. To be effective, then, we need to combine this second consequential dimension of the cross with its first and remember that the inevitability of suffering is a Christian's rationale for persevering throughout the effort to respond to it. This takes courage, but it also takes a unique perspective, so we want to close this chapter with a meditation designed to cultivate that peculiar worldview through the development of our Ignatian Realism.

Meditation: Exercising Ignatian Realism

At root, what Ignatian Realism describes is a way of beholding and being present to our world with senses attuned through the practice of discernment. It is a way of *becoming aware, understanding,* and *taking action* as persons committed to discerning how to claim one's place within the Christian narrative. It is not simply a theory *about* theology but a vision for practicing a theological way of life in a manner inspired by Saint Ignatius of Loyola.

In this exercise, we ask you to imagine the consequences *you* would face were you to commit yourself to living for God's reign as proclaimed by Jesus. To do this, we share a prayer written by Saint Ignatius and found at the end of *The Spiritual Exercises.* It is a prayer I (Ryan) committed to memory when I was in high school, and I have recited it countless times since then. It might be my favorite prayer because it demands that I take seriously that crucial question of Christian discernment: *Who does God desire me to become?* It is this prayer that, on a snowy February night in 2002, led me to abandon my plans to be a doctor and set me on a totally different journey. I have never regretted praying it, even if sometimes the shadow that falls on my life—like the shadow that falls on all lives—leads me to ask, "What if?"

1. Relax. Let today's concerns slip away. Call to mind a reason to feel grateful. Savor this moment as you step back and take stock of your life.
2. Read this next part slowly. Don't rush through it. If a word or phrase strikes you, linger over it:

Suscipe

Take, Lord, and receive all my liberty,
My memory, my understanding,
And my entire will. All I have and call my own.
You have given all to me.
To you, Lord, I return it.
Everything is yours; do with it what you will.
Give me only your love and your grace.
That is enough for me.

3. Our lives are often driven by a desire to take, to seize, and to grasp. The logic: "The more I have, the more I am." When we pray, we pray for God to *do* or *get* something for us. This prayer reverses that pattern and invites God to take from us. Note the danger this poses to the one who offers it sincerely. One surrenders one's freedom, one's past (memory), one's present (understanding), and one's future (will). The *Suscipe* (the Latin word for "receive") is a prayer of radical vulnerability. It is not the prayer of the roly-poly who turns inward in self-protection; this prayer asks one to be open and self-giving. *If* you were to make this prayer your own, what would *you* ask God to receive? Does entrusting yourself to God's will—again, the heart of discernment— bring you peace or anxiety. Why?
4. Can you identify places in the world where *your* gifts and talents are needed? Take some time to open your heart and mind to hearing how *you* might be called to dedicate your

whole self to responding to this need. What would happen if . . .

    a. Your skills as a teacher led you not to a wealthy suburban school but to a school where resources were scarce but the students hungry for knowledge?

    b. Your passion for scientific inquiry inspired you to find ways of addressing ongoing global health care challenges and inequities?

    c. Your commitment to justice gave you the courage to stand up and speak out on behalf of others who were voiceless and ignored?

    d. Your sense of God's reign informed and transformed your way of living within society?

5. If God's grace does not hold us back but propels us forward, where would God's grace lead you? As you survey the world today, do you have a sense of your own "mysticism of open eyes" that enables you to see what other people ignore?

6. How might this mysticism of "open eyes" turn into a mysticism of an open life, a life more concerned with giving of yourself than in grasping? Is there some area in life—choosing a major, an internship, a job—that terrifies and excites you because it requires you to be open in new ways? How might this discomfort and fear be a summons to growth?

7. "Give me only your love and your grace." It is precisely *because* of God's love and grace, made flesh in Jesus Christ, that even today disciples put their lives on the line as they work for God's Kingdom. *Because* of God's grace, how might you respond? How would this lead you to the Cross and how would you react?

8. As you bring this meditation to a close, take a moment to ponder: What, in this world, *would* be enough for you? Is there anything you could *possess* that would satisfy you fully? Or might it be that true fulfillment comes not from

grasping but from giving . . . a life lived and given in loving service patterned after Jesus Christ? Does this theological vision, this Ignatian Realism, offer a compelling way to respond to the reality of the world's suffering?

Key Terms and Ideas

- Passion: from the Latin for suffering (*passio*), the Passion is the term for the events immediately preceding Jesus's death on the cross in which he suffers virtually all the worst pains and indignities known to the human condition, from abandonment by his friends to physical torment.
- Ignatian Realism: a way of beholding the world that is rooted in St. Ignatius's vision for discernment, which allows someone to search for the deeper meaning of God's presence not only in positive experiences but also in painful ones.
- Dark grace: a peculiar way God works, according to Christians, in which Jesus's experiences of suffering (and death) allow one to experience the support and accompaniment of God when entering into and sharing the suffering of others.
- Mysticism of open eyes: term coined by the twentieth-century German theologian Johann Baptist Metz to describe the way Christians can find God even in the midst of suffering and darkness because of Jesus's solidarity with all those who suffer. The mysticism of open eyes allows a Christian to look at the world in its entirety—both good and bad— without losing faith.
- Atonement theories: theological interpretations of the "work" of the cross, atonement theories seek to explain how Jesus's Passion and death could save humanity from the legacy of sin and its effects.

Recommended Resources

Luke 22–23

Each gospel contains a Passion Narrative, or depiction of the events leading to Jesus's death, focusing on the suffering that surrounded his execution. Luke's account has the most overt emphasis on the political dimensions of Jesus's crucifixion, emphasizing the cross as an act of imperial power and thereby demonstrating the links between Jesus's ministry and his death, the first consequential dimension of the cross.

James Cone, "Strange Fruit: The Cross and the Lynching Tree," *Journal of Theology for Southern Africa* 14 (March 2014): 7–17.

Cone, an influential Black Christian theologian, has used his writings to overtly grapple with how a Black man in the United States might faithfully interpret the saving work of the cross in light of his experiences. This 2014 essay, which builds on ideas developed in Cone's earlier book *The Cross and the Lynching Tree*, argues both that the Black community in the United States needs the cross to make sense of the brutal history of slavery, segregation, and lynching and that Christians need the Black community's experience of those sufferings to make sense of the saving impact of the cross. The essay is therefore a text displaying the second consequential dimension of the cross in vivid fashion, with a vision of solidarity atonement on full display.

Anselm of Canterbury, *Cur Deus Homo* (full text available online at: https://sourcebooks.fordham.edu/basis/anselm-curdeus.asp).

The original source of one of the most prominent atonement theories in Christian theology, Anselm's treatise on "Why God Became Human" makes sense of the consequences of the cross for human salvation using a satisfaction model. A careful reading of the text will give a more nuanced account of the satisfaction theory and the theological problems it was meant to address.

The Dark Knight, directed by Christopher Nolan, Warner Brothers, 2008; *Gran Torino*, directed by Clint Eastwood, Warner Brothers, 2008; *The Green Mile*, directed by Frank Darabont, Warner Brothers, 1999.

These three films each have a "Christ figure," or a character who presents a narrative arc that imitates the gospel story of Jesus's life and death. The impact of this parallel varies, however, presenting different implicit atonement theories. Watch Nolan's *Dark Knight* for links to the satisfaction theory, Eastwood's *Gran Torino* for a moral influence interpretation, and Darabont's *The Green Mile* for similarities with the solidarity theory.

Notes

1. Karl Marx, *Critique of Hegel's 'Philosophy of Right'*, trans. Annette Jolin and Joseph O'Malley (New York: Cambridge University Press, 1977), 127.
2. Johann Baptist Metz, *A Passion for God: The Mystical-Political Dimension of Christianity*, trans. J. Matthew Ashley (Mahwah, NJ: Paulist Press, 1998), 163.

7

Ready for Action

As we conclude the "Understanding" part of the book, readers may feel as if they've been hoodwinked. "Wait! Explain to me how *any* of this theological stuff can impact my life? You said you were going to help me to figure out my major, internship, or career, but you keep talking about Jesus. Sure, the little exercises have given me some opportunities to reflect on my life, but I'm not certain what I'm supposed to get from this." If you're curious about how this all hangs together, let's take a step back and look briefly at the path we've followed.

Our goal is to help readers pause and examine their lives through a process we have described as the Ignatian B.U.T. (*become aware, understand, take action*). In part I, "Becoming Aware," we discussed how our own stories can fit into and "make sense" within the larger Christian narrative. Discernment, as we understand and practice it, is not about making decisions in a vacuum. Discernment demands that we become attentive to reality and stand before it—an idea, person, the world itself— and appreciate it on its terms. We suggested, in chapter 1, how practicing the *Examen* can help to put us in touch with our deepest desires. This led, in chapter 2, to a discussion about the telos, end, or "goal" of human life. One way of getting at this is to reflect on what David Brooks called "eulogy virtues." When we leave this life, do we want to be remembered for *what* we did or, rather, for *who* we were to, with, and for others? In chapter 3, we examined natural and moral evil. Theologians do not deny the world's brokenness; indeed, we know that sin causes a "crack" in everything. Nevertheless, we believe that through this "crack," divine light can still be glimpsed. In history's darkness, believers seek out and move toward this light.

As Christians and theologians, Conor and I struggle to "understand" how Jesus Christ is the "divine light" that pierces history's darkness. Without question, there's a lot of darkness in history, and it is an ongoing struggle to discern how, and where, God is to be found within it so that we can recognize how best to act in that darkness too. But as we examine how our lives fit into and make sense within the Christian story, we are inspired to continue this discernment. Even in the darkest hours, we open ourselves in prayer and expend ourselves in the service of Jesus Christ who speaks plainly: "I am the light of the world. Whoever follows me will never walk in darkness but will have the light of life" (John 8:12).

Thus, in chapters 4–6, we have looked at aspects of the Christian story. If my argument in chapter 4 was convincing, we can now envision that the Bible does not merely tell us *a* story but, more radically, reveals *our* story to us. In his words (parables) and deeds (miracles), Jesus hammers this lesson home: Our sinful organization of the world, its oppressive and dehumanizing structures and practices, are not of God's will. Through his whole person, Jesus makes present the reign of God. To the poor, infirm, and marginalized, this was received as Good News, but to those in power, it was a threat. Not surprisingly, Jesus met the outcome that awaits those who speak truth to power: death. Were we to conclude part II simply with Good Friday, with Jesus hanging on a cross outside of Jerusalem's walls, this would make for a bleak book. Christians do not believe the story ends there. To the eyes of many, the cross is foolishness; yet, for Christians, it is nothing less than a subversive sign of God's power at work in history. Saint Paul puts it this way: Jesus Christ was put to death, was buried but "raised on the third day" (1 Corinthians 15:4). In this chapter, we will explore the implications of this claim *both* for theologians and for those whose discernment leads them to follow Jesus's way of life.

The Tyrant Memory of Golgotha

Try as one might, it cannot be denied that Christianity is a religion founded on a loser. Jesus may have told good stories; he may have done some wondrous, if not miraculous, things, but when all is said and done, he lost in a spectacular manner. The wheel of history turned and crushed him beneath its weight, yet another victim added to a growing pile of those who have been pulverized for challenging the ones with power. Indeed, the gospels are unflinching in depicting Jesus's fate. On Palm Sunday, Jesus is a hero who enters Jerusalem and is greeted by a joyful and enthusiastic crowd. Days later, on Good Friday, the crowds that had welcomed Jesus by proclaiming "Blessed is the king" (Luke 19:38) now jeer at him and call for his death. The political and religious authorities who were threatened by Jesus's proclamation of God's reign are only too glad to accede to this request. Jesus is flogged as a criminal, mocked and humiliated, and then led out of the city where, naked, he was nailed to a cross. His death was brutal, shameful, and agonizing. The cross served as a warning to anyone tempted to follow Jesus: *Think again, for this is the fate that awaits those who threaten the system.*

For Jerusalem's Roman occupiers, crucifixion was an efficient and effective deterrent. And, for Jesus's fellow Jews, the cross was also theologically significant: "for anyone hung on a tree is under God's curse" (Deuteronomy 21:23). So, when Jesus, in an echo of Psalm 22, cries out, "My God! My God! Why have you forsaken me?" (Mark 15:34), this is a cry of a man who has lost *everything.* To any bystander, Jesus dies a failure, a criminal abandoned by both his followers and the God he claimed to serve.

Let's be honest: It *should* have been the end of the story. Jesus's own disciples—well, quite a few of them, at least—certainly thought it was. Some took refuge in an upper room; others quickly set off for other cities. They had seen the way the mob turned on Jesus and wanted to distance themselves lest the mob call for their deaths, too. This is the tyrant memory of the gospel: Jesus died outcast and, except for a few stalwart women, alone. Jesus failed. His closest associates failed. Humanity, it seems, failed. At the cross, Herbert McCabe writes, two terrible truths about human history are disclosed: "The first is that if you do not love you will not be alive; the second is that if you do love you will be killed."[1] Jesus embodies what it means to be fully alive and fully human. A world diminished by sin regarded his humanity as a threat, so it killed him.

Significantly, Jesus was neither the first nor the last to suffer this fate. History has a way of treating prophets in this manner. Step out of line, question the system, or stand in defiance against it, and those in control will silence you by any means necessary. It happened to the Old Testament prophets, it happened to Jesus and his Christian followers, it happened to Martin Luther King Jr., and many more. Turn on the television or the radio and you'll find it happening wherever and whenever someone dares to speak out for human dignity.

Even though the wheel of violence turned and crushed Jesus beneath it, his story did not end. On the contrary, Christians believe the events of Good Friday mark the beginning of an entirely new story. Briefly put, the new version goes like this. Two days after his death, Mary Magdalene rushes to the other disciples, who are hiding in fear, with an astonishing claim: "I have seen the Lord" (John 20:18). She had gone early Sunday morning to tend to Jesus's tomb but found it empty. She sees a man she takes to be the gardener and asks him where the body is. Then the "gardener" speaks: *Mary!* Suddenly, it is as though her eyes are opened and she sees Jesus. Not a hologram and certainly not a zombie. On Easter Sunday, Mary sees the same Jesus but in a new way, as glorified and alive with the power of God. For Mary—as for all those who continue to meet the Risen Jesus in their lives—this is not merely a new chapter to their life story. The Resurrection, accordingly, is nothing less than the event that rewrites and reshapes history itself.

Theologians, artists, and musicians have tried to express the meaning of the Resurrection in various ways, but like all efforts at human communication about the divine, they never quite capture it. Nor should they be expected to, for Jesus's Resurrection blows apart our logical expectations about the nature and meaning of human life. Indeed, you could say that the Resurrection, for Christians, gives a *new* type of logic (theo-logic) wherein good is stronger than evil, life conquers death, and the peace of God's Kingdom is more powerful than the violence of sinful history. For Christians, the Resurrection does not destroy history but, rather, holds out the promise that God is at work in history to heal and bring it to completion.

My favorite quote to this effect comes from Gandalf the White in *The Two Towers*. Having passed through fire and water as he battled his enemy the Balrog, Gandalf collapses and darkness seizes him. Yet he passes through death and is restored to a renewed and glorious form of life. His return does not mean business as usual. As he says to his astonished companions: "I come back to you now, at the turn of the tide." Gandalf the White does not deny the suffering of the past, nor does he promise that future victory will come easily. His return "at the turn of the tide" means that a Power greater than death itself has taken a stand in history and has chosen a side. Revealed through Gandalf, this Power stands in solidarity with those who struggle against the powers of darkness.

This phrase, to my mind, vividly captures the adventure of Christian life and underscores the need for ongoing discernment. For believers, the Resurrection is not just something we profess to believe on Sundays but, rather, something we live out in our daily lives. In a world broken by sin and hostile to authentic humanity, Christian hope is found in the Risen One who has triumphed over death and invites all of us to share in his victory. If the miracles were the "cracks" that give us a glimpse of how God's reign should look in history, the Resurrection makes these cracks into a doorway. Because of the Resurrection, Christians believe God "turned the tide" against sin and death, making it possible to live according to grace and forgiveness. By Easter morning's light, we see Jesus's life as the pattern of an authentic life; we can recognize the way he interacted with others in a self-giving way as the telos of a truly human life.

Many books have been written attempting to explain what Mary Magdalene meant when she exclaimed to the disciples on that first Easter morning, "I have seen the Lord." Allow me to offer two brief points and then a definition. First, as we survey the various "appearance narratives" found in the gospels, it becomes clear that the Risen Jesus could be encountered only at his initiative. A person walking down the street sees food vendors, the tax collector, and a woman by the well, but he will not glimpse the Risen Christ unless the Risen One reveals himself. Recall the Emmaus story in Luke 24. Two disciples encounter a stranger who joins them as they flee Jerusalem. Readers know this is Jesus, but the disciples are clueless until Jesus makes his identity known. This means, in effect, that the body of the Risen Jesus is not like the ordinary bodies we see every day with our physical eyes. "Seeing" the Risen Jesus requires a deeper vision through the "eyes of faith" that are opened by God's grace. Second, the New Testament insists that the encounters with the Risen Christ were objective and neither self-induced nor hallucinatory.[2] Post-Easter experiences of Jesus involve encountering a bodily presence that cannot be explained away. The extraordinary claim of Easter—"He is Risen"—is not a reflection of disciples who were hallucinating. Their testimonies agree that in their encounter with Jesus, they were encountering an objective and bodily presence, not a ghost, but a glorious and hope-giving presence that "breaks into" our reality not to destroy but to save.

Now for a definition. By Resurrection, I mean the *theological event whereby the Jesus who preached and enacted God's reign by word (teachings and parables) and deed (ministry and miracles), the Jesus who was crucified and really died because this reign threatened the status quo of sin (he died as a consequence of being human in an inhuman world), is now fully alive with God and continues to be known by and to interact with believers.*

For Christians, the Resurrection means that Jesus remains present to believers not simply as an "idea" or an inspiring figure from the past but as a real presence in history. Being alive with God means that the Risen Christ is not limited—like we are—to the here and now of space and time. The Risen Jesus is no longer bound by these constraints and, so, can be personally present in all times and places. The Jesuit and Ignatian impulse to seek God in all things is guided not by a quest for some holy "God goo" seeping out of everything but, rather, a fervent belief that the Risen Christ—the Logos or Logic—of God can appear wherever and whenever he desires. One can now encounter the Risen One in the celebration of the Eucharist with the church community, in silent adoration before a monstrance (the vessel used to carry and display a consecrated host), in the Word of God proclaimed at liturgy, and in the community of believers. Indeed, belief in the Resurrection should put one on high alert: Jesus is not present in *this place* or *that place* because now, after the Resurrection, Jesus can be encountered in *all* places. In Matthew 25, many at the "Judgment of Nations" are surprised to learn that they have been judged righteous because they didn't know they were serving the Lord: "Lord, when was it that we saw you hungry and gave you food, or thirsty and gave you something to drink?" (Matthew 25:37). The Lord's answer should both enkindle hope and a holy fear in Christians: "Truly I tell you, just as you did it to one of the least of these who are members of my family, you did it to me" (Matthew 25:40). Everywhere we go, everything we do, and everyone we interact with can be an occasion for us to encounter the Risen One.

When I was in the second grade—the year I made my first communion—my mom gave me a copy of *The Lion, the Witch and the Wardrobe*. To my mind, no piece of fiction provides a better allegory for the Christ story, which is precisely how C.S. Lewis intended it to be read. In Lewis's narrative, Aslan is the heroic Christ figure who willingly lays down his life for one of the children, Edmund Pevensie. Jadis, the evil White Witch who had seized control of Narnia, was only too glad to accept Aslan's offer. Indeed, she believed, this trade worked to her advantage: She could kill Aslan and, with him out of the way, could go on to kill *everyone* who defied her. The Witch's logic is cold and ruthless but hardly foreign to our world's way of conducting business. Jadis would be a natural on Wall Street *and* social media.

With macabre fanfare, Jadis conducts the ritual slaughter of Aslan. Susan and Lucy Pevensie look on with horror as the one they loved and trusted and followed dies a horrendous death. When the Witch's army departs, they creep over and shed tears over the body of their dead friend. They mourn. Aslan's story, as far as they are concerned, is over . . . and the Witch's army threatens to end Narnia's story altogether. They begin to walk away but a sudden cracking noise arrests their advance. They turn and see that the Stone Table where Aslan's body had lain is now cracked and broken. For a moment, they are blinded by the rising sun, and then they see him: Aslan. Not a ghost, not a zombie. But the dead-and-bodily-raised Aslan in their midst. They touch and smell and they *know* who it is: Aslan. He then reveals to them the meaning of this event:

Though the Witch knew the Deep Magic, there is a magic deeper still which she did not know: Her knowledge goes back only to the dawn of time. But if she could have looked a little further back, into the stillness and the darkness before Time dawned, she would have read there a different incantation. She would have known that when a willing victim who had committed no treachery was killed in a traitor's stead, the Table would crack and Death itself would start working backwards.[3]

Put in theological terms, the Witch's logic or understanding only reflected the world *after* the Fall, the world *after* humans had said "no" to God. Her logic is the tit-for-tat logic of vengeance, a logic where "might makes right" and power is everything. The motto of this logic is "Do unto others . . . before they do it unto you." Aslan, like Jesus, whom he represents, is inspired by and lives out a totally different logic. He is animated by, well, a divine *theo*-logic: he understands and shares with others an understanding of how the Creator intends and desires the world to be.

Simply *knowing about* this logic is not enough. Aslan had to put "skin in the game," and this put him in head-to-head competition with the Witch. He had to play her game by her rules. To the delight of her and her minions, this meant his death. To the cynical and jaded, this is the way the world works. Yet Aslan's return—his Resurrection—reveals that the Witch has been playing by the wrong rules all along. For her, the goal or telos of life is to accumulate and wield power. According to the Deep Magic, true power is gained only by totally giving oneself (Obi-Wan Kenobi noted this in *Star Wars*). Aslan's return does not erase the terrible events of the past. His return makes a new future possible for those who believe in the Deep Magic and fight with him. His return, like Gandalf's, "turns the tide" in the Battle for Narnia: the struggle is real and has consequences, but we are assured that the logic of life and love will overcome the logic of death and hate.

Back in the second grade, I grasped the implications of the return of Aslan—and, as I wrestled with the claims of Christianity, likewise came to realize that the Resurrection throws our understanding of history off balance. It ruptures our understanding of the "way things are" and gives us a glimpse of how creation should, and could, be. In a way, you might say that the Resurrection promises to fulfill our deepest desires. One may think happiness and fulfillment come from having great wealth or power. Certainly, these may bring pleasure, security, and satisfaction. Yet all of these are fickle and fragile. Can anyone ever have enough money or power? As a priest, I've been with people who have amassed enormous fortunes and wield great power but who are, beneath the glitter and glamor, deeply unsettled. Spending time with them has helped me to appreciate that, deep down, most of us do not crave things. Instead, our deepest desire is to know that, somehow, our lives are worth living and that our lives have purpose and meaning. As one wealthy pharmaceutical executive put it to me in an airport bar, "Ry, how can I believe in the Good News when there's so much terrible s—t happening in history?"

There is no denying that the stain of sin mars history. Nevertheless, for the Christian, it does not blot out the goodness of creation. Perhaps this is why I take consolation in the fact that in the Gospel of John, the Risen Christ still bears the wounds of the crucifixion on his body. Jesus's past and history are not erased by the Resurrection but transformed and glorified through it. At Golgotha (meaning "place of the skull") or Calvary—the hill outside Jerusalem's walls where the condemned were crucified—human history uttered the ultimate no to God with the violent execution of Jesus. In the Resurrection, God utters the ultimate "Yes" to humanity. "Yes, this is who I AM, a God of life and not death, a God of peace and not violence, a God of love and forgiveness and not hate and vengeance." The Risen Christ returns to history, not to seek vengeance but to redeem the goodness of creation. Christians believe Jesus Christ continues to extend his pierced hand to those trapped in the mire of sin, that he cleanses us of this muck and invites us to journey with him and to "go and do likewise" (Luke 10:37) with those we meet. Indeed, when we look at history with the eyes of faith, as Conor will now do, we can see instances of Christ's pierced hand at work delivering humanity from sin and gathering them into the Body of Christ.

Living as People of the Resurrection

Precisely because the Resurrection reveals who God really is, it helps us in our efforts to *understand* before we *take action*. Jesus's Resurrection reveals the power of God's victory over death and suffering. It confirms the inbreaking of the reign of God and demonstrates that it is possible to live according to the values of the right side up even in our otherwise upside-down world. The Resurrection therefore shows us how we can act if we want to discern a way of life that will allow us to flourish as human beings. Moreover, because the Resurrection represents the turning of the tide, it shows us precisely how we *should* act, giving Christians a new mission as a Resurrection people.

When interpreted as the completion of the story of the cross, the Resurrection helps us understand how to pursue the consequential life that we discussed in the last chapter. More specifically, the Resurrection teaches us two more things about the best way to live a life of self-gift in a world marred by sin. First, because Jesus rose from the dead not as a ghost but as a human being, the Resurrection reminds us that the body matters, reinforcing the importance of using our gift of self to respond to the pain and suffering we see around us. Second, because Jesus rose in a way that *totally* destroyed the power of death and replaced it with the theo-logic of the reign of God, the Resurrection indicates that we should prioritize a comprehensive solution to the pitfalls of this life instead of settling for partial responses that redress only a small portion of our lasting problems.

Consider first the body. Christians assert that Jesus's Resurrection was not merely a singular experience available only to Jesus of Nazareth and no one else for all eternity. Instead of viewing Jesus's Resurrection as the exception to the norm—people die, and that is the end—Christians insist that this turning of the tide ushers in a whole new norm. In the aftermath of that first Easter Sunday, Christians now anticipate the same fate for themselves, making Resurrection of the body the expectation rather than the exception. As a result, Christians need to take humanity's bodily existence seriously. Whereas some religious traditions emphasize a dualistic opposition between the body and the soul, Christianity maintains that these two aspects of our human nature are inherently linked. Thus, in his grand vision of heaven, the fourteenth-century Italian poet Dante Alighieri astutely portrayed the souls in paradise—those who live in the very presence of God—as still yearning for the day when they are reunited with their bodies and have the chance to bring their union with God and one another to an even fuller completion. A soul without a body, he was trying to explain, is always somehow incomplete, even when it is in the happy state of union with God.

The Christian vision of perfection thus entails a close connection between body and soul. In a Christian worldview, there is no need to downplay or overcome our embodiment so that we can somehow "free" our souls from the prisons of the material world. On the contrary, the material world can be a tool for spiritual development. As we will discuss in chapter 10, this is the rationale that has allowed "finding God in all things" to become an Ignatian term of art. For the moment, though, I want to underscore that this assumption about the spiritual prospects of bodily existence has practical implications, for one way to use the material world as a tool for our spiritual development is to take care of the bodily needs of those around us.

When Jesus appeared to his disciples after the Resurrection, he was clearly in bodily form, but his body was also somehow different. Ryan has already pointed to two illustrations of this point. The Gospel of John has Mary Magdalene mistaking Jesus for a gardener (John 20:15), and the Gospel of Luke has two of Jesus's followers completely unaware of who he is on the road to Emmaus (Luke 24:13–35). The traditional explanation for how this could transpire is that Jesus returned from the dead with his "glorified body." This is a body in all its glory, the perfection for which it was designed. It is not unmarked by suffering—as Ryan noted, Jesus's body still bore the wounds of his crucifixion—but it is also not subject to the pain of suffering itself. Because Christians identify this body as the proper destiny of all human bodies now on earth, they have a strong rationale to view physical suffering in the current realm as a departure from the divine plan. They are therefore motivated to take action to overcome the pain of suffering when it occurs. Caring for the body now is a logical extension of the conviction that the body is important enough to be part of the afterlife.

Christians from the earliest days took this practical corollary of their faith quite seriously. Rodney Stark, a scholar of Christianity's history, recounts how the initial Christian communities formed in urban environments and almost immediately set themselves apart from their pagan counterparts by embracing a new way of life. When horrendous plagues hit Antioch (one of the largest cities in the Roman empire at the time) in the late second century, for example, the normal course of action was to hunker down and hope that one's household would remain uninfected. Christians, however, went out into the streets to help those who suffered, offering what rudimentary medical care they could to ease suffering and save lives. Unsurprisingly, a number of the Christians died in the process, after becoming infected themselves. They were willing to do this because they believed in the Resurrection, which both gave them the assurance that addressing their neighbor's bodily needs was a worthwhile task and offered them the confidence that there could be a better reward for their own body in the next life if they succumbed to the plague in this one.[4]

As this early Christian example demonstrates, faith in the Resurrection properly entails caring for the bodily needs of others. The Resurrection thus helps to specify the kinds of suffering that demand a response from those who are discerning how to live their lives most fully as a form of self-gift. They cannot overlook bodily suffering but must instead respond to misery in the material world with the mercy that moves them to act for healing and transformation; otherwise, they would implicitly deny that the body matters enough to have a place in the perfection of paradise.

In addition to stressing *that* Christians ought to address the bodily suffering of their neighbor, the Resurrection also reveals something about *how* Christians should go about responding to this pain. Understood as the conclusion of Jesus's life on earth, the Resurrection reveals the totality of God's response to suffering, turning the tide in a way that leaves the most profound effect of sin—death—completely powerless (at least in the grand scheme of things). As a model for humanity's reaction to suffering, the Resurrection therefore countenances a commitment to a comprehensive response. We must seek to correct the bodily suffering we see in a lasting way; we cannot settle for temporary solutions to perennial problems or put minor band-aids on major wounds. Because bodies matter, there can be no half-measures in our response.

The best way to understand the practical implications of this commitment is to recognize the distinction between charity and justice. Ken Himes, a Franciscan priest and one of my theological mentors, uses the image of a broken bridge to get at this difference. If we imagine the bridge as an essential link for a small community—say residents live on one side of the river and work on the other—then we can easily envision a situation where a bridge collapses while people are crossing the river. They fall into the river and cry out for help so that they do not drown. These people have an immediate bodily need: they must get out of the water so that they can survive. If I am on the riverbank witnessing their plight, the most obvious response to their physical suffering is to jump into the river to save them. This, Himes explains, is the reaction of charity. It responds to an immediate need and addresses the suffering of one individual at a time. It is a way of loving my neighbor. It is also essential, for if I do not get the struggling swimmers out of the water, they will die. It is not, however, the whole solution.

In the case of the broken bridge, pulling one near-drowning victim out of the water saves that individual, but it does nothing about the bridge itself. If I am genuinely concerned about these townspeople, then I *must* do something about the broken bridge that is leaving them stranded in the water. In order to help them, I need to find a way to fix the bridge, so that the situation does not recur and their lives can return to normal. This represents the work of justice, for it addresses the root cause of the problem, removing the structural impediments that would otherwise make drowning a routine crisis. For each individual townsperson who has already fallen into the river, charity is indispensable, but for all the townspeople and their community as a whole, justice is required as well.[5]

By stressing the value of bodily existence, the Resurrection underscores the importance of charity as a direct response to the suffering of my neighbor immediately in front of me. At the same time, the Resurrection reveals that charity alone is not enough. Those who are committed to *taking action* in the world in a way that mirrors the fullness of humanity revealed in Christ must also pursue justice as a means of enacting the total transformation that the Resurrection promises. In his preaching, Jesus *did not* say, "Blessed are the poor *in theory.*" He said, "Blessed are the poor," and this means that the whole person—body and soul—matters. Charity and justice are, in a way, a full-contact sport.

In more concrete terms, this implication of the Resurrection means that our discernment must account for the structural forces shaping the problems we recognize through the first part of the Ignatian B.U.T.—that is, as we *become aware*—and refine our *understanding.* Certainly, we must find ways to care for those who suffer, but we must also identify the root causes of their suffering and *take action* to address those obstacles as well.

To give a quick example, consider food. A lack of food is a real problem for more than 800 million people worldwide, including almost 40 million people in the United States.[6] When someone is hungry, it constitutes a form of bodily suffering that merits a compassionate response. Christians routinely do this, donating to food pantries and organizing food drives throughout the world. This is an important effort, but it only gets at part of the problem because hunger persists in part due to larger structures that affect the distribution of food across the globe. In some areas, for example, hunger is the result of famines that are, in turn, caused (or at least exacerbated) by global warming. This means that the reliance on fossil fuels for everyday life in the richer countries of the Global North has a role to play in creating the conditions for devastating degrees of hunger in the Global South. The very structures of our society create some of the hardships we want so desperately to address. If we are truly concerned about the plight of those who are starving, then we will need to couple our efforts at charity with a renewed commitment to justice, so that we can change some of the structures that are creating the bodily misery we encounter in the world around us.

One tool that can help us in this project is the theological notion of structural sin. In its simplest form, structural sin captures the idea that the effects of human sinfulness (evil done) carry over into the systems and social structures that sinful humans create. In my own academic research, I define structural sin as the institutions and collective practices that reward selfish behaviors with social or economic incentives, making it harder for everyone to realize their part in the common good. When we think about hunger, this could include the way the institution of factory farming masks the real cost of meat production by dismissing animal welfare. This makes it less expensive for people in the United States to buy certain kinds of (factory-farmed, rather than organic) meat, creating an incentive for more people to purchase a product that is particularly damaging to the environment. (Studies indicate that meat-rich diets have the highest environmental impact.) Cultural practices, meanwhile, reinforce this dietary decision, suggesting that meals without meat are somehow incomplete, at least in the US mindset. If individuals are concerned about hunger—as the Resurrection's emphasis on embodiment suggests they should be—then they also need to think about these connections, and they need to complement their pursuit of charity with the promotion of structural reforms that would create a more just use of the earth's climate resources so that food might be more readily available for all.[7]

Notably, this is just one illustration. There are similar structures of sin at the heart of almost all our intractable social problems, so the point is that people need to consider *this kind* of analysis when they encounter suffering, not that these specific strategies are the perfect answer (although there is a good argument for eating less meat . . .). If we do adopt this structural perspective and work to develop structural solutions, we can offer a more comprehensive response to the pain of suffering in this world. Certainly, love of neighbor ought to prompt us to pursue justice in this way, for it is not enough to counter drowning by throwing a rope into the river when there is a broken bridge upstream; we must also find out what caused the bridge to collapse and fix the bridge if we care about the townspeople's well-being. The Resurrection helps us to understand the importance of this approach, inviting us to identify solutions that get to the heart of the problem so that we can provide a genuinely transformative response to suffering that breaks its power over our neighbors just as Jesus's Resurrection broke death's power over us. When we *take action* in our discernment, then, we must prioritize both the immediate benefits of charity's care and the long-term impact of justice's structural reform. Anything less would deny the Christian claim that Jesus is risen and that, through his victory over evil and death, the tide has turned in favor of God's reign as it unfolds on earth.

Meditation: An Invitation to New Life

Christians interpret the Resurrection of Jesus as a truly transformative event. Certainly, it was transformative for Jesus himself, who went from death to new life. As noted throughout this chapter, this new life was not simply a reanimation of his corpse, allowing a repeat of his old life. Instead, Jesus's new life involved a glorified body that represented a fulfillment of his earthly existence, amounting to an even better way of being in the world. At the same time, the Resurrection is also supposed to be transformative for those around Jesus. This is the point of insisting that the Resurrection serves as a summons for Christians to attend to the bodily needs of others—through both charity and justice—with a new confidence that they can put their own bodies on the line in the process if they need to do so. By turning the tide, Jesus invited his followers to recognize that they could live a new life, a fuller life, in this world now even before they experienced their own resurrection.

We close this chapter with a meditation that highlights these two transformative dimensions of the Resurrection. In *The Spiritual Exercises*, St. Ignatius structured the final section (the "Fourth Week") around the Resurrection appearances of Jesus recounted in the New Testament, inviting those on this retreat to focus on the immediate impact of the Resurrection for Jesus and his followers and then to connect this impact to their own lives. In that same spirit, we invite you to do the same through two distinct stories of how Jesus, after his Resurrection, walked with those who knew him in this life before his death.

1. Close your eyes for a moment to take five deep breaths.
   Inhale slowly, for a five-second count, each time. Hold that

breath for a three-second count, and then exhale slowly for another five-second count. Pay attention to your breathing during this process and allow this focus on your body to center your mind so that you can put your thoughts about the day's troubles aside for this brief exercise.

2. In the Gospel of Luke, Jesus appears to a small group of his followers as they walk from Jerusalem to a town called Emmaus. They do not recognize him at first but instead greet him as a stranger and talk to him about the pain they recently experienced at the loss of their friend. Try to imagine yourself watching this interaction on the dusty road. See this band of dejected travelers welcome a fellow pilgrim into their group and note the interactions as they tell this newcomer of their heartbreak and he "interpreted to them the things about himself in the scriptures" (Luke 24:27), offering them surprising reassurances that their loss was not in vain. You know this wise stranger is actually the very friend they mourn, but they do not. Why are they unable to recognize Jesus? What is it about his new way of being in the world that makes him different? Where can you see the transformation of the Resurrection in this unexpected appearance? What does this confusion tell you about the promise of new life after the turning of the tide?

3. Now, shift gears to a second appearance recounted in the Gospel of Matthew. This one occurs after some of Jesus's disciples had already seen Jesus in his resurrected body, so they have more context than the travelers on the road to Emmaus. In this instance, Jesus's followers immediately recognize him, although not all of them can understand what it means to see their dead friend alive again. As they converse with Jesus, he gives them a special set of instructions: "Go therefore and make disciples of all nations, baptizing them in the name of the Father and of the Son and of the Holy Spirit, and teaching them to obey everything that I have commanded you" (Matthew 28:19–20). Sit with this

exhortation for a moment. Note how Jesus is giving his
followers new responsibilities; he is transforming the idea of
what it means to be his disciple. How might you be called to
a similar mission? To whom are you being sent, so that you
can use your life as a form of self-gift? What forms of
suffering are you called to respond to, with both charity and
justice? What are the tasks of your new mission, and how
are you empowered to fulfill them?

4. Take a moment in gratitude to reflect on and appreciate the
insights of this exercise. Note one or two things you want to
take with you and identify a plan for how you will try to
respond to your own invitation to new life in the week
ahead.

Key Terms and Ideas

- Resurrection: the theological event whereby Jesus, who was crucified and
died because his ministry of the reign of God threatened the status quo of
sin, is now fully alive with God and continues to be known by and to
interact with believers.
- The turning of the tide: a phrase borrowed from Gandalf the White in
The Lord of the Rings, the turning of the tide refers to the powerful
cosmic consequences of Jesus's Resurrection, which represents a holistic
transformation of the sinful world and ushers in God's plan for the
world in much the same way that an outgoing tide comes rushing back
just after its lowest point.
- Charity and justice: the distinction highlights the importance of
responding to suffering at both the interpersonal level of its immediate
effects (charity) and at the broader level of its root causes (justice). Thus,
responding to the suffering of hunger requires providing food to those who
do not have enough (charity) and working to counteract the social
influences that lead to food insecurity (justice).
- Structural sin (sometimes called structures of sin): a term for the effects
of sin that extend beyond individual actions to the way social life is
structured more broadly. These effects can be seen in the institutions and
collective practices that reward people for doing selfish things and
discourage them from working for the common good.

Recommended Resources

N. T. Wright, "The First Easter," in *Simply Christian: Why Christianity Makes Sense* (New York: Harper Collins, 2006), 111–116.

In this excerpt from a chapter on "Jesus: Rescue and Renewal," Wright explores the theological implications of the Resurrection, arguing that it makes sense only within the context of a specific Christian worldview. Rejecting a complete unity between God and the world (found in ancient belief systems like "pantheism" that make the gods part of everything) and also a complete separation of God and the world (found in the "cosmic clockmaker" vision of "deism," which suggested God has chosen to leave the world to its own devices), this Christian worldview accepts a distinction between the infinite God and the finite world and yet still insists that God chooses to interact with—and as the Resurrection shows, even intervene in—this world. The excerpt also stresses the pivot to action Christians see in the Resurrection, which inspires them to live a new way in the world.

E.T. the Extra-Terrestrial, directed by Stephen Spielberg, Universal Pictures, 1982.

Spoiler alert! This film involves a resurrection scene that puts the transformative "turning of the tide" on full display and also highlights the Resurrection's power as a conquering of the forces that lead to death. The reactions of those who witness the movie's "resurrection" also display the contrasting emotions of triumph and fear expressed by Jesus's disciples in the gospels.

United States Conference of Catholic Bishops, "Two Feet of Love in Action," online resources available at https://www.usccb.org/beliefs-and-teachings /what-we-believe/catholic-social-teaching/two-feet-of-love-in-action.

A campaign created by the US Catholic bishops' Justice, Peace, and Human Development initiative, these resources stress the importance of combining both charity and justice in any human efforts to combat suffering in the world. The website includes handouts summarizing the distinction between charity and justice as well a short video explaining the necessity of working for change on both the interpersonal and the structural levels.

Daniel K. Finn, "Sin and the Social World," *Modern Theology* 39, no. 1 (January 2023): 114–120.

A technical, yet still accessible, article that gives more details on the concept of a "social structure" and explains how these structures can operate in "sinful" ways that frustrate the common good. While the article was written in response to a larger theological question (How can Christians talk about structural sin and still claim that Jesus was a sinless human being?), it includes a number of examples that help to explain the notion of sinful social structures.

C. S. Lewis, *The Lion, the Witch and the Wardrobe* (New York: Macmillan, 1950).

Written by C. S. Lewis as a children's book explaining the central claims of Christianity, this now classic text (part of the larger *Chronicles of Narnia* series) shows how Jesus's death and resurrection are truly transformative in a Christian worldview through the parallel experiences of Aslan the lion.

The Lord of the Rings: The Two Towers, directed by Peter Jackson, New Line Cinema, 2002.

This film adaptation of the second installment of Tolkien's famed *Lord of the Rings* trilogy includes dramatic battles between good and evil and shows Gandalf the White returning "at the turning of the tide." Watch the film for a visually rich enactment of all that Christians claim Jesus's resurrection accomplishes.

Notes

1. Herbert McCabe, OP, *God Still Matters*, ed. Brian Davies (New York: Continuum, 2002), 67.
2. Sandra Schneiders, IHM, *Jesus Risen in Our Midst: Essays on the Resurrection of Jesus in the Fourth Gospel* (Collegeville, MN: Liturgical Press, 2013), 13.
3. C. S. Lewis, *The Lion, The Witch and the Wardrobe* in *The Chronicles of Narnia* (New York: HarperCollins, 2001), 185.
4. Rodney Stark, "Antioch as the Social Situation for Matthew's Gospel," in *Social History of the Matthean Community: Cross-Disciplinary Approaches*, ed. David L. Bach (Minneapolis: Fortress Press, 1991), 189–210.
5. For the original analogy, see Kenneth R. Himes, OFM, "Poverty and Christian Discipleship," in *Poverty: Responding Like Jesus*, ed. Kenneth R. Himes, OFM, and Conor M. Kelly (Brewster, MA: Paraclete Press, 2018), 11–20, at 18–19.
6. "World Hunger Is Still Not Going Down after Three Years and Obesity Is Still Growing—UN Report," *World Health Organization*, July 15, 2019,

https://www.who.int/news-room/detail/15-07-2019-world-hunger-is-still-not-going-down-after-three-years-and-obesity-is-still-growing-un-report; "Facts about Poverty and Hunger in America," *Feeding America*, accessed August 12, 2020, https://www.feedingamerica.org/hunger-in-america.

7. For more on the impact of these food structures, see Julie Hanlon Rubio, "Toward a Just Way of Eating," in *Green Discipleship: Catholic Theological Ethics and the Environment*, ed. Tobias Winwright (Winona, MN: Anselm Academic, 2011), 360–78.

PART III

Taking Action

8

Finding a Place in It All

Readers familiar with Christian theology may ask, as we begin the "Take Action" part of the book, "Did you forget the Holy Spirit?" We've talked about God, we've discussed Jesus, but until now we haven't said too much about the Third Person of the Trinity: the Holy Spirit. In this chapter, I begin by looking at the scriptures to give a sense of the Holy Spirit's nature and activity. Next, I invite you to the karaoke bar. Using a karaoke analogy, I provide a sense of how Christians understand the Trinity's dynamic nature and its relevance to Christian life. In the chapter's second part, Conor develops Saint Ignatius's insight that God calls each person in a unique manner to note the work of the Spirit in ordinary life. To recognize and respond to this call, one needs to practice and hone one's skills in discernment. Thus, Conor will discuss how Christians understand the formation of conscience and the way the well-formed conscience directs one to the proper end, or telos, of a human life.

Working Backward

When Jesus prayed with his friends, they did not make the "sign of the cross," and they did not say, "In the name of the Father, and of the Son, and of the Holy Spirit." It took a long time and much prayer and reflection before Jesus's followers could appreciate the consequences of the Resurrection. The events of Easter Sunday forced Jesus's followers— almost all of whom were Jews—to rethink their understanding of God. Their experience of the Risen Lord was not like a new fact or bit of trivia that they could easily tuck into their religious beliefs. On the contrary, the events of the first Easter Sunday required the disciples to reexamine and rethink some of their most basic theological beliefs. Let me briefly describe the seismic shift caused by the Resurrection.

Each day, Jesus and his disciples would have prayed the *Shema*. The *Shema* (*shema* is Hebrew for *Hear!*) is a confession of Judaism's faith: "Hear, O Israel, the Lord is our God, the Lord alone" (Deuteronomy 6:4). Theologically, this set Jews apart from just about every other culture and religion around at the time. Romans, Persians, and Egyptians all had *many* gods they could pray to and worship. If you've ever read the Book of Exodus or seen *The Ten Commandments* or *The Prince of Egypt*, you may recall that Pharaoh refused to allow the Hebrew people to leave Egypt. This brings about the Ten Plagues (Exodus 7:8–12:32). In each plague, Israel's *one God* effectively takes down one of Egypt's gods. God +1, all other gods 0. For the early Jews, other nations could have their gods, but they insisted on pledging allegiance to and worshipping *only one God*. In good times and in bad (there were lots of bad times— read the Psalms!), the Jews are distinctive due to their fidelity to one Lord God.

The books of the Old Testament recall—in stories, poetry, prophecy—the history of how the Jews came to know and to serve their God. For the Jewish people, this is their sacred text in its entirety: the Hebrew Bible. When we start reading the New Testament, things do not seem to be going well for the Jewish people and their God. Jerusalem, their political and spiritual center, is ruled by a client king who is subject to the Romans. To the casual onlooker, it would have seemed that Israel's God had abandoned them. Nevertheless, Jesus, his disciples, and the rest of the Jewish people continued to profess belief in their God. In first-century Jerusalem, this religious belief had dire political consequences, for it created tension with the Roman authorities, who expected the Jews to worship the Roman emperor as a god. It is, then, of great consequence that after Jesus's very public execution, his believers claimed that he had been raised from the dead. Read John 20:24–29. This is the story of the so-called "Doubting Thomas" made famous by Caravaggio's painting. Thomas—who, let me remind you, would have prayed the *Shema* twice a day just about every day of his life—encounters the Risen Jesus and, in one sentence, puts a match to theological dynamite: "My Lord and my God!" He meets the Risen One and confesses *Jesus* as "Lord and God." For Christian believers, this is theologically and politically charged. Theologically: If Jesus is somehow God, we need to rethink God's nature. Politically: If Jesus is Lord, this means the emperor is not.

Jesus's disciples realized that this theological upheaval was not finished. The more they reflected on the Resurrection and puzzled over its meaning, they found themselves "caught up" and influenced by a force or power that was in continuity with Jesus but, somehow, distinct from him. Jesus had, during his ministry, promised to send the Holy Spirit to his disciples. In the Gospel of John, this was the promise to send the *Paraclete* who would guide Jesus's followers into the future. The "Spirit of truth" would be an active force, an Advocate, who would testify to who Jesus was and sustain and defend the movement he started. After his Resurrection, Jesus appears to his disciples in the locked upper room. He says to them, "Peace be with you. As the Father has sent me, so I send you," and he breathes on them, saying, "Receive the Holy Spirit. If you forgive the sins of any, they are forgiven them; if you retain the sins of any, they are retained" (John 20: 21–23).

In his version of the story, the evangelist Luke (who wrote both a gospel and the Acts of the Apostles) describes the Holy Spirit as arriving on Pentecost (a Jewish feast taking place fifty days after Passover) and depicts it as a violent wind that "filled the entire house" and appeared like tongues of flame on each of the disciples (Acts 2:2–3). Filled with the Holy Spirit, the disciples were empowered to speak in foreign languages so that they could go out to all corners of the world and spread the Good News. By the power of the Spirit, the early disciples were sent out to continue Jesus's mission of proclaiming the reign of God. Accordingly, Christians regard Pentecost as the birthday of the Church.

Nevertheless, there's a big theological wrinkle in all this. Remember: Jesus's first followers were monotheistic Jews who believed in *one God*. Suddenly, though, his disciples are confessing Jesus to be *Lord and God*.

Moreover, they had the experience of receiving the Spirit and being impelled out into the world to proclaim the Good News. In Jesus and in the Spirit, they came to know God not as a far-off deity but as a God who had drawn close to them. They kept professing belief in *one God* (they are monotheists) but discerned that God was, mysteriously, one-and-three—one God in three distinct persons: God the Father, God the Son, God the Holy Spirit. It took many years, a lot of debate, and a tremendous amount of prayer for Christians to come up with what we today call the "doctrine of the Trinity" to describe this mysterious reality. (In fairness, this could even be called "doctrine*s* of the Trinity" as there are slight variations in the ways different Christian traditions describe the Trinity; the fundamental claim of three persons, one God, however, has roots that predate the development of today's numerous Christian denominations, so we will refer to that unifying version as the Christian doctrine of the Trinity.) Significantly, learning to worship and describe God as the Trinity required the early church to undertake a process of discernment to gain some clarity about how the one God could be encountered in three distinct ways: God the Father, God the Son, God the Spirit.

One of the consequences of this discernment was that their framework for understanding God had to be revised. Why? Because they realized that in Jesus's preaching and teaching, and in their receiving the Holy Spirit at Pentecost, God was made known to them in a radically new manner. As a community, the more they prayed and reflected on their shared experiences (especially their regular sharing of a meal of bread and wine, just as Jesus had told them to do), the more they realized that Jesus was *Emmanuel*: "God with us" (Like the Christmas song, *O Come O Come Emmanuel*). As they worshipped together and prayed through their scriptures, they noticed that the Holy Spirit had been at work not only during Jesus's life and ministry but since the beginning of creation. Looking backward, they saw the Spirit at work in Jesus's miracles and as having a role in his Baptism in the Jordan River (Luke 3:21–22). Peering further back, they detected the Spirit at work from the origins of creation itself, seen even in the first words of the Book of Genesis: "In the beginning when God created the heavens and the earth, the earth was a formless void and darkness covered the face of the deep, while the spirit of God swept over the face of the waters" (Genesis 1:1–2). The Holy Spirit was not, then, a novel innovation or "invention" by Jesus's followers. The Spirit they received at Pentecost, they discerned, was the same spirit that had been at work in all of history. The more they looked *back* on their experiences, the more evident this became: the Spirit's presence was found in their songs and poetry, in their history, in their prophets. So, in addition to the opening of the Gospel of John, "In the beginning was the Word, and the Word was with God, and the Word was God" (John 1:1), the early church had to deal with the fact that the Holy Spirit was also eternally present with God and at work in history. God was not a lonely god but, somehow and mysteriously, eternally in communion with the Spirit and the Word.

It did not take long for believers to be struck by the earth-shattering importance of these insights. Within decades of Jesus's Resurrection, they saw that Jesus's life and ministry, his death and Resurrection, and his sending of the Spirit and the birth of the Church were all intimately connected. In fact, they recognized that what had happened in and through Jesus was in continuity with the whole of their religious history. For the Church, this was not simply an instance of getting new *information* about God. It was a moment of radical *transformation* because this insight into the work of the Father, the Son, and the Spirit reformed the community's self-understanding. The Spirit opened their minds, and they perceived that God was at work in their lives. God, who *is* relationship, was healing the relationships damaged by sin and inviting humans through grace to a new relationship with the Trinity. Saint Paul describes this insight when he writes to the Galatians: "Because you are children, God has sent the Spirit of his Son into our hearts, crying, 'Abba! Father!' So you are no longer a slave but a child, and if a child then also an heir, through God" (Galatians 4:6–7). Through the Spirit, believers become *by grace* what Jesus is by the Incarnation: children of God. This becomes the foundation of a new and revolutionary community (or, if you want to impress others, the Greek term for community is *koinonia*). This community is not based on wealth, or race, or power, or status. It is made of living stones—people like you and me—who allow the Spirit to pray in our hearts to our Father in heaven. By the Spirit's grace, we are made equal members of God's Kingdom. The consequence: to profess Jesus as Lord means one *cannot* go back to business as usual. *What* Christians believe must shape and reform *how* they live.

Peter, Mary Magdalene, and the other early believers *did not think* they had found a new God. As they contemplated their faith and tradition, they realized that God had revealed who God is and made God known in a new way through Jesus, whom they *now* saw as the Christ or Messiah. Remarkably, they discovered that the work Jesus began—announcing God's reign in word and deed—they could continue. They were drawn into a community whose focus was to proclaim and work on behalf of this "Good News." The Church, Christians believe, is not just a building one goes to on Sunday but, rather, a dynamic movement that continues Jesus's work today. The same Spirit who brought order to chaos in Genesis, the Spirit who at Pentecost empowered disciples to speak in foreign tongues, the Spirit who makes Christians children of God: this same Spirit gathers a community—the Church—and calls it to announce God's reign. The call to be a Christian is nothing less than a call to prolong the Incarnation; Christianity is a vocation to live here and now in a way that testifies and gives witness to the reign of God as it is breaking into history and reforming it in a new and gracious way.

Of course, there is no ready-to-hand blueprint for *how* God's reign or Kingdom works. Thus, from its humble beginnings, the Christian Church has been a community of discernment. Jesus's first followers discerned in his life and ministry that God was active in a new way. They discerned in the days and years after the Resurrection that the Holy Spirit continued to be active in their lives. They "broke open" the scriptures and prayed, they "broke bread" and shared a meal as Jesus did at the Last Supper, and they discerned that *this* community—people gathered into a new community—was *who* they were. They discerned that in Jesus and through the ongoing activity of Spirit, they were being called to an entirely new way of life. Every Sunday, Christians around the world profess this theological insight: "I believe in God, the Father almighty . . . I believe in one Lord, Jesus Christ . . . I believe in the Holy Spirit, the Lord, the giver of life." The words of the Nicene Creed preserve Judaism's monotheism—One God—with the distinctive Christian twist: God is a tri-unity of persons. Moreover, what these persons of the Trinity *do*—Create, Redeem, and Sanctify—is *who* they are: God is love. God, Christians believe, is not merely loving. God is a boundlessly effervescent event of love: the Lover, the Beloved, and the Love that they share. Jesus, God's beloved, reveals in our history what authentic love looks like in human flesh; the Spirit sent by the Father and Son continues to work in history to heal sinful hearts and gather a community of sanctified believers. Hardly an abstract bit of theological trivia, belief in the ongoing work of the Trinity is the "secret sauce" that transforms believers' lives. The Spirit who enkindles the hearts of the faithful, who inspires them to continue Jesus's ministry, is the Spirit of love grafting us slowly into the Love that we share. Through the work of the Spirit, we are invited to enter and be transformed by the realization that "God is love" (1 John 4:8).

I know: This is hard to grasp. Theologians recognize that we can't "make sense" of the Trinity like we can "make sense" of calculus. Even our best concepts fall short of God! This means theologians have job security, because we'll never *ever* say everything that needs to be said about God. Indeed, the fun of theological reflection is pushing the limits of the imagination. For instance, Saint Patrick used the image of the clover to explain the Trinity. I want to be hip, so let us go to Iggy's Karaoke Cave, where I will offer a way to imagine the Trinity using an analogy of music.

Three-in-One

The Christian doctrine of the Trinity states not simply that the *one* God is Triune: Father, Son, and Spirit; more technically, it asserts that the *one* God is in fact a relationship of three *persons.* The creative heart of the cosmos, accordingly, is the Trinity. If you think about the consequence of this idea, it is mind-blowing. The cosmos is not "just there" but exists because the Trinity creates and sustains it; all of creation is *because* of this divine relationship and has been created *to be in relation* with the Trinity. I think here of a beautiful line from the prophet Isaiah, "I have called you by name, and you are mine" (43:3). The Trinity of Divine Persons—Father, Son, and Spirit—is the divine relationship that creates us *for* relationship. Our creaturely vocation is to be in relationship. Indeed, we are most fully and truly ourselves when we are most in tune with other creatures, the natural world, and the Creator who has called the cosmos into being. Let me try to offer a way—admittedly an imperfect way—to think about the Trinity as the communion of love that calls each of us—by name—to love. Since we are in a karaoke bar, think about how every song is a unity-in-distinction. Using your Ignatian imagination, consider that each song reflects three realities: Author, Lyrics, and Music. Moved by a desire to create, the Author expresses herself through word (lyrics) and music (melody/ rhythm). A song's words are used to express *what* the Author feels. A talented songwriter—like a poet—has a knack for saying things that touch us deeply. Great lyrics speak *to* the human condition because they emerge *from* and reflect what it means to be human. On this analogy, the Author is fully present in and reflected by the Lyrics, but the Lyrics and the Author are not the same. They are united, yet distinct. When familiar listeners hear the Lyrics, they recognize the Author behind them; those familiar with the Author's work can, in turn, recognize how the Lyrics are expressive of the Author.

Likewise, every song is a dynamic event animated by melody. The Music enlivens the Lyrics and rhythmically expresses the desire of the Author. A composer does not just scatter notes across a page. Instead, she composes a melody intentionally and with a desire to move and, perhaps, inspire the listener. Just think of how a musical score affects the way we watch a film. No less than an Author's lyrics, the melody communicates the Author's desires. Of course, the Melody is distinct from the Author and the song's Lyrics, yet it is inextricably linked to both. As with the Lyrics, the Melody is the Author's way of extroverting and expressing herself through the composition.

A song is not a static thing. Every song worth singing is a living and dynamic reality, an "event" with three distinct yet inseparable parts. To finesse an image used by Saint Irenaeus, you might think of the Music and Lyrics acting as the Author's "Two Hands" that reach into history to make the Author known to listeners. If either hand is not operative, the song would collapse (imagine singing the lyrics of a Beyoncé song to the tune of "Baby Shark" and then clean out your ears). But when all three work together, when the Author's music and words express the Author herself, the result is transformative because they create a relationship between the Author and Listener. A song is not great because it *tells* us something new. It is great because it reaches into the soul and reveals new levels of meaning; it is great because it *transforms* how we feel, how we live, and how we see the world. When we experience a song that "speaks to us," when we sense that we "get" this Author, we try to share this discovery with others. We tell family and friends that they *must* listen to this artist, and we hope that, if they are open to it, they will be similarly touched. We are, understandably, excited to share new discoveries.

Likely, you have detected the analogy. The "Author" is God the Father, who expresses who God is in two distinct but intimately related ways: Word and Spirit. God's Word does not simply inform Christians about the Father like a report—a "word" that gives us more data about God. Instead, Christians believe the Incarnation is what happens when God speaks into and makes God known in history. God *is* what Jesus and the Spirit *do* in history. Thus, Jesus, the Word who "became flesh and lived among us" (John 1:14), might be thought of as the flesh-and-blood "Lyrics" that express in human language just *who* God is. When the Author (the Father) expresses God's self in human history, the result is Jesus Christ (God's Word made Flesh). Jesus's words and deeds reveal who God is and what God wants so perfectly that, as Jesus's disciples reflected on their experience, they realized that Jesus *was* the Son of God. In like manner, the Spirit is akin to the Music that supports the words and transforms the text-on-the-page into the song-that-is-sung. Although we cannot "see" or "touch" music, we feel the way a melody gives life to a song's words, the way the rhythm moves us to sing and to dance. The Spirt *is* God's rhythmic and musical self-expression that makes God the Father known to us in our innermost depths. For Christians, the very Spirit who animated Jesus's life has been poured into our hearts. But instead of turning us into solo artists, the Music gathers a community—the Church—who sings and dances according to its tune. And, as Jesus's disciples prayed about this experience, they came to understand that the Spirit *was* the Spirit of the love proclaimed by Jesus and poured into their lives, making them children of God.

The history of Christian theology is riddled with the corpses of bad analogies for the Trinity: the three-leafed clover, two men and a bird, a triangle, and I once saw someone use a Dorito to try to get at this Mystery. We must admit that no image or idea can adequately capture the Mystery of the Trinity. We can use our analogies, though, as launch pads to vault us into reflection and discussion. My karaoke analogy is likely heretical (if taken literally) and certainly imperfect, but I hope it makes a little clearer how one dynamic reality (a song) can have three distinct but intimately related parts. Yes, the analogy limps: in music, the Author composes songs, but neither Lyrics nor Music exercise any agency or have a personality. For Christians, however, the Word and Spirit do because Jesus and the Spirit are distinct Persons. God, for Christians, is not a monad but is, rather, a joyful community of persons, Father, Son, and Spirit.

On a related note, the traditional language used to describe the Trinity falters due to the imperfections of human language too. There are, for example, limitations to speaking of God as Father. God, in the sense of the first person of the Trinity and also in the sense of the divine essence, does not, after all, have an XY chromosome (although Jesus, the second person of the Trinity, must have). But, as the early Church reflected on how Jesus related to God, they were struck by the relationship's tenderness (Jesus, at times, calls God *abba*, which in modern Hebrew means "daddy"). After Jesus's Resurrection and through the Spirit, the disciples discovered that they, too, could relate to God in this profoundly intimate way. Indeed, it is this intimate relationship that Christians acknowledge when they pray the Lord's Prayer (the "Our

Father") and when they profess their faith on Sundays: "I believe in God, the Father Almighty, maker of heaven and earth."

The language of "God the Father" captures these nuances, but like all human language used to describe God, it remains analogical, which means it reveals some things about God, but it never fully captures all that God is. When Christians lose sight of this fact, dangers emerge. Feminist theology, for instance, has noted that the tendency to take the traditional language of God as Father literally has supported an implicit association between maleness and divinity, facilitating the subjugation of women in very real ways throughout history. To highlight this tendency and to critique it, the Catholic feminist theologian Elizabeth Johnson has called attention to the ways that even the Bible's metaphorical language for God is hardly limited to male imagery and instead incorporates rich female metaphors as well. She makes the case that Christians must be more conscious of the ways their language about God might be communicating unintended associations if taken too literally.[1]

Readers may not have noticed, but throughout this text, we have taken Johnson's insights seriously by avoiding gendered language when speaking about God, in the broad sense of the divine essence, although we have used male pronouns when referring to Jesus given that in the case of the second person of the Trinity, God appeared in a particular human form. The traditional language of Father, Son, and Spirit is still the language of the Church and is the language that connects today's believers with their ancestors in faith, going all the way back to the time of Jesus. We therefore still use that language, but we want to be careful not to extend the metaphors beyond their limits. All that we say about the Trinity here thus requires the same degree of caution as the traditional language itself.

In light of these limits, if the musical analogy is useful, it is so because it helps us to understand how God, a Trinity of Boundless Love, makes God's very self known to believers and transforms their lives. Just as we come to know a song's Author by listening to the song's words and being moved by the music, so also do Christians come to know God through the work of Jesus and the Spirit. Moreover, Jesus and the Spirit both have a divine mission that they have been sent to accomplish. Jesus proclaims the gospel in word and deed; the Spirit gathers a community (the Church) to continue Jesus's work. Jesus is like a music performer who is the definitive model for how a song is to be sung. The Spirit, in turn, is the same rhythm that energized Jesus's performance and now, within the Church, animates our own. We cannot perfectly replicate *what* Jesus did but, enlivened and inspired by the Spirit, Christians try to follow the way of life he revealed. Whether we are musically talented or tone-deaf, the Spirit gives believers the courage to enter the chorus of Christian discipleship as they try to find their place within the Author's song. The Spirit opens our eyes to recognize the way that Jesus is the "Way" and gives us the courage to take our own place in the song and, in so doing, to be a part of the divine Song's own life.

To extend the analogy just one step further, we can say that the Christian life is like karaoke. In place of something from Taylor Swift, Post Malone, or Beyoncé, the "song" of Christian life is the Trinity. Having prayed and reflected on Jesus's ministry, and having been moved by the Spirit to see him as the "way, and the truth, and the life" (John 14:6), we can sing his "Lyrics" ourselves with our lives. Drawn by the Spirit's rhythm, the Christian tries to "sing" as Jesus sang, to imitate the way he acted and performed. Yet no one is as good as the original. Sure, there are standout performers (the saints), but the rest of us struggle to get the words right, to stay on key, to keep tempo. Yet here's the remarkable thing about Christian karaoke: even though each believer must take up the mic, no one ever sings alone. For the Church is the community who, gathered by the Spirit, struggles together to perform as Jesus performed. His show "goes on" through our lives, and all our gifts and talents can serve this performance, but only if we have the courage to open ourselves to the music and take our place on stage. And here we come to the place of discernment: How does the Spirit move *you* to take your place in this performance? How are you called by grace to discover your voice *in* the Trinity as you relax into the rhythm of the Spirit and find yourself "singing" your life in a way that more and more resembles the life of Jesus? To answer this, I hand the mic to Conor.

Discernment in the Spirit

Although I am certain he never used the analogy ("Iggy's Karaoke Cave" notwithstanding), Ignatius affirmed the idea that the secret to a life well lived was to add our voices to the karaoke version of God's song. In fact, he based his evaluation of discernment—arguably the most uniquely Ignatian element of his *Spiritual Exercises*—on this idea. This approach to the spiritual life was quite novel, for he fully embraced the doctrine of the Trinity in a way that took all its implications seriously, resulting in a dynamic vision of the Christian life that can help us *take action* in pursuit of our own human flourishing. In this half of the chapter, then, I am going to give you some sense of the theological distinctiveness of Ignatius's approach to discernment and then demonstrate how his vision fits within the broader Catholic account of conscience as the place of moral discernment and the heart of the spiritual life.

To understand the theological roots of Ignatius's take on discernment, we need to appreciate the impact of the doctrine of the Trinity, especially its claim about the work of the Holy Spirit. As Ryan explained, Jesus's earliest followers came to understand the role of the Spirit from Jesus's own promises to send the Paraclete as an advocate or helper. After Jesus died, rose from the dead, and then returned to heaven, Christians found that they were still inspired to do the work of the reign of God, and they slowly realized that this was because the Holy Spirit was with them, guiding their efforts. Ignatius recovered this early experience of the Spirit and taught not only that God could continue to guide individual human persons in this way but also that God *did* continue to act in the life of the believer through the guidance of the Holy Spirit. While most of his contemporaries emphasized the necessity of a mediator, like a priest or the structures of the Church, to facilitate any conversation between God and the individual, Ignatius radically maintained that God spoke directly to the human soul.

This claim created some conflict with the religious officials of Ignatius's day, because it had the potential to undermine their authority by setting up the individual as an arbiter of God's plan in their own life.

Nevertheless, Ignatius persevered in this belief, and a faith in the expansive work of the Spirit has been a hallmark of Jesuit spiritualty ever since. As we shall see in a moment, these assumptions about the Holy Spirit do not need to call into question the value of religious authorities, and they do not contradict anything the Catholic Church teaches on this point. Ignatius's vision did, however, challenge many of the prevailing *practices* associated with religious belief in his time, and for this reason, they were controversial. Even today, some Christians find the claim that God would communicate meaningfully with an individual soul to be too risky to avow, so it is worth remembering that Ignatius's understanding of the power of the Spirit can still require a shift in worldview (much like Jesus's own ministry) to this day.

By accepting early Christian understandings of the work of the Spirit and assuming that God could move the human soul without requiring mediation, Ignatius elevated the importance of discernment. It was not enough for someone to be simply told what to do by a parent, supervisor, or other authority because there was always space for God to guide that person directly. This is clear in Ignatius's instructions, or "annotations," given to those preparing to start the retreat in his *Spiritual Exercises.* The Fifteenth Annotation reminds directors that within the context of the retreat, they must not impose their will on the exercitants and try to sway their decisions. "For though, outside the Exercises, we can lawfully and with merit" encourage appropriate ways of action and even life plans, "in the Spiritual Exercises, when seeking the Divine Will, it is more fitting that the Creator and Lord Himself should communicate Himself to His devout soul . . . disposing it for the way in which it will be better able to serve Him."[2] In other words, Ignatius taught that we can trust God to guide the soul, meaning that the principal task of the director (or any other mentor, really) is to encourage genuine discernment rather than an arbitrary deference to some external set of assumptions.

In this way, Ignatius reveals how the Christian account of the Trinity, particularly its vision of the Holy Spirit as the Advocate given by the Son, creates the expectation that each of us needs to find our path for ourselves because these theological convictions establish that God works with each of us directly. Discerning God's will does not mean the replacement of one external authority (a parent, a sibling, a set of social conventions) with another (God), however. As the systematic theologian Michael Himes reminds us, the doctrine of the Trinity means that "God is not another person out there" but the Spirit of love that constantly calls us to the self-giving life that will bring us true fulfillment. "To find the will of God," he explains, "don't look 'out there'; drill down to the deepest depths of your own will. . . . Discover what it is that you most really and deeply want when you are most really and truly you. When you are at your best, what is it that you most truly desire? *There* the will of God is discovered."[3]

Discernment, then, invites us to understand ourselves ever more deeply, so that we can each become the person we most deeply long to be. It allows us to find the best way to give ourselves for and with others, so that we can fulfill our telos as human beings in the way that most clearly matches our own unique gifts and talents. We will say more about how to do this in the next chapter, when we explore Ignatius's rules for discernment. For now, suffice it to say that the Trinity provides the theological basis for asserting that discernment involves greater attention to the desires that move us and to our affections so that we can find what we genuinely want—which is not the same thing as what we *think* we want. When we find this, we are not responding to an outside imposition but instead finding an opportunity to be most authentically the human being we were created to be.

Before we can get to the next chapter's discussion of how this process of discernment plays out in some of our "big" life decisions (like selecting majors, planning careers, and pursuing relationships), we need to take a moment to appreciate how this same process plays out in the day-to-day, small-scale decisions of our ordinary lives. As I said in the introduction, all our choices make us who we are, and this means that all our choices merit some discernment. The Catholic theological tradition affirms this reality through its teachings on conscience, which the Catholic Church recognizes as the seat of moral discernment. It is the faculty that allows us to determine the right thing to do in particular circumstances, facilitating a thoughtful discernment before we act so that we can use our individual choices to become the person we most deeply desire to be. It is, in this way, the Catholic Church's parallel to Ignatius's remarkable claims about the possibility and power of God's unmediated movement of the soul.

Typically, when people first think about their conscience, they conjure up the pains of a guilty conscience, those uncomfortable feelings deep in our gut that prompt us to acknowledge that we have done something wrong. Unquestionably, this is an element of conscience, but it is only a tiny slice of what the conscience is supposed to do in the moral life. Beyond judging our actions after the fact, conscience is also supposed to help us discern the right thing to do *before* we act, so that we can avoid the wreckage of a guilty conscience altogether. The Catholic definition of conscience therefore focuses less on the judgmental elements of what we might call the judicial conscience and instead depicts a much more powerful, and spiritually enriching, human capacity. The Second Vatican Council, an authoritative gathering of all the leaders of the Catholic Church from around the world that took place in the 1960s, declared, "Conscience is the most secret core and sanctuary of a man. There he is alone with God, Whose voice echoes in his depths."[4] This gives conscience a much more expansive role in the moral life than being an *ex post facto* arbiter of poor decisions. It makes conscience the primary resource for the regular discernment process Ignatius described because this is the place where we can hear the movements of the Spirit.

The Catholic Church realizes the importance of conscience for personal discernment, underscoring its power as the secret core and sanctuary of a person with an official teaching on the primacy of conscience. Just as Ignatius stressed that directors must allow directees to come to their own conclusions about where God might be calling them in the *Exercises*, so the Catholic Church insists that the human person must listen to the voice of God when it echoes in their depths. "In all his activity," the Second Vatican Council proclaimed, "a man is bound to follow his conscience in order that he may come to God, the end and purpose of life. It follows that he is not to be forced to act in a manner contrary to his conscience. Nor, on the other hand, is he to be restrained from acting in accordance with his conscience."[5] From a Catholic perspective, one must always obey the dictates of one's conscience, and no authority, not even a religious one, can supersede those dictates. Moral discernment is therefore essential for the life well lived because we cannot rely on other people to make our choices for us.

While some might bristle at the suggestion that people should be free to make their moral judgments, fearing that the world will rapidly deteriorate into a state of complete moral relativism in which each person gets to decide what is "right for me," I want to clarify why this is not going to be the case—at least, not if we take the Catholic view of conscience and moral discernment seriously. Built into the teaching about the primacy of conscience are two presuppositions that hedge against the threat of arbitrary morality. The first is the conviction that discernment in conscience is not about deciding what is right *for me*. The power of conscience comes from its role as a connection point with God. What one discerns in conscience is therefore what God wants, and this is not some capricious whim but an objective constant. By understanding the nature of God—whose identity as selfless love (1 John 4:16) is manifest in the Incarnation and revealed through Jesus's Passion, death, and Resurrection—one can recognize that certain things cannot genuinely come from God. If we imagine that we are called to act in a way that violates this core identity of the Lord, then we are not listening to our conscience but are instead betraying our own identity. You might even say that it is at the point of conscience that our deepest desire for God intersects with and can be informed by God's deepest desire for us to be drawn into the Trinitarian song.

The second guard against a relativistic "anything goes" morality is the expectation that everyone must take the time to rightly form their conscience. Certain standards can guide everyone's actions, and thus the Bible is full of moral norms, or rules, to direct personal choices. The Ten Commandments, for example, explain that one must not lie or kill (among other things). Jesus's antitheses, discussed in chapter 5, meanwhile, similarly exhort people to act in a particular kind of way. Outside of these religious sources, there are also moral norms that people can readily agree are worthwhile preserving. The Ten Commandments may prohibit murder, but I would like to think that anyone opening the Book of Exodus for the first time already had that pretty well figured out and did not need to read a specific verse to conclude that killing innocent people is wrong. In theological terms, we call these universally recognized moral norms the natural law, because they are rules that all humans can affirm naturally through reason.

The natural law gives us some basic guidance, and scripture can reinforce and clarify its conclusions for believers, but neither of these sources provides the definitive determination of how to act in every conceivable circumstance. Part of moral discernment is therefore establishing which rules apply where and how. Learning about moral norms is thus an indispensable aspect of the formation of conscience, but it is not all that this process entails. One must also complement an understanding of moral norms with the cultivation of virtue.

The virtues are the good character traits that help us make good choices more easily. Traditionally, these include things like prudence (the trait of making wise choices), justice (the trait of seeking fairness), temperance (the trait of moderating our impulses), and fortitude (the trait of persevering in pursuit of the good). Theologically, they include faith (the trait of trusting in God), hope (the trait of looking for higher spiritual goods), and love. There is also another list that characterizes the virtues as the traits we need to perfect our relationships: justice to guide all our relationships (so we can recognize what we owe to all humans and even to all creation), fidelity to shape our particular relationships (so we can be true friends, siblings, and partners), self-care to inform our "unique" relationship with ourself (so we can ensure we are not burnt out), and prudence to adjudicate conflicts between the demands of these three categories.[6] What these lists all have in common is that they imagine virtues as a necessary component of the moral life, helping us both to make better decisions and then to follow through on them once we have identified the right thing to do. When combined with norms, virtues create the conditions that keep moral discernment in conscience on task, so that we can make the choices that will allow us to flourish as human beings.

The takeaway from this chapter, then, is that the Christian doctrine of the Trinity provides the foundation for prioritizing discernment in our vision of the good human life. By presenting the Holy Spirit as an advocate, or counselor, this theological account allowed Christians to recognize not only the possibility but also the certainty of God's direct communication with the human soul. Once he adopted this insight, Ignatius imagined that the first step in *taking action* would always be for an individual to look for God's direction in the unique circumstances of their own life. His sixteenth-century vision remains alive and well today in the Catholic description of conscience as the secret core and sanctuary of a person where God speaks directly to the soul. When formed properly, this conscience can embrace the freedom that comes with living a life animated by the Spirit, so we can craft our own karaoke versions of the song God authored for us all to share. As we do this in our little choices, through our moral discernment in conscience, we can progress toward the person we want to become, and we can prepare ourselves for a more intensive discernment around the major decisions that make their impact on our identity and life course profoundly evident.

Meditation: An Invitation in Conscience

Given the importance of conscience, we would like to close this chapter with an exercise that focuses on attuning one's conscience. To work well, one's conscience must be formed, as noted above, but we also must form ourselves to pay attention to our well-formed conscience, and this is where Ignatian insights can be valuable. Toward the center of *The Spiritual Exercises*, Ignatius included a famous meditation known as "The Two Standards." A former soldier, Ignatius used the imagery of a battlefield, with two armies lined up in opposition to each other, preparing to fight, to highlight the contrasts between good and evil. The two standards, then, are the battle flags of these competing groups, each one proclaiming the values for which their army will fight. Ignatius asks the person meditating to imagine themselves caught in the midst of these preparations and insists that they must look at these two standards and decide on which side they will stand.

While there are definite limitations to battlefield imagery (war, after all, is not pretty and its implicit glorification in battlefield metaphors can often mask this fact), Ignatius employed the illustrations he knew, and in this instance, he was stressing a cosmic battle rather than a human war. Significantly, Ignatius's discussion of these two standards shows not simply the attractions of goodness but also the subtle, albeit deceptive, appeals of evil. For this reason, "The Two Standards," despite the constraints of its imagery, is a valuable foundation for a meditation on the formation of conscience because it highlights the very real tensions that conscience must navigate. The voice of God echoing in our depths will always be calling us toward the good, but it is not always easy for us to appreciate what is truly good in the concrete particulars of our everyday lives where even the things that are ultimately bad for us can appear, at first glance, to bring a benefit. Sit with the Two Standards, then, and see what it feels like to have your conscience moved between good and evil so that you might better prepare for the complex task of moral discernment.

1. Sit quietly and take a moment to focus yourself. Close your eyes and breathe deeply, concentrating on your breathing for at least three deep breaths. Then, open your eyes and read slowly through this meditation.

2. Imagine two rival armies preparing for battle. Let your imagination take the lead. You might envision a massive battle scene from a movie like *The Lion, the Witch and the Wardrobe* or *The Lord of the Rings*, or another film. However the scene looks, note two competing groups arrayed on a gigantic battlefield, troops extending on both sides as far as the eye can see. On one side, the leader is the champion of goodness (Ignatius asked the exercitant to imagine Jesus as this side's general); on the other side, the leader is a defender of evil (Ignatius envisioned the devil in this role).

3. Turn to the side fighting for evil and you will realize that everyone here looks more or less the same, covered in gleaming armor that masks any difference between them, presenting a unified front. Next, witness the leader summoning the troops to lay out their battle plan.

"My followers," this leader proclaims, "let me tell you our strategy to bring more souls to our side. We begin by tempting them with riches and possessions, making them believe that if they just accumulate enough goods, then they will have security and autonomy, no longer needing to rely on others for their well-being. As they acquire these riches and build their confidence in their own capacities, they will become attached to these goods and think increasingly of no one but themselves. As they become used to prioritizing their own interests, they will become divided from others and then, in their isolation, they will fall into our service."

With that, the leader waves a gruesome hand, and a soldier raises a dark flag, or standard, that will guide this side into battle. Embroidered on the flag in vivid gold letters are three simple words: Riches, Honor, Pride. The crowd cheers, ready to fight for the riches that lead to honor and the honor that comes from the pride of self-sufficiency, placing their side on top at all costs.

Pause for a moment to consider how you feel as you witness this scene unfold. Are you ready to fight under this standard? Is this an army you want to join? Focus on the three words of the standard. Can you see, at least on some level, the allure of riches, honor, and the pride of security and autonomy that these goods promise?

4. Now turn your attention to the other army preparing for battle. On this side, the soldiers look like a motley crew. There are no uniforms; everyone is wearing whatever they could find, and many of them look ill-prepared for a fight. There is no single model for these soldiers, as the members of this side represent every demographic you can imagine. You suddenly hear the leader calling the troops to attention and laying out their battle plan. "My friends," this leader starts, "I have called you each by name and I now invite you on a mission. Go out into the world and offer yourselves in service to others. You will each need to do this in your own

way, using your unique strengths, but you should all pour out what you have to improve the lives of others. You will not need riches for this task; on the contrary, you will be poor if you do this right. Be warned, though, that your poverty will alarm others, who have been taught by the enemy that they are only as good as the goods they have acquired. They will lash out at you, but do not fight back. Instead, accept these humiliations as a sign that you are getting through to them, and remember: your worth comes not from what you have but from how you serve."

Immediately, the standard of this side appears by the leader's side. This bright flag has three silver words emblazoned across the front: Poverty, Contempt, Humility. The soldiers on this side pause, link arms, and bow their heads. Then, a moment later, they look up, their eyes alive with determination.

Step back for a moment and consider your reaction to this side's display. What would it mean to join this strange group? This leader does not promise success but rather offers assurances only of meaning. Is this an army you want to join? Where can you find the appeal in this leader's message? Are you apprehensive about anything this side offers?

5. Finally, ask yourself how you feel as you meditate on the two camps together. Ignatius presented these competing sides in stark contrast. There is no middle ground, and each of us must choose where we will serve. Look at your life and consider your experiences, your passions, your hopes, and your dreams. Can you see yourself joining the ranks of one side over the other? Do you want to live a life under the banner of Riches, Honor, Pride, or do you see yourself under the banner of Poverty, Contempt, Humility? Are you summoned to be a solo player or a part of a team based on solidarity with others, especially those who have the least? Which way of life inspires you most deeply?

Key Term and Ideas

- Paraclete: a Greek term used to describe the Holy Spirit in John's Gospel, the Paraclete is an "advocate," or someone who is on our side as a counselor or trusted advisor and who makes our case for us (think of a lawyer in a courtroom). This understanding allowed the earliest Christians to emphasize God's continued presence in the life of the believer through the Spirit.
- Author, Lyrics, Music: an analogy meant to show how Christians believe God can be both three persons (Father, Son, Holy Spirit) and still one God. With a song, we can understand how one Author communicates the same message through the Words of the song and the melody that accompanies them. Like all analogies, this one is imperfect, but it highlights the interrelated work of the three persons of the Trinity and emphasizes that we are all called to join the song and make it our own through discernment.
- conscience: the "most secret core and sanctuary" of a person, conscience is more than just a judge of the rightness or wrongness of past actions (though it can certainly do this); it is also the place of discernment where Christians believe one can hear the invitation of the Holy Spirit revealing God's guidance for the particular circumstance of one's life. In the Catholic tradition, a person is bound to follow their conscience first and foremost, but they are also bound to form their conscience through resources like the natural law and the virtues.
- natural law: universally accessible moral truths that are meant to help all humans understand right and wrong at the most fundamental level. Traditionally, the natural law is known by reason and leads to many of the same moral commands found in scripture (for example, humans can use their reason to recognize that it would be wrong to murder, much as the Ten Commandments prohibit this crime).
- virtues: described as the "perfection" of a power, the virtues are the character traits that make someone a good person by helping them recognize right from wrong and then empowering them to act on that judgment. The cardinal—or foundational—virtues are usually listed as prudence (judging rightly), justice (acting rightly and fairly), temperance (rightly controlling one's desires), and fortitude (persevering in the face of difficulty to do what is right). Christians also talk about fidelity and self-care as virtues that support relational well-being and faith, hope, and love as essential theological virtues.

Recommended Resources

Andrew M. Greeley, "The Mystery of the Spirit," in *The Great Mysteries: Experiencing Catholic Faith from the Inside Out* (Lanham, MD: Sheed and Ward, 2003), 25–38.

Greeley, an explicitly Catholic author, turns his prowess as a storyteller to the fundamental questions at the heart of Catholicism, including this chapter in which he reflects on the Holy Spirit, using a similarly musical analogy to capture the Christian claim that the Holy Spirit is indeed God.

Michael J. Himes, "Exploring the Mystery of God in Relationships," in *Doing the Truth in Love: Conversations about God, Relationships, and Service*, with Don McNeill, Andrea Smith Shappell, Jan Pilarski, Stacy Hennessy, Katie Bergin, and Sarah Keyes (Mahwah, NJ: Paulist Press, 1995), 1–21.

This chapter, which launches Himes's excellent introduction to the core beliefs of the Christian faith, describes the practical implications of asserting that God is a Trinity of Persons, connecting this claim to a way of life grounded in relationships of selflessness and love.

Elizabeth A. Johnson, CSJ, "A Theological Case for God-She," *Commonweal* 120, no. 2 (January 29, 1993), 9–14.

This short article, written for a general-audience Catholic periodical, summarizes the central claims of Johnson's landmark book, *She Who Is*, cited in this chapter. The article provides a sharp reminder of the limitations of all human language for God and makes the case for using broader gendered analogies when attempting to conceive of who God really is.

James F. Keenan, SJ, "Who Are We to Judge? How Scripture and Tradition Help to Form Our Consciences," *America* (March 23, 2016): https://www .americamagazine.org/issue/examining-conscience.

This accessible article from the Jesuit-sponsored periodical *America* magazine effectively summarizes Catholic teaching on conscience. Noting important distinctions, like the difference between a retrospective "judicial" conscience (that judges past actions to put us on the right path going forward) and a forward-looking "legislative" conscience that helps us discern the right thing to do, this article shows the consequences of interpreting conscience as the "most secret core and sanctuary" of a person.

Yiu Sing Lúcás Chan, SJ, "Common Characteristics of Virtue Ethics," and "The Four Dimensions of Virtue Ethics," in *Biblical Ethics in the 21st Century: Developments, Emerging Consensus, and Future Directions* (Mahwah, NJ: Paulist Press, 2013), 82–92.

These short excerpts from a chapter in Chan's volume on the role of scripture in Catholic ethics provide a succinct overview of the main ideas involved in virtue ethics, an approach to moral discernment that focuses on the goodness of the person and not just the rightness or wrongness of a particular action (although those choices are still very important for how they shape the person who acts in that way).

On the Waterfront, directed by Elia Kazan, Columbia Pictures, 1954.

This classic film (starring Marlon Brando in his "I coulda been a contender" role) puts the power of conscience on full display and illustrates the hard work of moral discernment, especially when social pressures (think structures of sin) push in the opposite direction.

Notes

1. Elizabeth A. Johnson, CSJ, *She Who Is: The Mystery of God in Feminist Theological Discourse* (New York: Crossroad, 1992).
2. Ignatius of Loyola, SJ, *The Spiritual Exercises and Selected Works*, ed. George Ganss (New York: Paulist Press, 1991), 125.
3. Michael J. Himes et al., *Doing the Truth in Love: Conversations about God, Relationships, and Service* (New York: Paulist Press, 1995), 55, 56.
4. *Gaudium et Spes* (December 7, 1965), no. 16, http://www.vatican.va/archive /hist_councils/ii_vatican_council/documents/vat-ii_const_19651207 _gaudium-et-spes_en.html.
5. *Dignitatis Humanae* (December 7, 1965), no. 3. https://www.vatican.va/ archive/hist_councils/ii_vatican_council/documents/vat-ii_decl_ 19651207_dignitatis-humanae_en.html.
6. James F. Keenan, SJ, "Proposing Cardinal Virtues," *Theological Studies* 56, no. 4 (December 1995): 709–729.

9

To Give and Not to Count the Cost

To conclude the book's third part, we want in the next two chapters to explore practical ways *you*, the reader, might "Take Action" by applying the skills of discernment to your life. Discernment never takes place in the abstract or in a vacuum. On the contrary, theological discernment requires one to *become aware* of one's situation, to *understand* how God actively calls each individual into service, and to *take action* by committing oneself to this call. As discussed in the last chapter, the triune God does not invite humans "in general" but, rather, addresses each one of us specifically. Recall the karaoke analogy: God calls us *through* the music (Spirit) to sing *with* the lyrics (Jesus Christ) and to discover, as we do so, that we are performing this heavenly song in the company of others who challenge and support us (Church). Whether we have perfect pitch or are tone-deaf, Christians believe that the Spirit works to draw each one of us into this Trinitarian event.

In this chapter, we want to equip you with some tools to assist you in *becoming aware* of the Spirit's action in your life, in *understanding* how it is calling you into service, and in accepting this invitation by *taking action*. To put this in another way, this chapter intends to assist you in discovering and embracing your *vocation*. Rest assured, it is not our intent to woo readers into seminaries or convents. The word "vocation" comes from the Latin *vocare* and means "to call." Long before we are called to *this* job or *that* career, Christians believe that God has been at work in our hearts and leading us through our desires to embrace *who* we are invited to become. *What* we do—teacher or nurse, doctor or programmer, musician or athlete—does not define *Who* we are. In fact, the opposite is more accurate: *Who* we are gets expressed in and through

What we do. Thus, by drawing on Saint Ignatius's "Rules for Discernment," we hope to provide readers with an opportunity for examining and sifting their deepest desires as they discern *how* God calls them, *who* God desires for them to become, and *what* they should do to put this vocation, this calling, into practice.

Saint Ignatius's Rules for Discernment

If you think about it, our daily lives are littered with rules. Whether we are visiting our parents' home, driving, working in a laboratory, showering, or cooking, a rule is in place. For instance:

- Parents: "We expect you to be back before midnight."
- Highway: Speed limit is 75 mph
- Shower: Lather, rinse, repeat.

Some rules, like our parents' and speed limits, can seem arbitrary but are intended to ensure safety. Others, in the lab or shower, are evidence based. Still other rules—like cooking or playing an instrument or a sport—function like guidelines to enable the cook, the musician, or the athlete to perform well. These rules develop the skills necessary for one to do what one desires to do. Saint Ignatius's "Rules for Discernment" fall into the latter category. His rules are meant to make those who use them more sophisticated in their understanding of the spiritual life. These rules are not plug-and-play equations but ways of *becoming aware*, *understanding*, and *taking action* on the heart's desires. Allow me to explain how they work.

If we only ever heard the voice of the Holy Spirit calling us, discernment would be easy. We are pulled, however, in many different directions throughout our lives. When I went to college, I felt torn between two starkly different paths: I wanted to be a special education teacher or a chemist/doctor. One part of my heart was drawn to teach children whose mental and physical disabilities required special attention. Another part of my heart was drawn to the rigors of chemistry and felt called to heal the sick. Sometimes I would daydream about being a lawyer, or going into business, or dropping out to be an Irish musician (of these, this one endures: I still play professionally). I had a really hard time settling on a major or finding a direction. Psychologist Kenneth Gergen calls this *multiphrenia*, the condition of being pulled in many different and often conflicting directions all at once.[1] So many options, so many choices, and so much pressure to choose. But how?

I felt, for a long time, anxious and uncertain. Each day, I seemed to change my major twenty times. Having discovered a real passion for science, I started to think more seriously about being a doctor. But as soon as I settled on this, some new idea would creep into my mind. My inner turmoil was worsened because I felt alone. To my inexperienced eye, everyone appeared calm and certain while I was a hot mess. After Christmas break of sophomore year, I needed to fulfill a requirement for the college's core, so I enrolled in a New Testament course. The course was incredibly challenging and, more importantly, life-changing. The instructor, a wise Jesuit priest, quickly identified my spiritual crisis. One day, he pulled me aside and invited me to take a walk with him. He had read one of my papers and wanted to give some feedback. I was disappointed he didn't offer a solution and, honestly, pretty annoyed when he gave me this assignment: *For the next week, spend fifteen minutes a day imagining yourself as a doctor.* I did as I had been told, and a week later, we walked again. We took many walks that term.

Each week, he listened as I shared not what I *thought* but how I *felt*. I shared my hopes and fears, named strengths, and found the courage to acknowledge weaknesses. Over time, I noticed patterns. Whenever I imagined myself—as a doctor or a teacher—helping and healing others, I experienced peace, joy, and excitement. But the longer I spent imagining myself *as a doctor*, those feelings cooled. As the semester drew to a close, he gave one more assignment: *Imagine that you had decided firmly and completely on going to medical school.* Oddly, I felt torn. On one hand, I was drawn by a desire to help others; on the other, I felt cool and ambivalent about the medical profession. I was attracted to the rigor of science and the prestige of medicine, and I wanted to love and help others. But I felt as if, somehow, I was being moved to help others in a way other than through medicine.

Without using the word, he was guiding me through discernment. What he helped me to identify were two movements crucial to Ignatian spirituality: *consolation* and *desolation.* Using Father Gallagher's translation, let me share some elements from Ignatius's Rules:

> *Third Rule.* The third is of spiritual consolation. I call it consolation when some interior movement is caused in the soul, through which the soul comes to be inflamed with love of its Creator and Lord, and, consequently when it can love no created thing on the face of the earth in itself, but only in the Creator of them all.

> *Fourth Rule.* The fourth is of spiritual *desolation.* I call desolation all the contrary of the third rule, such as darkness of soul, disturbance in it, movement to low and earthly things, disquiet from various agitations and temptations, moving to lack of confidence, without hope, without love, finding oneself totally slothful, tepid, sad and, as if separated from one's Creator and Lord.[2]

Even if the language is foreign, I suspect all of us have had experiences of consolation *and* desolation. When we feel consoled, everything seems to "fit" together, and even if we're struggling to achieve a task, we are inspired to persevere. In a state of consolation, it is as though we are being energized and empowered. When we feel desolate, by contrast, we feel uneasy and uncertain, cold and confused. In a state of desolation, it's as though a sinister voice whispers to us, "Oh, forget about it. Give up—you're only going to fail. There's no hope for you."

Similar to the Two Standards meditation that closed the last chapter, Ignatius saw the human soul as a battleground where two opposite forces were engaged in constant struggle. He called these opposing forces "spirits." The Good Spirit or Holy Spirit comes *from* God and leads us *to* God. This spirit gives hope and ignites our hearts with love. Where the Good Spirit is present, we find integrity and wholeness. The Good Spirit encourages us to resist evil and to work for God's Kingdom. It gives us the courage to find and take our voice in the Trinity's song.

The "Evil Spirit" does the opposite. This force opposes the Good Spirit and actively works against it. It discourages us, beats us down, and breeds self-doubt and cultivates hatred of self and others. It is the agent of an enemy who wants nothing more than to thwart and frustrate our participation in God's Kingdom. It impedes our spiritual progress by sowing suspicion, urging us to "give up," and reminding us of all the times we've tried before and failed. What the "Good Spirit" unites and makes whole, the "Evil Spirit" fragments and divides. At its most elemental level, Ignatian "discernment of spirits" tries to (1) become aware of these forces, (2) understand how they affect us, and (3) choose the way of action that embraces the Good Spirit and rebuffs the lies of the Evil one.

A good cinematic illustration of the conflict between the Good and Evil Spirits is found in *Harry Potter and the Order of the Phoenix*. At the climax of the magical duel between Dumbledore and Voldemort in the Ministry of Magic atrium, the Dark Lord disappears in a column of pulverized glass. But as the dust settles, we realize Voldemort has one final, and most deadly, attack. He invades Harry's body and takes control of it. Harry's eyes change and Voldemort taunts Dumbledore: "You've lost, old man." Internally, Harry is tormented by flashbacks and visions of pain and suffering. The death of his mother and father, feelings of loneliness and isolation, pain and doubt. The Dark Lord—like the Evil Spirit—works from within Harry's heart and coaxes him, "Give in to despair and hopelessness. Surrender." At his side, Dumbledore kneels and whispers encouragement, but Harry's fate seems to have been sealed: in the battleground of Harry's heart, Voldemort has the upper hand. He is just too powerful.

And then . . . Harry's friends arrive. As his body contorts, wracked by the Dark Lord's presence, he sees Hermione and Ron. Memories of happiness and friendship, joy and solidarity, turn the tide against Voldemort. "You're the weak one, and you'll never know love or friendship. And I feel sorry for you." The Dark Lord's hold over Harry is broken, and in a cry of agony, he flees Harry's body.

Were Ignatius to view the clip, I think he'd recognize the two spirits at war with one another. The Evil Spirit, personified by Voldemort, will triumph only by convincing Harry that he is alone and unwanted. This spirit divides in order to conquer. The Good Spirit's approach is different. Here it is personified in the community of Harry's friends. This Spirit encourages by drawing one deeper into communion. Instead of threatening harm or doing damage, the Good Spirit arouses love and empowers Harry to speak against the dark one. For even if Harry has not the same power as Voldemort, he knows and is in touch with a power that Voldemort cannot claim: the power of solidarity, friendship, and love. It is this power, wielded not by wands but by the heart, that will guide Harry and his friends toward their final victory over evil.

Admittedly, *Harry Potter* is a little more dramatic than our regular spiritual lives. Nevertheless, the film nicely illustrates how the Good Spirit—the Holy Spirit—works. It does not impose something foreign on Harry's imagination. Rather, it exposes and brings to light the sources of Harry's joy and love. Unlike the Dark Lord, who covets power, Harry's power comes from love and friendship. Where Voldemort seeks conquest, Harry seeks communion. Harry's path is seldom easy, and he makes many mistakes along the way. Indeed, when we read the books—or watch the films—through an Ignatian lens, what we find most compelling is not *what* Harry is ("the boy who lived," a wizard) but the journey of discernment he undertakes as he embraces *who* he is to become. He can, so to speak, embrace the Spirit of Light and Truth, of Communion and Peace, *or* he can opt for the Spirit of Darkness and Lies, of Isolation and Violence.

Ignatius has more rules meant to assist in discernment, but we can't address all of them here. I can share that, given time and practice, one can become really good at distinguishing the Good from the Evil Spirit. It takes a long time and a lot of talking (perhaps on walks) with people one can trust, but this is a skill all of us can develop. In my case, it took years to sift through my desires and to discover that I could better serve as a healer and a teacher by becoming a priest. Conor discerned that his way of serving God was as a husband, a father, and a theologian (and as a friend to this Jesuit; he has been a great companion). None of us is called in the same way, but it is a Christian conviction that we are—every single one of us—called to dedicate our gifts and talents, our strengths *and* our weaknesses, to the service of God's Kingdom. Animated by the rhythm of the Spirit and inspired to perform our faith as followers of Jesus, *who* we are will continue to direct, inform, and find its fullest expression in what we do. God calls us through our greatest passions not merely to have "a job" but to say yes to the great adventure that is a life dedicated to seeking out and saying yes to God's invitation to be who we are called to become.

This is not easy. I've been actively discerning my vocation for over twenty years . . . and, for as much light and joy I have experienced, I certainly know the shadow. It comes as a niggling, gnawing feeling. Almost a whisper, but one whose sinister words slice into the heart and deflate peace: *Don't kid yourself. You're not a good teacher. Your music is boring. Oh, the people in the pew . . . yeah, they know you're a hypocrite. That book you wrote? Total waste of time.* Sometimes, this voice comes from real people—family, friends, associates, critics—who dismiss me or call my life and ideas into question. The Holy Spirit may be a reliable guide, but in the chaos of daily life, it's easy to be led astray! In such times, I find quiet and pray on the movements in my heart. Instead of running from them, I confront them head-on to see where they are leading. Sometimes, even a painful voice can be healthy because it "wakes us up" from spiritual complacency and stirs us into action. Other times, prayer helps me to see that this naysaying voice is not of God's spirit but is working, instead, to tear me down. When I notice this spirit at work, I smile to myself and say, "Ah, well, nice try. It's not going to work. I see what you're up to, so go away." The light of prayerful meditation both scatters the shadows and illuminates the path we are being called to walk.

Given my penchant for charts, allow me to offer the following to illustrate how the Good and Evil Spirits operate in our lives (see page 201).

Notably, the general actions of the Good Spirit and the Evil Spirit remain a constant—they each have their "trademark" orientation—but our experience of these general actions can vary greatly depending on where we are situated. When we are on the right track, the Good Spirit inspires us further and reassures us, while the Evil Spirit pulls us in unpleasant ways. When we are already moving in the wrong direction, however, we experience the Good Spirit's interventions as an

	Good Spirit	Evil Spirit
Origin	God, who is love, seeking to draw us into relationship.	The "Enemy" who seeks to subvert God's reign.
General Action	Brings healing and hope; enflames a deeper love of God and a commitment to serve; leads toward communion.	Inflicts discouragement and suspicion; undermines confidence and leads to self-absorption; fragments the community.
Operation—Situation A In this situation, a person is making spiritual progress (trying to get one's life together). Their spiritual trajectory is movement *toward* God.	Encourages the person to keep going, even when this is difficult; inspires faith, hope, and charity. One is moved to be life-giving, desiring to serve God's reign. Removes obstacles; strengthens and heartens.	Discourages progress; reminds person of past attempts and failures. Makes growth or success seem impossible. Throws up obstacles; whispers "You're not good enough, you're a hypocrite."
Operation—Situation B In this situation, a person is *not* making spiritual progress (think of a self-destructive lifestyle). Their spiritual trajectory is movement *away* from God.	Pricks the conscience to awaken it. Steady voice saying, "You're called to more than this. Turn away from this path." Stirs feelings of guilt, sorrow, and shame that make us yearn for healing.	Encourages self-destruction. Insists one keep an eye on immediate pleasures while ignoring long-term consequences. Stirs feelings of false confidence that only remain as long as one refuses to acknowledge any critical thoughts.

uncomfortable reminder that we could be doing something more, and any sense of reassurance we have in this instance comes from the Evil Spirit that is trying to shield us from the deeper awareness that this is not all we are capable of attaining. To discern well, then, we need to know not only how these competing Spirits operate but also where *we* are on our journeys.

To help illustrate the operation of these competing Spirits, I want to close with a discussion of one more movie scene. If you have watched 2019's *Captain Marvel*, you might recall the film's climax when Captain Marvel confronts the Supreme Intelligence. The Supreme Intelligence effortlessly tosses Captain Marvel around. Icily, she directs Captain Marvel's attention to her own frailty: "Remember: Without us, *helpless.*" Memories of past failures flood her mind. Yet, seemingly against all odds, another movement stirs. Captain Marvel resists and stands against her foe as she embraces *who* she is: Carol Danvers. In claiming her name, in owning her past, she becomes who she has always had the potential to be. "I've been fighting with one arm tied behind my back," she says. "But what happens when I'm finally set free?"

To an Ignatian imagination, this scene captures nicely how the Good Spirit works in the midst of our specific context. This Spirit does not erase the past but makes it possible to move on from it into a new future. Whether we are moving in the right direction or the wrong one, the Good Spirit always helps us to see that a new path forward into a better future is possible, and the Evil Spirit continually tries to convince us that there is no hope for change. By putting us in touch with and giving us a part in God's own life, the Good Spirit empowers us to resist the Enemy's voice as it tempts us to give up and accept failure. The Evil Spirit, like the Supreme Intelligence, insists, "You, as you are, are simply not good enough. Why bother?" The Evil Spirit's ploy is to make us despair, to doubt that we are capable of being loved, to reject our humanity. The Good Spirit, by contrast, says, "You don't need to be anything other than yourself. Stop running from who you are called to become. Embrace your identity and let my power, my Spirit, transform you and your life." The Good Spirit may not give one the power to lift cars or fly, but it does empower one to participate in God's reign and to work heroically on its behalf.

Because practice makes perfect, let's try our hand at recognizing and responding to the movements of consolation and desolation in a case study. It should be obvious that elements of the case come from my life. But, even if you've never struggled to settle on a major or a profession, there is no question that you have at some point felt torn between choices. Learning to negotiate these tensions through discernment will, I promise, prove invaluable. For once you understand how your heart is being moved and the ways you could live this out, you will be able to say "yes" to who you are called to become and embark upon the exciting adventure that awaits.

Case Study: Corrinne

Corrinne is a senior at a Midwestern college majoring in chemistry and theology. She grew up in a churchgoing family, but weekend sports and other events became her focus in high school. During her first year of college, she became friends with some students who attended Sunday evening Mass. While she would not call herself a "holy roller," she has grown committed to her faith and its practice. A robust spirituality, she has come to realize, cannot be lived apart from a community of fellow believers but only as a part of it.

Corrinne has always known that she wanted to be a surgeon. She excels in pre-med courses and works in a chemistry lab. During sophomore year, because of her deepening interest in religion, she decided to double-major in theology. This, it turns out, was a great decision: during her medical school interview, several interviewers were intrigued by her second major and commented that this was something that made her application "stand out." Not surprisingly, she has already been admitted to five schools. Everything, it seems, is going according to her master plan.

But, as she left church a few weeks ago, she was struck by a strong desire to do a year of service. During Mass and after, she felt a gentle tug within her heart and a feeling of excited hopefulness at the idea. Initially, she tried to push the idea out of her mind, saying, "Are you nuts? Medical school first and then service." But the idea of service keeps revisiting her, and she has found herself daydreaming about it more. When she daydreams of her life in medical school and as a surgeon, she feels content and satisfied. When she daydreams about doing a year of service, however, it's different. More intense. More exciting. More . . . inspiring. And the more she daydreams and prays about what she should do, the more she feels as though she's being called to take a gap year between graduation and medical school. Just last week, her roommate saw her looking at a service website and said, "Are you interested in that? My brother did it—he worked with gang members in Los Angeles—and said it was the hardest but best thing he ever did. You know, you'd be good in a program like that." For Corrinne, the year of service doesn't just seem to be something she wants to do. It feels like she's being called to do it.

There is a catch: her parents. They have sacrificed for her to attend college. It took some convincing when she told them she wanted to double-major. Her father tried to stop it, saying, "Are you serious? What are you going to do with a degree in theology? It's not going to get you a job. It'll just clog your schedule and eat up the time you need for important classes." Luckily, Corrinne didn't heed her father's advice. Her theology courses offered her a holistic and well-rounded academic formation that made her medical school application distinctive and gave her a different way to think about what it means to be a doctor. Her parents appreciate this now, they love and support her, but Corrinne is sure that they will discourage her from doing the service year.

Corrinne is torn and feels like she could go either way. In her head, she knows the "rational" decision is to go to medical school and start her career as soon as possible. This is, after all, the job she has always wanted. But in her heart, she feels something else, a sense of being called to follow a different path . . . at least for a year. When she prays, when she discerns, she feels excitement, nervousness, and peace when she imagines the service year. When she thinks about going to medical school, the enthusiasm isn't as vivid.

You and Corrinne meet up for coffee. You notice how her energy and enthusiasm shift when she goes from talking about service to discussing medical school. She trusts you and asks for your help in sorting out these spiritual movements. After she tells you about her struggle to discern, she says, "The other day, I went to Mass on campus. One line from the reading really grabbed my attention. Jesus said to his apostles that true greatness does not come from power but from service, something like, 'whoever wishes to be great among you shall be your servant.' When I heard that line, it felt like the Holy Spirit was talking directly to me. But then there are times when a shadow falls on my heart and I think that it's all pointless, that I'm just doing this to avoid having to be an adult, that I should go to medical school and prioritize my future career. Pushed in one way, pulled in another; attracted most of the time, repelled at other times. I wish there were one clear path forward, but I feel pulled . . . called . . . in various ways. Can you help me to discern whether and how I'm being called?"

How would you help her in this discernment process? How might you interpret the movement of the Holy Spirit in her life? What counsel would you give her?

Discernment in Practice

Reading this case likely generated a number of responses, but if we try to work through it with an Ignatian lens, we begin to see how the rules for discernment can help us navigate the challenges of concrete decisions. Indeed, if we pause to step back and apply the method developed through the Ignatian B.U.T., we can see how we might give some productive, substantive advice to Corrinne. In the process, we can also get a clearer sense of how we might help ourselves with similar decisions. With that end in mind, let me walk through the Ignatian B.U.T. in light of what we have learned so far in the book to show how this approach can help Corrinne *become aware, understand,* and *take action.*

First, part of *becoming aware* involves framing what is really at stake. On the surface, Corrinne is trying to decide what to do next year, but below the surface, something else is about to be determined. As I argued in the introduction to this book, it is our choices that make us who we are. Corrinne is not just making a decision about what to do immediately after graduation; she is also making a decision about who she really wants to become. Answering that question, of course, gets us back to the discussion of God as the human person's ultimate concern. If Corrinne is the kind of person who has taken the time to determine her overarching commitments, then she will find that she can flip this question and ask herself, "Which option best aligns with who I *really am?*" After all, one of the points we emphasized in the last chapter was that the will of God is not an external imposition but a longing for our own fulfillment. Flourishing is about living up to our true potential, and the point of discernment is to become the best possible version of our truest selves.

One of the keys to identifying this true self is to take stock of our inner desires. To help with this process, Ignatius's rules for discernment emphasize consolations and desolations. The things that bring us consolation and reassurance are the things that resonate in our core. They inspire us, fill us with hope and excitement, and sustain us when we face difficulties. Meanwhile, the discomfort of desolations emerges from the disconnect between what we are considering, on one hand, and who we really long to be, on the other. In this way, desolations work to discourage any movement toward our true telos.

If Corrinne refocuses on her identity, she can begin to see that the choice in front of her is not as overwhelming as it first appeared. Often when we confront a major decision like this one, we can become paralyzed in fear, unable to decide out of a deep-seated sense of alarm that we might pick the wrong choice. The venture capitalist Patrick McGinnis, who first proposed the term "FOMO" (fear of missing out), has a name for this paralysis: fear of a better option. "FOBO," as he calls it, leads people to resist committing to a choice because they worry that they may be closing themselves off to a path that could, in theory, be even better.

On one level, it is easy to imagine how this fear of a better option might afflict someone like Corrinne trying to decide between two different postgraduate trajectories: "Do I really want to do a year of service? What if medical school would actually be more fun, allowing me to meet some important friends?" The striking thing about FOBO, however, is that it often prevents people from selecting a real course of action because they are holding on to unrealistic hopes for theoretical choices. Thus, Corrinne might say to herself, "How can I decide between a year of service and medical school when I could become a lawyer?" even though she has never planned to go to law school, has not taken the LSAT, and frankly dislikes reading complicated legal texts. Although it may seem reasonable to weigh our choices carefully with the intent to pick the better option, if we let FOBO run the show, we can quickly spiral down a path of total indecision.

The way to overcome this "analysis paralysis" is to dissect the motivations involved. The fundamental fear in FOBO is the "fear of letting go." As McGinnis, the man who coined the term, explains, "In order to choose something you must let go of another thing and it's the fear of having to mourn the road untaken [that overwhelms us]. So we would rather not decide at all and keep all of our options open."[3] However appealing it may sound to "keep all our options open," this is no way to live a life. We must make decisions and commit to our choices if we are going to craft a life worth living. This is, in essence, what *becoming aware* is all about. From identifying our ultimate concern to establishing our eulogy virtues, the "B" in the Ignatian B.U.T. requires taking the time to craft our commitments so that we can make choices with a confident assurance that we are on the right path, even when we are tempted to compare our real-life options against a set of hypothetical ones.

Now, this discussion of FOBO might seem like I am saying that Corrinne needs to become a doctor because that was her original plan, and she should stick with her decision instead of indulging in the FOBO-driven evaluation of a year of service. This interpretation misunderstands the nature of the commitments we make when we *become aware*. The point of identifying our deepest values and determining our true telos is not to decide *what* we will *do* but, as we have said throughout this book, to bring clarity to *who* we will *be*. Corrinne's true commitments are not to a particular career path but to a life that will allow her to flourish through service to others. When we recognize this orientation as her true identity, then FOBO begins to lose its power, because there is no such thing as a better option. Both a year of service and a direct dive into medical school can allow Corrinne to craft the life of self-gift that is so essential for human fulfillment. She does not need to fear letting go of one option or the other because she can still find ways to pursue her proper telos on either path.

At first, this evaluation could sound like a copout. "What do you mean she can choose either option?" we wonder. If that is the case, we seem no better off than when we first began. But take a minute to appreciate what is going on. Corrinne is having a hard time deciding between two options in part because she is worried about making the *wrong* choice. She is afraid that the road untaken really would be the better option. She is, in effect, held captive by fear. By taking a step back and *becoming aware*, however, she develops the perspective that leads to Ignatian indifference, which in turn gives her the freedom to decide. She no longer has to focus on what is the "right" choice, with all the indecision and fear (of a better option) this framing implies. Instead, she can think about what she genuinely *desires* to do. Far from leaving Corrinne without any assistance, the first step in the Ignatian B.U.T. allows Corrinne to give herself permission to decide, something she has been hesitant to do until this point.

The challenge, of course, is that Corrinne still has to determine what she really wants, and it is not entirely clear that she has this figured out. This is where the next phase of the Ignatian B.U.T.— *understanding*—becomes so important. As we discussed throughout part II, the life of Jesus helps with the task of *understanding* by providing a model for how humans might act to pursue their proper telos in a world colored by the effects of sin and evil. The message of accompaniment in God's decision to become Incarnate, the values embodied in Jesus's ministry of the reign of God, the consequential nature of Jesus's Passion and death, and the transformative power of the Resurrection all offer tools for those attempting to discern how to live meaningful lives in a fallen state. Corrinne can rely on these tools to examine the choice before her, asking more substantive questions about the options she is considering.

To begin, if Corrinne thinks about the *understanding* that emerges from the Incarnation, she can probe which path will allow her to embrace the humble and compassionate form of accompaniment with those who suffer that God's appearance in the flesh represents. She might be able to make a case for either option, but she will at least have a sense of the type of case she needs to make. She has new resources to arrive at a concrete choice.

When Corrinne turns to the insights of Jesus's ministry, meanwhile, she can add two new dimensions to her discernment. First, she can think about the efficacy of Jesus's own deeds, which should prompt her to prioritize the option that will yield the most significant impact on others. This means analyzing her particular skills and background, her talents and gifts, to determine where she—this unique woman named Corrinne, who is not the same as anyone else in the world—can succeed in accompanying a world in need. Second, she can consider the reversals involved in Jesus's words about the reign of God, searching for the best way to embrace the new values, expectations, and vision encompassed in Jesus's teachings and parables. In more concrete terms, this means asking about her motivations. Is she driven to become a doctor because this is a particularly poignant way of helping others, or is she drawn to that profession because of its prestige? Is she thinking about a year of service as a way to grow into a more loving person who can better pursue her telos of self-gift throughout her life, or is she looking to add an attractive credential to her résumé? In other words, do her motives align with the values of the Kingdom? Obviously, the reversals of the reign of God would give her more reassurance for the first set of motivations rather than the second in each case, and this might give her greater clarity right away. Nevertheless, it is possible that she might find genuinely good intentions behind her interest in both options, in which case she will benefit from the two remaining elements of Jesus's ministry.

The message of Jesus's death, at least with respect to discernment, hinged on the issue of consequences. People must be ready to face the consequences of their decisions to live a life of service to others, and they ought to expect that some of those consequences will be negative, for Jesus showed what can happen when people pursue goodness in the face of worldly power. This fact means that Corrinne should not fear any unfortunate or unpleasant aspects that might accompany either decision. She should focus on the choice that actually aligns with her deepest values and steel herself to bear whatever challenges her ultimate choice may entail. At the same time, she can also think about the consequences of Jesus's sacrifice—as represented in the various theories of atonement—to determine which course of action will allow her to make a more meaningful sacrifice so that she can be confident that the challenges she faces are not in vain.

Finally, Corrinne can use the *understanding* that emerges from the Resurrection to ensure that she is evaluating her decisions from a more holistic perspective. One crucial element of Jesus's victory over death was its vanquishing of sin *and its effects*, a holistic victory that implies a concomitant responsibility for humans to challenge unjust structures alongside any isolated effects of evil suffered and evil done. With this broader perspective in mind, Corrinne can analyze which path will better equip her to fight for a more just ordering of affairs while she pursues a life of self-gift. Significantly, this fight is not won on a short-term timeline, so the question is not which decision challenges structures of sin most directly but which set of experiences will give her the resources she needs to contribute to this fight effectively over the long haul. Given the ways that a firsthand encounter with the underside of oppressive structures can ignite a passion for justice and structural change, she might find great value in something like a year of service, even if she then goes on to medical school the next year.

Like the first step of *becoming aware*, this second step of *understanding* can give Corrinne a way of moving forward in her evaluation of her postgraduate plans. These two elements of the Ignatian B.U.T. help her recognize what is at stake so that she can make a decision with greater confidence. While necessary to help Corrinne recognize what is at stake and commit to a choice without FOBO's lingering regrets, neither *becoming aware* nor *understanding* alone offers a definitive answer for which path to choose. In order to make that final choice, Corrinne will need to build on these insights and embrace the final component of the Ignatian B.U.T. She must *take action*, something she will be able to do successfully if she recalls two additional insights from Ignatius's rules for discernment: the importance of context and the trademark operation of the Evil Spirit.

First, Corrinne must appreciate the way that context informs discernment in Ignatius's rules. As Ryan explained, Ignatius stressed the importance of our affective responses when discerning. He talked broadly about consolations—positive affective responses of reassurance or satisfaction—and desolations—negative affective responses of discomfort or dissatisfaction. Buried within the details of Ignatius's rules for discernment, however, is the specification that these affective responses tell us different things in different contexts. This is the point Ryan highlighted in his chart, which notes that the promptings of the Good Spirit are experienced positively when one is making spiritual progress and negatively when one is engaged in a self-destructive lifestyle. As Corrinne evaluates her affective responses to the two possibilities in front of her, she therefore needs to consider the broader context in which she is discerning. Is her big-picture trajectory moving her toward spiritual growth or away from it?

Given the details included in this test case, one can safely say that Corrinne is progressing in her spiritual life rather than declining. She is not engaged in a self-destructive lifestyle but is instead taking the time to figure out who she is and what she values. She has surrounded herself with a real community of friends who genuinely care about her well-being and "she has grown committed to her faith and its practice." By taking the time to examine this larger context, Corrinne can develop the right framework to evaluate her affective responses. Consistent with Ignatius's rules for discernment, she can imagine that the feelings that bring her comfort are reflective of an alignment with her deepest desires, whereas those that generate unease are likely indicative of a departure from her true identity. In this case, Corrinne's feelings of excitement and the persistence of her desire to do a year of service are both revealing, particularly when they are coupled with a marked decrease in her enthusiasm for medical school (at least right away). When she puts these feelings into the larger context of her movements toward spiritual growth, she can rest assured that they are propelling her toward her deepest desires and not leading her astray.

These assurances can be further reinforced when Corrinne remembers the typical workings of the evil spirits. According to Ignatius's careful evaluation of the influence of the Good Spirit and the Evil Spirit, each one has its own standard way of proceeding, its own modus operandi (MO). By remembering the Evil Spirit's MO, Corrinne can distinguish the movements that are helping her decide from the ones that are clouding her judgment.

As Ryan's examples from *Harry Potter* and *Captain Marvel* illustrated, the Evil Spirit's conventional approach is to stir up unrealistic fears and to feed on doubts. The Evil Spirit spreads a false narrative that hits just the right notes to trigger our subconscious anxieties about the ways we might not be good enough, worthy enough, or strong enough to handle the great plans we imagine for ourselves when we are at our best. These doubts are effective precisely because they speak a language we have already spoken to ourselves, for no one is completely immune from self-doubt. As a result of this resonance, we often fail to notice that the voice is no longer our own but rather an echo of a more nefarious influence. When we walk into discernment with the eyes of the Ignatian B.U.T., however, we come anticipating this tactic, and we can remove the power it normally achieves through stealth.

In Corrinne's case, if she anticipates the Evil Spirit's machinations, she can more easily see that the fears that are currently halting her discernment are not genuine concerns. Remember, the catch in this example is her parents. She worries that they will be upset by her decision to commit to a year of service. But will they? Will they really be upset in a way that damages Corrinne's relationship with them? Obviously, we do not have all the details of her family dynamic, but we at least know that her parents care for her enough to make sacrifices for her to attend college. The Evil Spirit spins a web of lies in which these sacrifices are only justified if Corrinne "repays" them by becoming a doctor. The truth is that these sacrifices—assuming they are genuine—are acts of love. Rather than revealing a concerted effort on her parents' part to dictate Corrinne's future, these sacrifices are a tangible reminder of how much they want what is best for her. If this is indeed the case, Corrinne's fears that her thoughts about a year of service will cause her parents to explode suddenly seem less convincing. Surely the parents who wanted to give up so much to send their daughter to college will be happy to listen to her hopes for her future, especially once she takes the time to explain the discernment process that led to this new path in more detail. She only has to fear her parents' reaction when she doubts their love and sincerity. This is a telltale sign that these reservations are the work of the Evil Spirit.

And now, we can imagine a final decision for Corrinne. Given her identity as it emerges from her efforts to *become aware*, her hopes as they are informed by her efforts to *understand* how to craft a meaningful life, and her affective responses as they are analyzed in an Ignatian effort to *take action*, Corrinne has every reason to conclude that this year of service will offer her an opportunity to make more progress in her efforts to become the woman she most deeply longs to be. She will know for sure when she examines her affective responses in the days and weeks following her decision. She should feel a sense of peace, knowing that she has discerned well and that she is headed toward her true telos. Of course, this does not mean that there will never be times when she second-guesses herself or thinks, "What am I doing here?" When this happens, she can trust in her careful discernment and return to the experiences of consolation that led to her choice, proclaiming confidently, "Even though the future is uncertain, and even though I am a little nervous now, I trust that this is where I am called to be." The "Yes" to a year of service she reached through her discernment process will prove to be an abiding source of peace and joy.

At this point, I need to be clear about two things from the analysis of Corrinne's case. First, this assessment does not mean that everyone considering a year of service after graduation must make the same decision. The assessment of Corrinne's choices was made on the basis of Corrinne's particular (albeit fictional) circumstances. It cannot be translated word for word to another person's situation. Anyone can use the process we just walked through—that's the whole point of this book! Yet this is a far cry from assuming that because the process led to one outcome in one set of circumstances, it must always lead to the same outcome regardless of circumstances. We are actually preaching the exact opposite message: the process can lead to multiple outcomes, depending on the circumstances. Consequently, those who are looking to discern practical choices like Corrinne's on their own should use the tools of the Ignatian B.U.T. without presuming the results in advance.

Second, although we may have helped Corrinne discard her FOBO in favor of a decision in this case, we have not ended her discernment process. Discernment is an ongoing task because it aims to craft a *life* worth living. Corrinne's decision about her postgraduate plans is just one step on her longer journey, and she will have plenty of opportunities to correct her course along the way if necessary. After all, she was only trying to decide if she should take the time to do service *for one year*. Yes, a year is a big commitment, but in a lifetime, it is ultimately only a tiny part. Corrinne's decision to do a year of service does not close her off from any of the other paths she might consider, including medical school. Of course, as she nears the end of her service, she will need to discern what to do next, and that might be medical school and her original pathway, or it might be something else she had never considered before. The beauty of recognizing discernment as an ongoing project is that it allows us to make one decision at a time. Corrinne will one day have to decide what comes after her service, but she does not need to make that decision today. Significantly, when she does make that choice, she will have the benefit of the careful discernment process that led to her service. Precisely because discernment is an ongoing project, it is a skill that we can build over time, meaning that each decision gives us new insight into what it means to discern well. If we take the time to review our past decisions, we can sharpen our discernment process and strengthen our future decisions.

Meditation: The Freedom of Commitment

The next chapter examines what it means to integrate discernment throughout our lives, drawing on the Ignatian notion of "finding God in all things" to explain how to habituate discernment and spiritual growth. However, we close this chapter with a meditation on another Ignatian notion. This one is a short prayer attributed to Ignatius (although likely not written by his own hand) that highlights the freedom for commitment that indifference and discernment provide.

1. Take a moment to center yourself. Breathe slowly and deeply, paying attention to your inhaling and exhaling in order to calm yourself. Be in the moment.
2. Read through this Ignatian prayer slowly:

"Dearest Lord, teach me to be generous. Teach me to serve you as you deserve; to give and not to count the cost; to fight and not to heed the wounds; to toil and not to seek for rest; to labor and ask not for reward, save that of knowing that I do your most holy will."

3. How is this possible? For what purpose would anyone "toil and not seek for rest," "labor and not ask for reward," or "give and not count the cost"? What sort of goal or telos could inspire such selflessness? What sort of confidence in our decisions do we need to commit to something and ignore external rewards?
4. Consider how these insights can translate into your own life. How might you develop this kind of confidence in the decisions you make? How can you reject the fear of a better option in order to focus on the path you want to take? How can you use discernment to free yourself to commit to something meaningful?
5. Take a moment to be grateful for any past decisions you have made that have given you this kind of confidence, and then ask yourself, where are you being called to discern a course of action now?

Key Terms and Ideas

- Good Spirit/Evil Spirit: the two competing influences that Ignatius believed were at work in every discernment process; the Good Spirit (aligned with the Holy Spirit) calls us toward God and the life we most deeply long to live while the Evil Spirit deceives us into settling for a life that has some apparent benefits but leaves us unsatisfied at the deepest level.
- Consolations and desolations: the two types of affective responses (emotions) that Ignatius presented in the *Spiritual Exercises* as signs of the work of God in our lives. Consolations are feelings of comfort, reassurance, and peace when we reflect on who we are and where we want to go with our lives; desolations, meanwhile, are feelings of discomfort, anxiety, or unease during this reflection process. Consolations and desolations are crucial for discernment, as they are the emotional blips that call our attention to the issues that need further consideration when we are working to figure out our deepest desires.
- Rules for discernment: Ignatius crafted a list of "rules" for those looking to discern well; the rules were meant to capture the typical tactics of the Good and Evil Spirits and to help discerners recognize the different experiences of consolations and desolations depending on their context. In this chapter, we stressed that one of the most important insights from Ignatius's rules for discernment is the claim that the larger context of growth versus decline in one's spiritual life can shape whether we feel the resonance of consolation in the hope of continuing on our journey (growth) or the pangs of conscience (decline).
- FOBO: "fear of a better option," a form of analysis paralysis that prevents people from committing to a plan of action in discernment because they worry that as soon as they commit, they will find that there was another, more appealing path that they can no longer take. FOBO is typically rooted in unrealistic expectations that stop someone from doing what they *can* do concretely now while they hold out hope for something they think they *could* do in the future, but only in theory.

Recommended Resources

Samuel Wells, "Rethinking Service," *The Cresset* 76, no. 4 (Easter 2013): 6–14, available online at: http://thecresset.org/2013/Easter/Wells_E2013 .html.

This accessible article from an Anglican priest explores the theologically significant impact of a distinction between service "for" others and service "with" others. Given discernment as a process for identifying how one can best give their life selflessly in service to others, Wells's analysis of these categories is an indispensable resource for those looking to apply the insights of the Ignatian B.U.T. to their own lives.

The Autobiography of St. Ignatius (multiple editions and translations are available).

This short text recounts the major moments shaping Ignatius's own discernment process, highlighting how he came to see the Good Spirit and the Evil Spirit at work in his own life, providing one way of witnessing what eventually became his rules for discernment in action.

Warren Sazama, SJ, "Some Ignatian Principles for Making Prayerful Decisions," *Marquette University*, https://www.marquette.edu/faith /ignatian-principles-for-making-decisions.php.

A detailed summary of the most important resources for discernment found in Ignatius's writings, this website from Marquette University (the Jesuit university where the two of us teach) provides some additional context for the rules of discernment explored in this chapter.

Star Wars (a.k.a. *Star Wars IV: A New Hope*), directed by George Lucas, 20th Century Fox, 1977.

One of the most important science fiction movies of all time, *Star Wars* depicts a galactic battle between the forces of good and evil. From the perspective of discernment, the film is especially valuable for its effective presentation of the deceptive tactics of the Evil Spirit (seen in the temptations of "the Dark Side"), its illustration of the need for formation to discern well (note Luke Skywalker's training process), and its reminder that a community of support can help us be our best selves.

Groundhog Day, directed by Harold Ramis, Columbia Pictures, 1993.

This comedy, which tells the story of a TV newscaster caught in a time loop that forces him to relive February 2 (Groundhog Day) on repeat, has a number of theological themes. In relation to discernment, the film is particularly poignant for the way it shows the contrasting experiences of the Good and Evil Spirits depending on context; the things that bring Phil Connors, the newscaster, "reassurance" at the start of the film are actually the deceptive affirmations of the Evil Spirit, and he only experiences the Good Spirit's interventions as positive consolations once he has had a change of heart.

Notes

1. Kenneth Gergen, *The Saturated Self: Dilemmas of Identity in Contemporary Life* (New York: Basic Books, 2000).
2. Timothy M. Gallagher, OMV, *The Discernment of Spirits: An Ignatian Guide for Everyday Living* (New York: Crossroad Press, 2005), 7–8.
3. Coco Khan, "Do You Take Hours to Make a Simple Decision? You May Have Fobo," *The Guardian*, November 24, 2019, https://www.theguardian.com/global/2019/nov/24/fear-of-missing-out-fomo-making-decision-biology-fobo-christmas-turkey.

10

Finding God in All Things

As Conor and I envision it, the Ignatian B.U.T. describes a committed practice, a willingness to pause and take stock of one's life in a deliberate and discerning way. Instead of acting impulsively or out of routine, one asks oneself, "*But* what if God is calling me to something more? Inviting me to walk another path?" The B.U.T. is a way of pausing to take stock of one's situation (*become aware*), of trying to recognize how God is at work (*understand*), and of responding to God's invitation to live as a follower of Jesus (*take action*). Although this is now the final substantive chapter (the crowd goes wild), we don't consider it a "Conclusion." Instead, we see it more as a launching pad. For centuries, those influenced by Ignatian spirituality have described the fruit of discernment as an enhanced ability to "Find God in All Things." To be sure, Ignatius's insight that God is present in everything is not novel. Many religions share a belief that the divine can be encountered within the world. What Ignatius provides is akin to a form of "spiritual education" that tutors practitioners to perceive the world in a new manner. The gift of this practice is an enhanced ability to recognize and respond with one's entire self to the God who is in, and communicates through, all things. In this chapter, then, we want to examine this fruit of the practice of discernment (and thus the study of theology) more fully.

Knowing in the Spirit

As discussed in chapter 7 (and revisited in the last chapter), Jesus's Resurrection demanded an entire rethinking of how his followers understood and related to God. Even though it took decades for the early

Christians to express this in official creeds and teachings, Jesus's earliest believers tried to put this experience into words. The man Christians today know as Saint Paul of Tarsus was enormously influential in this process. A prodigious letter writer, Paul wrote the following to the Christian community that had taken root in Corinth. As you read, observe the role both spirits play in a human being's life.

> For what human being knows what is truly human except the human spirit that is within? So also no one comprehends what is truly God's except the Spirit of God. Now we have received not the spirit of the world but the Spirit that is from God, so that we may understand the gifts bestowed on us by God. And we speak of these things in words not taught by human wisdom but taught by the Spirit, interpreting spiritual things to those who are spiritual.

> Those who are unspiritual do not receive the gifts of God's Spirit, for they are foolishness to them, and they are unable to understand them because they are discerned spiritually. Those who are spiritual discern all things, and they are themselves subject to no one else's scrutiny.

> "For who has known the mind of the Lord so as to instruct him?"

> But we have the mind of Christ. (1 Corinthians 2:11–16)

As has become my custom, let me make a chart to distinguish "the spirit" from "the Spirit" before discussing why this difference is vital (see page 221).

What Saint Paul describes is how God's Spirit—the music of Trinitarian karaoke—draws believers into its depths and transforms them. The Spirit does not transport recipients to a different world; it enables them to live within the world differently. The Spirit tutors those who receive it to perceive the world with senses attuned to God's presence rhythmically pulsing in the depths of creation and to take part in that world in a new way. If God's act of creation is like a musician who sings and sustains a musical note, then it is the Spirit that frees us to hear and dance to creation's Trinitarian melody.

	Spirit of the World	Spirit of God
Reveals	Human matters	Divine matters
Describes reality	In human words and concepts; stays at surface level	In spiritual terms; provides insight into reality's hidden depths
Comes from	The customs of this world	God and draws us into the Trinity
Effect	Permits us to dwell in and make our way securely within our world. We "make sense" to other humans. It is reflected in our worldly logic.	Endows us with spiritual judgment. The Spirit lets us share in the way that Jesus Christ knows and empowers believers to live according to a new, spiritual logic.

Now, this language of "receiving" and "taking part" may strike the reader as odd, even presumptive. After all, shouldn't an introductory book objectively lay out "the facts" and leave it to the reader to decide what to do with them? When Conor and I set out on this adventure, that was exactly the route we opted *not* to take. We wanted our book to be an experience of theological education. The word "education" comes from the Latin *educere* and means "to lead out." If we've been successful, we've led students to see that the Christian tradition provides a framework in which the "facts" of theology—and, indeed, of life—fit and make sense. Another way of putting it is to say that this has been an exercise in show-and-tell. So instead of *telling* readers what Christians believe, we've tried to *show* how and why two theologians find faith so meaningful. This is because we have experienced theology as training us (1) to *become aware* of the ways God is made known through the world, (2) to *understand* how each person is addressed by God, and (3) to discover ways to *take action* on this call and respond to it with our lives.

When people learn I'm a theologian, they often have questions. Some ask "Big Questions" about life: *Does life have meaning and purpose? Is there a God?* These, of course, are the type of questions I think about a great deal. The theological vocation is to discover and describe how theology provides a credible framework for reflecting on our world. As a guy with a lifelong interest in chemistry and science, I marvel at the intricacies of biochemistry and the awesome scope of the universe. When I read about nanoparticles, a breakthrough in particle physics, or when I hold one of my nephews, I am regularly overcome with a sense that my theological training has given me a privileged access to appreciate reality's innermost depths. There is more to reality than meets the eye; creation, to my eye, pulses with a secret mystery that, for those with ears to hear, sings of its creator. For those who have grown in the discipline of attentiveness, the finite acts as a passageway to the infinite.

This is the core of Ignatian realism. Theological education never discourages rigorous or critical investigation. On the contrary, a theologically astute person insists on looking at reality in its entirety, in its lights *and* shadows. A good theologian gets life and excitement from standing in the space between wonder and horror. Wonder: *Everything that is, is, because it is being created by a loving Creator. Everything that we see around us is a result of love.* But, at the same time, the theologian is not blind to the horrors of history. Horror: *The reality of sin offers searing testimony to the many ways we have "failed to love." Abuse, hypocrisy, terrible violence, prejudice, discrimination: our world is broken.* When we see the worst that the human race can do, when we consider the violence we perpetrate against each other and our world, it is easy to wonder, "What kind of God is running the show here?"

The theologian does not rush to give easy answers. Instead, we try to take very seriously the reality of pain and suffering within the world. But Conor and I really do believe that in every era, humanity's "No" to God is still graciously met with God's "Yes" to us. As Catholics, this "Yes" is most vividly apparent on Easter Sunday. On Good Friday, sinful humanity silenced the Word of God by executing Jesus on the cross. By all accounts, Jesus's story *should* have ended then and there. Yet at dawn on Easter Sunday, a new light pierced history's darkness and opened the eyes of believers to see the world in a new way. This light erupts with the Good News that Jesus has been raised from the dead, a revelation that galvanizes a community—the Church—and empowers it to live the values of God's Kingdom. Thus, Christian justice, animated by the Spirit, attempts to reenact Jesus's words and deeds, which drew the margins to the center as the reign of God broke into history. At its best, Christian life and action is energized not by an ideology or an agenda but by the Spirit who gives us "the mind of Christ" and sends us into the world not only to preach, but *to be*, the Good News.

A Sacramental Vision: Matter *Matters*

Ignatian discernment challenges us to consider our role within this story of the Kingdom's unfolding. For the Spirit does not free us *from* the world and its demands but liberates us *for* service to the world as a response to God's summons. Simone Weil, the twentieth-century mystic, understood how creation serves as the locus for this calling: "The essence of created things is to be intermediaries. They are intermediaries leading from one to the other and there is no end to this. They are intermediaries leading to God. We have to experience them as such."[1] To those with Spirit-opened eyes, the world is never "just there." On the contrary, the world is an arena of encounter where, for those with senses attuned to it, God can be sought and found. It is easy to forget that from its understanding of Creation to the Incarnation, from the Resurrection of the body to the Church's sacraments, Christianity insists that matter *matters*.

Catholics acknowledge seven Sacraments: Baptism, Eucharist, Confirmation, Penance, Anointing of the Sick, Holy Orders, and Matrimony. (Other Christian denominations recognize sacraments too, although they differ on how many sacraments there are.) Sacraments are visible, physical "rites" that symbolize and make God's accompaniment of humans tangibly present in the world. The word "sacrament" comes from the Latin verb *sacrare* meaning "to hallow" or "to consecrate." Sacrament is also the word used to translate the Greek *musterion* (where "mystery" comes from). The Sacraments are not magical incantations; they are privileged liturgical acts that reconfigure Christian life. Through the material elements of daily life—water in Baptism, bread and wine in Eucharist, oil in Confirmation and Anointing of the Sick, laying on of hands in Holy Orders, mutual consent in Matrimony—God reaches into and transforms how Christians live. These liturgical Sacraments (note the big "S") are administered by the Church, providing the physical ways one is drawn into the believing community as a member of the Body of Christ.

Sacraments, as symbols, are the material ways God continues to make our reality God's reality. Even though Christians often say they "got" baptized, "got" married, or "got" Holy Communion, it would be better to say they were "gotten" by the Sacraments, as these are the concrete liturgical ways God "reaches out" and draws us into communion with other believers. In this, the Sacraments live up to their Greek heritage as *musteria* because they are profound moments of encounter with a God who, through the material reality of this world, mysteriously re-creates us as a community. It might be helpful, then, to think of Sacraments not as static "things" you get but as dynamic events where God takes the initiative to reach into our lives. Instead of getting the Sacraments, you must undergo and be transformed by them.

Nevertheless, as Ignatius and Simone Weil understood, the world itself has a sacramental character (small "s"). To return to an image we introduced in chapter 3, there is, if you like, a "crack" in everything through which the Creator's Divine Light shines through. As mentioned earlier, when we practice *attentiveness*, we allow the reality that stands before us to be present on its terms, not ours. We *reverence* what we encounter when we behold it as a unique expression of God's creation. This happens when we marvel at a baby's fragile beauty, when we gaze into a loved one's eyes, when we open ourselves to the ways God awakens a sense of calling, of vocation, within our hearts. This happens, too, in moments of darkness and crisis: in the cry of the poor, in battered and broken bodies of history's victims, in the earth's plight. *Attention* and *reverence* lead to one being moved to *devote* oneself to collaborate with the God who has been found. For some, this will be a call to married life and parenthood; others to serve as a religious sister, brother, or priest; still others to serve as single adults. Regardless of how one is called, each of us can discern within one's vocation a mission to serve God according to the pattern revealed by Jesus.

Within the framework of Christian theology, every single person has a vocation. The practice of discernment equips us with tools to help discover *how* we are being called. What is especially distinctive about Christian discernment is that it always thrusts us into the chaos of our world because matter *matters*. Christian life can never take seriously enough the implications of John's Prologue: "And the Word became flesh and lived among us" (John 1:14). Jesus's life and ministry sought not to destroy but to redeem human history so that we might "have life, and have it more abundantly" (John 10:10). Ignatian realists possess a sacramental way of seeing, with senses attuned to the many places within our world where God calls to us and asks us to commit ourselves in service. The vocation of the Ignatian realist, in a way, is to see with eyes opened by God's love. For Catholics, every Sacrament is a privileged event that reveals in a concrete way what God is *always trying to do*. Baptism: wash us and give us new life. Confirmation: share the Holy Spirit with us and strengthen us. Eucharist: feed us for our journey. Marriage: join us in a covenantal relationship where we come to know, love, and serve the Lord through our beloved and our family. Holy Orders: calling individuals to serve the community as leaders in prayer and worship. Anointing of the Sick: when we need physical health, restoring our vitality. Reconciliation: welcoming us home not as "wicked sinners" but as beloved sons and daughters. Every Sacrament is an invitation to receive and be transformed by what God is trying to do always and everywhere: make God's reign present in history by transforming who we are into the people God desires us to become.

We have only scratched the surface of theological inquiry. Could we do anything more? In place of a definitive conclusion, let me gesture toward an opening. As I said earlier, we have tried to show how Christian belief can provide a credible and compelling framework for living one's life. Christianity is not a program. It is a pilgrimage. Paul Elie defines "pilgrimage" as follows:

> A pilgrimage is a journey undertaken in light of a story. A great event has happened; the pilgrim hears the reports and goes in search of the evidence, aspiring to be an eyewitness. The pilgrim seeks not only

to confirm the experience of others firsthand but to be changed by the experience. . . . Each [pilgrim] must be changed individually; they must see for themselves, each with his or her own eyes. And as they return to ordinary life the pilgrims must tell others what they saw, recasting the story in their own terms.[2]

Conor and I are glad to have been your companions in this journey. We remain with you as fellow travelers, but as Elie notes, the next part of your pilgrimage is for you to discern. We hope that you do *discern*, that you do make use of theology's tools to assist you as you become who you are called to be. And if you find your life "making sense" because of the Good News preached and enacted by Jesus, we hope that you share your stories with others and encourage them to "Go and do likewise" (Luke 10:37).

Progress on the Journey

For my portion of this closing chapter, I'll discuss how to progress on this unfolding journey. Ryan has just explained that a theological approach to the world steeped in Ignatian Realism primes people to see the world differently. The journey of discernment is therefore one wherein the pilgrim strives to find God at work in the world—to look through the darkness for the cracks of light that reveal a constant call to both recognize that matter *matters* and to act so that it continues to matter for all. This is a complicated task, however, especially in a world that serves up ubiquitous reminders of the horrors that can impede our sense of wonder.

By way of closing, then, I am going to explore how one can continue to cultivate the unique perspective of Ignatian realism that allows one to acknowledge the challenges without losing sight of the positive contributions each one of us is called to make and the good people we are still called to become. To do this, I will unpack more of the theological underpinnings behind the Ignatian notion of "finding God in all things" that Ryan outlined and then explain how this vision relates to discernment so that we can leave you with a better sense of how the

Ignatian B.U.T. can shape a whole way of life and not just serve you in an isolated moment of crisis.

Let me begin with the theological vision and Ignatian roots of the idea of finding God in all things. This phrase, of course, is closely associated with St. Ignatius of Loyola and is often portrayed as a pithy summation of Ignatian spirituality. In fairness, the idea does represent a helpful way of carrying the insights of Ignatius's *Spiritual Exercises* beyond the four "weeks" of the retreat because Ignatius did design the *Exercises* to help people discover how God was at work in the immediate context of their own lives. Given this alignment with the central premise of the *Exercises*, I never gave much thought to the origins of the phrase and was not much concerned about whether it came from Ignatius himself or represented a later attempt by the Jesuits to craft a quick precis that they could use to explain their work to others. My indifference changed one day when a colleague asked me if I could point him to the exact quote Ignatius offered to introduce this idea. I had to admit that I was at a loss, but I promised I would do some research. After a bit of digging, I discovered the actual source, and it has had a profound impact on my interpretation of this common catchphrase.

The place where I found Ignatius's own contribution to the idea of finding God in all things was in a letter he wrote to a Portuguese priest named Antonio Brandão, who was new to the Jesuits. Still in the early stages of his Jesuit formation, he wanted to know how he could better prepare himself and other scholastics (new Jesuits) for their life in the Society of Jesus. He therefore sought out Ignatius's advice and asked, among other things, "What method of meditation more in keeping with our [unique] vocation [as Jesuits] should be followed?" Ignatius responded (through a secretary) by saying,

> Over and above the spiritual exercises assigned for their perfection ... they should practice the seeking of God's presence in all things, in their conversations, their walks, in all that they see, taste, hear, understand, and in all their actions, since His Divine Majesty is truly in all things by his presence, power, and essence. This kind of meditation, which finds God our Lord in all things, is easier than

raising oneself to the consideration of divine truths, which are more abstract and which demand something of an effort, if we are to keep our attention on them.[3]

After sitting with this Ignatian source material, I arrived at two conclusions that I think are essential for anyone who wants to make further progress on the journey of discernment with the eyes of Ignatian Realism. The first concerns the central task of that journey, and the second has to do with the presuppositions embedded in that task.

First, even though there is a reference to how Ignatius's unique spiritual strategy can allow someone to "find God our Lord in all things," the actual practice he encouraged was the "*seeking* of God's presence in all things." Although this may seem like mere semantics, there is a difference between finding and seeking, and this distinction creates a nuance that should not be overlooked. The task for Jesuits—and, by extension, for anyone who wants to live a discerning life—is to prioritize the seeking of God in all things. The emphasis is not on the discovery, which "finding" might imply and which could easily allow one to assume that the work was done as soon as they found at least one good illustration of God's presence. Instead, the emphasis is on the act of continuing to look for God. It is, quite simply, a way of life and not a mere one-and-done project. It is an ongoing journey, not a destination.

Significantly, these distinctions connect back to discernment because, as Ryan and I explained at the outset of the book, discernment is about identifying our ultimate concern—again, the value we place above all others as a matter of faith; that which is our God—and then determining how to act in a manner that is consistent with that ultimate concern in all that we do. Discernment is therefore an intrinsically dynamic task that is much better characterized by our perpetual seeking of new ways to pursue our proper end in each changing circumstance than it is imagined as an answer we are simply hoping to find.

Ignatius's call to be seeking God in all things is thus quite consistent with the task of discernment, especially in a theological context. As our whole book has tried to explain, Christians identify their ultimate concern as the God of love who is a Trinity of persons revealed most fully and most directly in the person of Jesus Christ. If, as a matter of discernment, one desires to act in a manner that is informed by and consistent with this vision of God in all that one does, then it is very important to have a good grasp of this ultimate concern. Naturally, one way to strengthen that grasp is by continually looking for God and God's actions in all the elements of ordinary life, so that one can arrive at an ever-clearer vision of who God is and how God might be calling us to act. Prioritizing the seeking of God in all things thus allows the person who has defined their ultimate concern in these theological terms to better ensure that they have that vision at the center of their lives while they discern how to act day in and day out. Without that emphasis, it will be too easy to go astray and fail to become the person one most deeply longs to be.

Beyond this clearer account of the specific task shaping a lifelong journey of discernment in an Ignatian vein, the second insight I have come to appreciate in Ignatius's original quote is that the seeking he exhorts only makes sense based on the assumption that God can in fact be found in all things. This assumption is reflected in the sacramental character that Ryan explained above, which is an essential feature of the Catholic defense of the conviction that matter *matters*. That approach appeals to the biblical belief that God created and redeemed the world and argues that God, the creator, can be found in that which the creator has created. Thus, people adopting this perspective look at the world in a unique way, expecting to find little "clues" pointing back to God's presence and power in all that has been created.

While Ignatius was undoubtedly rooted in this sacramental vision, I believe his summons to seek God in all things makes the most sense with an even more precise rationale for the expectation that a careful discerner will always be able to find God in the routine tasks of everyday existence and not just in mystical experiences. Certainly, he was not promoting some vague pantheism that says everything is God. The point is not to make enough mental leaps, from seeing a wood chip to thinking of a tree and then imagining the cross to transform a playground into a reminder of God. Instead, I think Ignatius's vision moved in the opposite direction. That is, he could encourage the seeking of God in all things because he started with a deep recognition of who God really is, which gave him an intimate enough knowledge of God to be able to see God in the world around him. Like an astronomer who has carefully worked to acclimate her eyes to the darkness before turning to her telescope, Ignatius had done the work to adjust his vision so that he could pinpoint the cracks of light no matter how small.

In other words, Ignatius started with the assumption that "the world is charged with the grandeur of God" (as the nineteenth-century Jesuit priest and poet Gerard Manley Hopkins famously asserted) and began to search for God in all things as a result of that belief. The best way to convey how this starting point changes the dynamic from "finding" to "seeking" is to speak about the experience of being in love. When people are head-over-heels madly in love, especially in the earliest stages of this feeling, they cannot stop thinking about their beloved. Because they love this person so much, and because they have come to know them so intimately, they quickly discover that almost every interaction becomes an opportunity to "find their beloved" in the world around them.

One might step into a coffee shop and hear their beloved's favorite song on the sound system, and instantly the café becomes a place to find their beloved even when the person they love may be busy at work miles away. Later, if they walk down the street and see someone with a jacket in their beloved's favorite color, they bring that person to mind and have found them on the sidewalk in the middle of the day despite their distance. And so on. (As an aside, this is often how I, as a father, experience the presence of my children when I am away from them while traveling for a conference or other work obligation—I can see them in a pair of rain boots on a traveler, a bowl of frosted wheat at breakfast, or a bow in a little girl's hair because these are the details I know about my own children from being their dad.) When we know someone with the depths that we associate with an intimate relationship, we can expect to find constant signs of their abiding presence in our lives, no matter how mundane our interactions are when we are away from them. This, I believe, is the same foundational vision that informs Ignatius's plan for seeking God in all things. Only after knowing something about God does it become possible to seek God around us in anything, let alone all things.

For Ignatius and his fellow Jesuits, the knowledge of God they needed to start this process came from the *Spiritual Exercises* and other forms of prayer. For the rest of us, such knowledge can come from the same exercises and any other spiritual practice we undertake to come to terms with what we believe. Spiritual practices like this are thus an essential part of discernment, particularly as we have described it in this book. The Jesuit theologian Howard Gray, whom we mentioned in the introduction, was fond of describing spirituality as a quest to answer three interrelated questions: Who is your God? How have you come to know your God? What does your God ask you to do? Discernment obviously underscores the third question, but note how it only emerges because of the other two. Only once we have taken the time to answer the first question—to really understand what we believe and what it means to establish this belief as our ultimate concern—can we then begin to answer the second question. Likewise, we can only sufficiently address the third question by building on the knowledge of our God gained in the process of answering that second question. In effect, we need to begin with a sense of who God is, and then we need to practice the seeking of God in all things, so that we can finally arrive at a clearer sense of what it means to *take action* in a meaningful way. Ignatian Realism demands nothing less.

Seeking God in the Discernment of Things

Hopefully, both insights from Ignatius's original vision can help you see how the idea of finding (because you have been seeking) God in all things can inform a process of careful discernment in the world. Before concluding this chapter, however, I want to give you one more thought about how this aspect of Ignatian Realism can strengthen discernment in a particular way. Obviously, the notion of seeking God in all things can help us come to a better understanding of God, our ultimate concern, and thus help us arrive at a clearer sense of what it means to embody our commitment to that God in our ordinary lives. That is the first benefit of discernment just described. Beyond this broader assistance to discernment, however, the Ignatian dictum can also be used to improve our process of discernment itself. In other words, it not only helps us identify our ultimate concern but also assists us in the practical task of aligning our choices with our guiding commitment.

Understanding this second benefit requires expanding our vision of exactly what we are looking for when we start to seek God in all things. If we are actively seeking God in all things and beginning with the expectation that we will be able to find God in those things, then we do not need to confine our search for God just to the material world around us (that is, in "things" as we normally think of the term). We can also look for and expect to find God in the lives of the people around us as well. With this Ignatian perspective, we can look to the example of others who have discerned well and acknowledge that their lives show us something of how God is active in the world through their discernment processes. We can see their pathways of careful discernment as a model for what it means to *become aware, understand,* and *take action* in the messy context of the real world.

In all honesty, this more expansive vision could take us in numerous directions. We might look to someone like Dorothy Day, a US Catholic from the twentieth century who is currently being considered for sainthood. She was appalled by the poverty she encountered in New York City during the Great Depression and, in response, opened a "house of hospitality" for the hungry and the homeless as a way of living out Jesus's call to love one's neighbor as oneself. In the process, she started what is now the Catholic Worker movement, which has led to similar houses of hospitality across the world. By seeking God in all things, we can see God's activity in Day's life, meaning that her example can provide us with a better sense of what it takes to live a life of radical commitment to God, making this God one's actual and consistent ultimate concern.

Day's example is beautiful and challenging, but it is not the only one. The lengthy list of officially recognized Catholic saints certainly offers a host of illustrations to inform our own discernment process. Learning from the example of others, however, is not just limited to those who have been singled out as prime examples by a particular religious tradition. We can also practice the seeking of God in all things whenever we identify inspiration in the strength and convictions of anyone who responds to the problems of evil suffered and evil done with the sort of vigor and hope that defined Jesus's proclamation of the reign of God. Again, this perspective could lead us to myriad illustrations, but the people who I think can teach us the most are the ones who have confronted the oppressive weight of evil done in its systemic manifestations of structural sin and fought the urge to despair.

Recently, I have seen this courage most explicitly, and most movingly, in the examples of the Black men and women in this country who have felt the weight of centuries of rejection and discrimination—much of it, like slavery, Jim Crow, and redlining, explicitly codified in law and enforced by the government that purportedly served them—and yet refuse to give up the hope that this nation will one day live up to its professed ideals. Certainly, to pick up a thread from the introduction, Rosa Parks would fit into this category, as she felt the oppressive power of the structural sin of legalized racial segregation firsthand and yet went forward in hope and helped to change the structure itself. Yet I also want to highlight how I have seen this same determination, and thus insight into discernment, from the men and women who unfortunately have had to demonstrate the same strength in the face of even more recent manifestations of American racism.

To give but one example, consider the words of Breonna Taylor's mother in the aftermath of her daughter's tragic killing by police officers in Louisville, Kentucky. Keenly aware of the way in which her daughter's death was emblematic of the larger systemic problem of the police's excessive use of force, Taylor's mother rejected the idea that she should just accept this dark reality as the way of world. Instead, she penned these words to be proclaimed by her sister, "You can take the dog out of the fight, but you can't take the fight out of the dog. For lack of better terms, 'Bark, Bark' for being the dog still standing to fight."

What does it take to face this tragedy, to internalize this pain, to know the depth of sin and suffering in the world so personally and yet to refuse to give up? It takes the courage of one's convictions. It takes the power of discernment and the assurance that one's ultimate concern is worth fighting for. It takes the grace of God. When we seek God in all things with an eye toward strengthening our own future discernment, then we can begin to see how that grace is active in the face of deeply challenging manifestations of evil suffered and evil done. We can spot the cracks that let the light into the darkness.

As Ryan pointed out, the ability to see in this way is most fundamentally about adopting a different worldview. It is about allowing the work of finding God in all things, the spirit of Ignatian Realism, to create a new way of seeing. One of the most thoughtful theologians on the reality of sin, evil, and suffering in the world, Gustavo Gutiérrez, OP (who is known as the father of liberation theology), explained this way of seeing effectively in his book *On Job: God-Talk and the Suffering of the Innocent*. Reflecting on the biblical account of Job, a faithful man who is tested with all kinds of suffering and afflictions, Gutiérrez insisted that a theologian's way of seeing is not about denying the reality of suffering or abandoning all hope because suffering is real. Instead, the theologian's more realistic vision starts by recognizing that it could just as easily have been the case that suffering was all there is to know. The remarkable thing is that, despite all the suffering that is real, there is still some goodness shining through.[4]

I found a slightly more poetic presentation of Gutiérrez's main point about how one ought, from a Christian perspective, to handle suffering in the HBO series *True Detective*. The show's first season focuses on two Louisiana detectives, played by Woody Harrelson and Matthew McConaughey, trying to solve a vicious crime. At the end of their endeavors, these investigators meditate on the horrors they have seen, and Woody Harrelson's character expresses the reasonable conclusion that there is little hope in fighting crime when it seems so monstrous and pervasive. If the battle is about darkness versus light, he argues, then we are all in trouble because, he explains as he points to the night sky, "it appears to me that the dark has a lot more territory." Disheartened, McConaughey's character initially agrees but, after ruminating a bit more, counters with Gutiérrez's—and frankly, any committed Christian's—basic realization, insisting, "You're looking at it wrong, at the sky. . . . Once, there was only dark. If you ask me, the light's winning."[5]

The Ignatian practice of seeking God in all things gives us the power to stop "looking at it wrong," so that even in the darkest points of our lives—the loss of a loved one, the shock of a pandemic that upends everyone's lives—we can recognize that light is still winning and therefore can find the strength to discern how we can contribute to that fight. This is what we learn not just from seeking to understand more about who God is but also about how others have discerned their ways to live a life with this God as their ultimate concern. If we keep our eyes open, we can continue learning throughout our journey, so that our pilgrimage will not be in vain. Instead, it will lead us ever more fully to become the person we most deeply wish to be. If you can continue to chart that course, not only will this book have been useful, but you will also have become your own proof of that fundamental Christian conviction: the light is winning!

Meditation: Open My Eyes

Back in chapter 1, I (Ryan) described my own experience of finding God in all things, when I was standing by the Atlantic Ocean and had a powerful experience of allowing God's presence to be made known to me. The older I get, the more I grow convinced that we don't need "arguments" for God's existence. We need, instead, the courage to practice attentiveness because God will be made known to us first not through logical proofs but through the ways we are hospitable to what is other to ourselves. In the New Testament, the "righteous" are shocked to discover that when they fed the hungry, clothed the naked, and cared for the sick, they were doing this for Jesus (Matthew 25:31–46). Now that is a summons to the "seeking of God's presence in all things!"

For this practice to be truly effective and truly *transformative*, we need to be willing to extend our seeking to the bad as well as the good. Conor's discussion of how we can learn from the perseverance of others in the face of darkness is a fine illustration of this holistic strategy, which embodies the Ignatian Realism we described in chapter 6. Yet we need a bit of preparation to apply this Ignatian lens to those dark situations in a way that allows us to see something more than just the thing we want to condemn. It is not enough, for example, to be antiracist or antisexist. It is too easy to say what we are against. It is far more difficult to say what we are for.

The key insight that allows us to link these two things—the bridge that helps us move from what we oppose to what we want to champion—is the recognition that we need to practice attention as a spiritual exercise because this is the way we grow in love. The British novelist and philosopher Iris Murdoch has a powerful definition of love: "Love is the perception of individuals. Love is the extremely difficult realization that something other than oneself is real," or, as she added more succinctly, "Love . . . is the discovery of reality."[6] *Becoming aware* is an invitation to love, and we can only be "for" love in this way if we practice a deep form of attention that allows us to see what is really there in front of us and then use that attention to discern how we are moved and called by what we discover.

Unfortunately, one of the most frequent obstacles to this cultivation of attention is us. As fallen human beings, we tend to be selective in our attention, developing biases—some intentional, many unintentional—that tell us certain things, certain issues, certain *people* do not deserve our attention, and so we look away. Or, more honestly, we do not even bother to notice in the first place.

This tendency is inadequate for a spirituality grounded in the Ignatian B.U.T., which asks one to *become aware, understand,* and *take action* chiefly by embracing the seeking of God's presence in *all things.* For this chapter's closing meditation, then, we offer an exercise that asks you to meditate on the "blind spots" in our spiritual vision. We invite you to consider, where do we struggle with some sort of *-ism* that prevents us from seeing others lovingly? It is a tough question but also a crucial one, especially if we are to take Ignatian realism seriously, for then we can learn from a new look at the darkness—not only as it appears in the world, but also as it hides within us. By taking time to meditate on the ways we evade and avoid hearing the voices of others crying out to us, we open ourselves to being healed and to becoming, in turn, healers in our broken and divided world. The goal of this meditation is not to make anyone feel bad but, by confronting our shortcomings and failures, to help us find ways to become better.

Let me put this task into perspective with one final observation linked to the sacramental practices I introduced at the start of the chapter. Catholics believe that, in the Eucharist, Jesus Christ comes to us through bread and wine. The priest and the people offer the gifts of bread and wine for consecration and, Catholics believe, God's Spirit makes them the food and drink that we truly need: Jesus. The simplicity of these materials should not be glossed over: communion bread tastes stale and communion wine would not be served at any party, but Catholics believe that God so desperately loves us and desires to feed us that even unleavened bread and cheap wine can become the One for whom the heart longs. I mention this because it strikes me as wondrous that *if* God can do this with bread and wine, what can God do with a human heart—with a human life—that opens itself to welcome God? Like communion bread and wine before consecration, our lives can seem to be good for nothing. But what would happen if we made an offering of even the undesirable aspects of ourselves, the parts that might seem shameful and embarrassing, and invited God to transform us through *those* parts of ourselves? If Jesus can become present in food, what might he do through us?

1. As usual, begin by sitting upright in your chair. Take a few deep breaths and allow the day's tension to fade away. There are always important things that need our attention, but right now, practicing attention is the most important thing you can do.

2. Now, think of any places in your life where you can notice a temptation to deny the "reality" of others, as Murdoch would put it. Open your eyes to those times and places when you refused to see the other. Places where you turn people into objects or things. Times when you used and abused others. Moments when you trivialized others' experiences or ignored them altogether. Times when you failed to bother to love. Don't shy away from the shameful

and embarrassing moments: let them come to the surface.
Be specific as you consider things like:

a. Occasions of malicious gossip that tore another down
b. Racist or sexist jokes told to amuse others
c. Victim-blaming without bothering to consider the
   person's journey or struggle
d. Ignoring the needs of others because of selfishness

In all of these times, note how, as with all forms of evil
done, there has been a total loss: the other has suffered from
what you have done, and you have become less human for
doing it.

3. Do not rush from this. Even if it is painful, stay with the
   reality and allow it to become apparent to you. See with the
   eyes of the mind and allow this moment to become real to
   you. Do not *do* anything. Indeed, it is often our rush to *do*
   that gets us into trouble. Use your energy to open yourself in
   hospitality to this other reality. From the depths of your
   being, say "Welcome" and bid the other to enter into your
   reality. Allow yourself to see the humanity you ignored
   earlier. How would reality appear if you saw with eyes of love?
4. Notice how judgments, prejudices, words, and deeds all
   work against our flourishing. We were not created to
   objectify others or dominate them. We were created, if
   Ignatius of Loyola is right, to serve them. How does *this*
   reality call you into action? How will *you* respond to the cry
   of the poor you hear in *this* person?
5. As you conclude this meditation, imagine yourself putting this
   resolution into practice. How would your life be different if you
   were to follow through on your resolve? What would you need
   to sustain this effort? Can you name the gift, the grace, that
   would give you strength enough to do it? Here is an invitation
   to a new arena where you can, and should, expand the seeking
   of God's presence so that you truly find God in *all* things.

Key Terms and Ideas

- Sacrament: a visible, physical "rite" that symbolizes and makes God's accompaniment of humans tangibly present in the world. The practice of liturgical Sacraments (Catholic Christians identify seven among rituals like Baptism and the Eucharist; other Christians have different numbers) undergirds a "sacramental" worldview that envisions God active in the world below the surface and allows for the finding of God in all things.
- Pilgrimage: "a journey undertaken in light of a story," a pilgrimage is a trip—either literal or metaphorical—that is less about the destination and more about the process of transformation that the journey itself facilitates. This is an apt metaphor for the journey (or pilgrimage) of discernment at the heart of the study of theology.
- Seeking God in all things: Ignatius's guidance for a distinct form of spiritual growth invited Jesuits to practice the "seeking of God's presence in all things," later yielding the "finding God in all things" catchphrase associated with the Jesuit order today. The differences between seeking and finding, however, highlight the active nature of the process and the level of awareness that makes the search theologically rich (and revealing).
- Seeking God in discernment: the idea that we can find lessons for honing our own discernment process from other people's efforts to *become aware, understand,* and *take action* in their lives. This is especially true when we see others modeling discernment in the face of suffering and evil in a way that leads to action and counteracts despair with perseverance in hope.

Recommended Resources

Michael J. Himes, "'Finding God in All Things': A Sacramental Worldview and Its Effects," in *As Leaven in the World: Catholic Perspectives on Faith, Vocation, and the Intellectual Life,* ed. Thomas M. Landy (Franklin, WI: Sheed and Ward, 2001), 91–102.

This essay includes some of the same fundamental claims about the nature of God (as love) found in earlier Himes texts recommended in this book but then uses those convictions to explain the impact of the sacramental principle at the heart of Catholic theology that lies behind the assumption that one can plausibly seek, and ultimately find, God in all things.

Tobias Wolff, "The Rich Brother," *Vanity Fair*, June 1985, available online at: https://archive.vanityfair.com/article/1985/6/the-rich-brother.

This provocative short story can be used to practice honing the skills of seeking God in all things. Wolff, who was raised Catholic, incorporates numerous Catholic themes into his writing, including many of the theological themes outlined in this book. By reading the story and actively searching for those theological connections, one will embark on a mini-pilgrimage built around the seeking of God in another arena (i.e., literature). You might start the process by asking, "Who is the rich brother here?"

Entertaining Angels: The Dorothy Day Story, directed by Michael Ray Rhodes, Paulist Pictures, 1996.

An independent film (starring Moira Kelly and Martin Sheen) that tells the story of Dorothy Day's slow transformation toward a life of service in which she persevered in the face of the enormous suffering wrought by the Great Depression and countless structural injustices beyond. Watch the movie for a powerful discernment process in action.

About Time, directed by Richard Curtis, Universal Pictures, 2013.

One of my (Conor's) all-time favorite movies, *About Time* is built around a young man who can travel back in time to any prior day in his life and then live his life again (and again and again) from that point. The way the main character chooses to use this unique "gift" evolves over time, ultimately teaching him crucial lessons about what it means to cultivate attentiveness to the deeper meaning in everyday life, just as the seeking of God's presence in all things invites.

Notes

1. Simone Weil, *Gravity and Grace*, ed. Gustave Thibon, trans. Mario von der Ruhr (New York: Routledge Classics, 1999), 145–46.
2. Paul Elie, *The Life You Save May Be Your Own: An American Pilgrimage* (New York: Farrar, Straus and Giroux, 2004), x–xi.
3. "Ignatius of Loyola to Father Antonio Brandão on Aspects of the Spiritual Life," June 1, 1551, available online at https://www.library.georgetown.edu/woodstock/ignatius-letters/letter15.

4. Gustavo Gutiérrez, OP, *On Job: God-Talk and the Suffering of the Innocent*, trans. Matthew J. O'Connell (Maryknoll, NY: Orbis Books, 1987).

5. *True Detective*, season 1 episode 8, "Form and Void," directed by Cary Joji Fukunaga, written by Nic Pizzolatto, aired March 9, 2014, on HBO.

6. Iris Murdoch, *Existentialists and Mystics*, ed. Peter Conradi (New York: Penguin Books, 1997), 215.

Conclusion

Where Are You Now?

As much as we have tried to say within these pages, much more remains—and, frankly, deserves—to be said. We don't see ourselves as having written *the* book on theology or discernment. We hope, instead, to have provided readers with an engaging introduction to a field we are passionate about. Theology, as we teach and try to practice it, is not something we simply think about. It's something we live.

At the start of this book, we introduced the idea that theology is valuable precisely because it can inform a new way of life, or, more accurately, it can *form* us for a richer way of living in this world. This was the point of discussing those "two choices behind every choice," which again were:

1. What do I really value?
2. How do I live up to those values in this moment?

Theology, we argued, is crucial for the first question because it is the discipline that helps each person identify and evaluate their ultimate concern. It helps people discern if the thing they say they value above all else is really worth their time and effort. But, of course, theology does not stop there. When practiced through the art of discernment, theology also helps people understand how they can enact a genuine commitment to their ultimate concern in their ordinary choices.

The study of theology, then, is not simply meant to inform, or even just to form, but ultimately to *transform*. The most important transformation in the study of theology is the change that this critical reflection invites in us, as the people who embark on this journey and who ask the questions that define the two choices behind every choice with more intentionality. As we have tried to show throughout the book, however, that transformation is not self-serving. It does not stop with us but rather begins with us so that we can then work to transform a world haunted by the pains of evil suffered and evil done and yet nonetheless suffused with the presence of a loving God who, having determinedly entered into the "horror story" created by sin, can be found in all things—even the darkness. Or, to put this claim in the terms that we have used throughout the book, the process of *becoming aware* and increasing in *understanding* has always been ordered to *taking action*.

Here at the end of the book, we hope that you have deployed the Ignatian B.U.T. so that you can continue moving closer to the life that you most deeply long to live. If Ignatius—and, indeed, the broader Christian tradition of which he is a part and which we, Ryan and Conor, have found so personally formative—is right, then this will be the life that allows you to fulfill yourself by serving others.

For all this lofty talk, we are not haughty (at least not as far as the book is concerned . . .). We realize this book by itself is not going to make any of these grand transformations a reality. In fact, this very realization is why we have presented this book, and the study of theology itself, as a practice. It only works if someone engages in it and dedicates the hours and the effort to letting the practice do its formative and transformative work. No one gets better at soccer by learning *about* the drills; one has to *do* the drills to develop the skills. So it is with theology. This book is dead unless you have decided to use it not merely to learn *about* the practice of discernment but to *do* it.

Even if you have embraced the vision of theology as a personal activity that we have promoted throughout the book and tried assiduously to put these skills into practice, we are not delusional enough to suggest that you have reached the fullness of your potential and realized the deepest of your desires by the end of this text. After all, the work of transformation that we have been describing is properly the work of theology as a whole, and we have written but an introduction to theology. There is much more the field can offer for those willing to wrestle with the two choices behind every choice. Consequently, even in the best-case scenario, there is space for a lot more depth in the transformative journey that we have argued theology can inspire.

Beyond the added content, the fact remains that this process of transformation is itself a journey and one that will continue throughout a person's life. If there are life choices to be made, there is discernment to be done. This book represents not the end of that journey but the starting point—or, as we described it at the start of the last chapter, the "launching pad"—for the next step.

In the hopes of making this launching pad as useful as possible for your impending liftoff, we would like to close the book with one final meditation. This is one that we hope will call attention to the work of transformation that, however incomplete, has also started in a meaningful way. With this description, we mirror the theological discipline of eschatology, or the study of the "end things" (as in the end of time), which holds out hope for the day when God's reign will be fully realized. Christians believe this transformation is *not yet* complete but *already* ongoing. We similarly hope that your transformation, even though not yet complete, has already begun. To help you discern where you are going, we take a moment to invite you to consider how far you have come. To do so, we want to pick up on the challenging question that Ryan identified in chapter 1 as God's first question in the Bible: "Where are you?"

As you may recall, in that first chapter, we asked you to sit with that question so that you could identify where you were at the start of this book. We asked you to consider how your choices—the good ones and the bad ones—had led you to the place you were in when you chose (or were required by your class) to pick up this book. Here, at the end of this book, we want to recall your answer so that you can assess how things may have changed for you through the work of theology and the practice of discernment. To invite you to see the beginnings of a transformation, we want you to compare where you were then with the same question posed anew, to answer, "Where are you . . . *now*?"

A Closing Meditation

1. Take a moment to center yourself and consciously direct your attention. Close your eyes and focus on your breathing for at least three slow breaths so that you can be more present to the moment.

2. Recall your initial response to the question in chapter 1, "Where are you?" You may wish to use your Ignatian imagination to remember what it was like to sit with that question the first time. What was unsettling about posing this question for yourself? What was illuminating? Finally, what was your answer? How did you position yourself at the start of this book?

3. Now, imagine yourself having a conversation with a friend, a family member, or other close confidant. Pick someone with whom you would be comfortable having an honest, even intimate, conversation. (In the *Spiritual Exercises*, Ignatius often proposed these imagined conversations, or "colloquies," as a private discussion with Jesus, so you could also envision a discussion with the divine if that is consistent with your faith convictions and easier than identifying a specific friend or relative.) Use your imagination to immerse yourself in a scene where you are walking slowly with this partner and telling them about your life. You bring up your experience of reading this book and they ask for the highlights. What two or three things do you tell them were your favorite elements—the parts that resonated the most with you? What two or three things do you raise as your least favorite aspects—the things you found yourself resisting?

4. After listening to your descriptions, your conversation partner says, "What does this say about you, that you were drawn to (and pushed away from) these specific elements? Why are these the parts that are so significant for you?" How do you respond?

5. Now, reflect on your responses. What have you learned about yourself in this process? Compare those lessons to the way you initially explained where you were in chapter 1. How do you see changes in your thinking, in your assumptions, in your commitments and values, or in yourself? How would you answer the question, "Where are you, now?"

6. Finally, return to the conversation with your partner and tell them what you hope to do with this new self-understanding. If they simply said to you, "Given what you told me, what's next?" what would you tell them? Use your response to identify one or two specific things you would like to do differently going forward and plan to start making changes in the week ahead.

INDEX

ABOUT THE AUTHORS

RYAN G. DUNS, SJ, is a Jesuit priest and theologian whose scholarship bridges theology, philosophy, and cultural studies. He is the author of *Spiritual Exercises for a Secular Age: Desmond and the Quest for God* (University of Notre Dame Press, 2020) and *Theology of Horror: The Hidden Depths of Popular Films* (University of Notre Dame Press, 2024). He has published articles on the thought of Karl Rahner, William Desmond, Iris Murdoch, and Charles Taylor. He currently serves as an Associate Professor and Chair in the Department Theology at Marquette University. In addition to his scholarly interests, he is also a professional Irish musician and teaches "Introduction to the Irish Tin Whistle" as part of Marquette University's Irish Studies Minor.

CONOR M. KELLY is an associate professor in the Department of Theology at Marquette University. His teaching and research focus on moral discernment in ordinary life. He is the author of *The Fullness of Free Time: A Theological Account of Leisure and Recreation in the Moral Life* (Georgetown University Press, 2020) and *Racism and Structural Sin: Confronting Injustice with the Eyes of Faith* (Liturgical Press, 2023), along with numerous articles on social ethics, health care ethics, and Catholic higher education.